Acclaim for Nancy Schulman and Ellen Birnbaum's

PRACTICAL WISDOM *for* PARENTS

A *Publishers Weekly* Best Book of the Year

"[Parents] will find comfort here. . . . These authors are keen observers of kids and know what makes toddlers tick." —*BookPage*

"A warm and commonsensical guide to this period of rapid growth. The authors have years of experience . . . and it shows." —*Newsday*

"Rewarding. . . . [Schulman and Birnbaum] cover all the contemporary issues." —*The Boston Globe*

"We've long benefited from the calming wit and considerable wisdom of Nancy Schulman and Ellen Birnbaum. . . . Nancy and Ellen's insights and advice have helped us to not only survive each of our children's journeys, but also truly savor them. Do yourself, your family, and your child a favor: read this book." —Tracy Pollan and Michael J. Fox

"If you ever wished your child had come with an instruction manual, this is it! . . . Schulman and Birnbaum have covered all of the topics you need to know about (and didn't know who to ask or trust). *Practical Wisdom for Parents* offers great insights, useful tips, and the most thoughtful advice out there. If you are looking for a book to help you get through the tricky preschool years and come out with great kids, this book is a *must-read*." —Jane Buckingham, author of *The Modern Girl's Guide to Life*

Nancy Schulman and Ellen Birnbaum

PRACTICAL WISDOM
for PARENTS

Nancy Schulman has been the director of the 92nd
Street Y Nursery School since 1990. She is also on the
board of the Independent School Admissions Associa-
tion of Greater New York, the Syracuse University
School of Education Advisory Board, and the NYU
Child Study Center Educational Advisory Board.

Ellen Birnbaum has been at the 92nd Street Y Nursery
School since 1981, first as a teacher, for ten years as
camp director, and as the associate director since 1997.

www.practicalwisdomforparents.com

PRACTICAL WISDOM

for PARENTS

Raising Self-Confident Children in the Preschool Years

NANCY SCHULMAN • ELLEN BIRNBAUM

Vintage Books
A Division of Random House, Inc.
New York

FIRST VINTAGE BOOKS EDITION, MAY 2008

Copyright © 2007 by Nancy Schulman and Ellen Birnbaum

All rights reserved. Published in the United States by Vintage Books, a division of Random House, Inc., New York, and in Canada by Random House of Canada Limited, Toronto. Originally published in hardcover as *Practical Wisdom for Parents: Demystifying the Preschool Years* in the United States by Alfred A. Knopf, a division of Random House, Inc., New York, in 2007.

Vintage and colophon are registered trademarks of Random House, Inc.

The Library of Congress has cataloged the Knopf edition as follows:
Schulman, Nancy.
Practical wisdom for parents / by Nancy Schulman and Ellen Birnbaum.—1st ed.
p. cm.
Includes index.
1. Parenting. 2. Parent and child. 3. Preschool children. I. Birnbaum, Ellen, 1949–
II. Title.
HQ769.S3355 2007
649'.123—dc22
2007006349

Vintage ISBN: 978-0-307-27538-7

Author photograph © Elena Seibert
Book design by M. Kristen Bearse

www.vintagebooks.com

147468846

TO OUR PARENTS

MARILYN AND ARTHUR MOTZKIN,
EVELYN AND ABE GREENBERG,

WITH OUR PROFOUND LOVE, RESPECT, AND GRATITUDE

Contents

Contents

Part Two **HOME**

Contents

PRACTICAL WISDOM *for* PARENTS

Introduction

When your child was born, your life changed beyond recognition. You became a parent. But this was just the beginning. Parenthood is a job that constantly evolves and presents different challenges with each new phase. When you were the parent of an infant, you were totally absorbed in meeting your child's daily needs from moment to moment. You had to figure out if she was hungry, tired, or wet, or if she wanted to be held or stimulated. Your own needs became completely secondary to this tiny new arrival in your life. When your child grew to be a toddler, your role changed. With her new-found mobility, she began to explore and discover her world, presenting you with a very different set of challenges. She was in constant motion and often in potential danger, needing your supervision at all times.

Now that your child has reached preschool age, your role is changing again. Your energetic toddler has turned into a curious, adventurous, social, assertive, and physical preschooler. She has language to express herself and will tell you exactly what she thinks. She'll begin to deliberately disobey you and needs you to be clear, firm, and consistent so that she can feel safe. For a child at this age, everything is new and needs to be learned—making friends, toilet training, gaining a baby sibling, sharing toys, putting on clothing. As she grows and becomes ready to venture into the new world of school, teachers, and classmates, she'll be experiencing an unprecedented degree of independence. You'll need to take a half step back so that she can take one step forward. You'll constantly have to adjust your expectations for your child and for yourself. This can be an exciting yet mystifying time, requiring you to find your voice as a parent and to make decisions about your child's education for the first time. From now on, the choices you make—who you are and what you say and do—are going to have a profound influence on your child.

Introduction

Like all parents of children this age, we struggled with guiding our children through each new experience and relished the rewards when they reached the next stage. As we write this, our children, Michael and Alissa (Nancy's son and daughter) are twenty-six and twenty-two, and Alice and Charles (Ellen's two) are thirty-one and twenty-six, but our experience of being their parents continues to inform the work that we do. Since 1997, we've worked side by side running the 92nd Street Y Nursery School on the Upper East Side of Manhattan, as its director (Nancy) and associate director (Ellen). Founded in 1938, the nursery school was one of the first early childhood programs in New York City and has since grown to accommodate 175 children and a faculty of thirty-five. Despite its large size, we're happy to say it still retains a feeling of warmth and intimacy, a place where children's imagination, creativity, and intellect is nurtured.

We first met in the spring of 1981, not as educators but as neighbors, in the lobby of the Manhattan apartment building where we both live and where we brought up our families. At the time, Ellen already had a five-year-old daughter, Alice, and was expecting her second child. Nancy was pregnant with her first. We were getting the mail one day when we noticed that we were both pregnant and asked the obvious question: "When are you due?" In June of that year, Ellen gave birth to Charles. The following month, Nancy's son, Michael, arrived. As busy mothers, we didn't meet again until a year later, when the boys were invited to the birthday party of a neighbor's son. It was here that the two of us first got to know each other. Our friendship developed naturally from that point, as it does for so many young mothers, through playdates and our children's friendships.

From the beginning, we took pleasure in sharing the newfound joys and frustrations of parenthood with one another. Often, the early childhood years can be an isolating time for parents, but we were fortunate. As neighbors, we never had to go far when we were feeling uncertain of ourselves or needed to let off steam. Our children were such similar ages, growing up together, going through the same stages of their development. We could count on each other. If one of us doubted our instincts, we could go to the other and talk it through. As we discussed our experiences, we recognized that we came from similar backgrounds and shared a similar approach to child rearing. We'd both grown up in somewhat traditional households where rules and routines were consistent and with parents who were affectionate and firm. Now that we were mothers, we were learning to rely on our parents' brand of common sense, adapting the structure of our own childhoods to suit our needs as working women. We were convinced of the practical wisdom of setting solid expectations for our children. As they grew to be preschool age, we sensed the increased importance of discipline in their young lives. And while we acknowledged the inevitable hard work that came along with parenthood, we also appreciated the fun of it—our children engaged us, made us laugh, allowed us to see the world through fresh eyes. Nearly twenty-five years later, we still look back on this period as one of the happiest in our lives.

At the time that we were bringing up our young families, we were both already working in the field of education. When we first met, Nancy was a teacher and admissions director at the Horace Mann Lower School in New York. After Ellen's son Charles was born, Ellen began teaching part time at the 92nd Street Y Nursery School. When Charles and Nancy's son Michael were old enough, they were enrolled in the school. Alissa, Nancy's youngest, soon followed. In 1990, the year that Alissa was about to graduate and go on to kindergarten, Nancy was offered the nursery school's directorship. Then, in 1997, after seventeen years as head teacher in a prekindergarten classroom and after a decade as director of the nursery school's summer camp, Ellen became associate director, and our daily working partnership began.

From day one of working together as nursery school directors, we were in agreement that our job wasn't only to educate children but also to support families. The early childhood years are a uniquely challenging period in the life of a family, as we'd learned from firsthand experience. We wanted to offer families the kind of basic guidance and support system that we had given each other when our children were young. After all, we could certainly relate to parents' need for reassurance and information during these years. What *is* an appropriate bedtime for children at this age? At what age should children dress themselves? How do you get children to clean up their toys? When and how do you teach manners? What are appropriate expectations for learning? How do you establish rules, consequences, and routines? At no other time in your child's life (with the exception, perhaps, of the teenage years) will you be faced with so much uncharted territory. Even when you have a second or a third child, each child is different and will require you to adjust your expectations and approach.

In the twenty-five-plus years since we've been working in education, what we've seen is that parents of preschoolers continue to deal with the same issues families have always had to deal with: toilet training, bedtime battles, sibling and discipline issues. In this same time period, however, we've watched the pressures that families are facing increase substantially. The pace of family life has become much more frenetic. It's not just parents who are busy; it's the children too. Many parents feel that they must keep their very young children occupied and productive, that it's essential to schedule them in a variety of after-school activities and to expose them to early-learning products, in order to give them the "best possible start in life." Parents often seem unsure of themselves, and in need of guidance, deferring to the experts in order to avoid making mistakes or harming their children in any way. Meanwhile, we've been witnessing behaviors in the classroom that weren't typical ten years ago—children who seem more anxious, less able to accept limits and adult authority, and who become more easily overstimulated. Around the time we began working together we started asking ourselves what had changed. Why were many parents lacking in the essential confidence necessary to be a good parent? Why were the children failing to benefit from the kind of parental care they were receiving? When we spoke to other early childhood educators, we discovered that they were encountering similar issues.

The more we spoke about this with parents and our colleagues, the more we were able to identify three main causes for this change:

- Pressure on parents. In the past decade in particular, great emphasis has been placed on the importance of early learning and development. This has put tremendous pressure on parents, without necessarily always benefiting their children. From the moment a child is born, parents are encouraged to begin the learning process in order to promote academic potential. The prevailing attitude seems to be that if children are given the correct stimulation, if they get into the "right" nursery school, and take multiple after-school activities before the age of five, they'll somehow be on track for a place at an Ivy League school. Many parents feel they must give their children these advantages so that they won't fall behind their peers. We live in a time in which job insecurity is a given and adults need to have multiple skills and qualifications to stay competitive. It's understandable that parents would believe that even their very young children should compete in order to "get ahead." Many parents apply the lessons they've learned in the workplace to family life, only to find that these principles don't translate. Of course, everyone wants the best for his or her child. Every parent wants a child who's stimulated and interested in learning. But by seeking to give their children a head start over others, many parents take on the role of managing children's busy schedules rather than actually spending time with them. Days are programmed tightly and the pressure to be productive has caused increased stress for the whole family, especially for children. We tell parents that quality early childhood school experience is enrichment enough for a young child. At school, we've seen that children who have been overstimulated by too many other activities actually have great difficulty concentrating and doing well in the classroom.

• A rapidly changing world. If parents have begun to feel less confident, then this has been as a natural response to the increased risks and dangers of modern life. In most parts of the country, it's no longer possible to have your child play in the street with other children or walk half a block home from a friend's house. Social circumstances have played an enormous role in undermining parental assurance. In previous generations, women in particular were prepared for the role of parenthood from girlhood. Now men and women are more likely to share the daily tasks of parenting with one another and with caregivers, but without the benefit of guidance or role models from an older generation. Extended families are often fractured, with grandparents, aunts, and uncles living in different parts of the country, so parents don't always have an instant community on which to rely when they're in need of support. Increasingly, schools, playgroups, mommy groups, and online chat rooms are the places where community is created, where parents can seek advice and meet other parents.

• A lack of confidence in parental intuition and authority. It's true that many parents no longer consider themselves to be sufficiently knowledgeable about the job of parenting. It isn't that parents care any less—in most cases, parents are extremely attentive toward their children, placing them at the very center of family life. But even so, many parents seem to have lost faith in their inherent potential to positively guide and influence their child's development. These parents want children to be happy but are finding that this doesn't always translate to a happy home. They tell us they don't want to say "no" to their children because they fear stifling their creativity or damaging their self-esteem. In fact, children need the adults in their lives to be definitive so that they can learn to cope with disappointment, to become resilient, to feel confident in their ability to solve problems for themselves, and to get along well with others. Over the past twenty-five years, however, families have been bombarded with confusing and conflicting information from experts as to how to be a parent. Hundreds of books and articles have been written with the purpose of trying to make the lives of families easier. In fact, much of this expert advice seems to have had the opposite effect—parenting has never seemed more complex. No wonder many parents feel confused. When you're terrified of doing the "wrong thing," of course you won't be able to rely on your own instincts as a parent. It's very easy to lose touch with your intuition and authority when you are being told that if you don't follow a set of rules, you'll be placing your child at a disadvantage or potentially doing her harm.

When we first began working together as nursery school directors, we realized there was a real need to address some of these issues affecting families. We decided to hold regularly scheduled meetings for parents. One of the great advantages of working in a nursery school—rather than an elementary or high school—is that teachers, directors, and parents speak almost daily. In fact, early childhood educators and families must form these kinds of partnerships in order to work together in the best interests of each child. The idea behind the meetings was to create a forum for discussing children's experiences at school and any issues or concerns parents might have at home. We wanted to create a warm and comfortable setting where we could talk about typical development at each age and about the various dynamics we saw occurring within the classrooms. The meetings were grouped by classroom so that parents of children of similar ages could share common concerns. In these meetings, we talked about practical parenting approaches and how to maintain age-appropriate expectations that would be consistent with the school's. More often than not, we found ourselves simply in the position of empowering parents, encouraging them to get in touch with their own instinctive common sense judgments and allowing them to trust in those instincts with a greater degree of confidence. We used our experiences (good and bad) with our own children to help highlight and reinforce what we were discussing. Clearly, these meetings fulfilled a need for parents, and we learned something at every meeting.

When we talk to parents, we remind them that, as a parent, you're at the very center of a young child's universe. You have a natural authority to positively influence her development that no one else possesses. Although parenting is hard work, it's usually much simpler than many parents assume. When you spend time with your child, rather than scheduling her in structured activities, you learn so much about her and about how to be her parent. You can find out what's on her mind, her likes and dislikes, the things that make her happy. You learn what your child really needs. In the rush to the finish line, many parents forget to place enough importance on childhood's simplest pleasures—playing alone or with others, spending time with a parent doing something fun, or creating special family traditions. When children have this time to be with you, to be solitary, and to be with others, they learn, gain confidence, and have time to relax. They enjoy themselves, and all of this is vital to their well-being and ability to function within their families and in the group environment of a classroom. During our meetings, we often ask parents to remember what made them happiest when they were children. They usually answer, "playing with my friends in the park," "creating imaginary worlds on my own," "cooking with my grandma." No one says, "going to violin lessons" or "learning French." We remind parents that the things that are memorable to them are the same things that their own children will take pleasure in, will learn from, and will grow while doing. We continue to encourage parents to schedule fewer activities and to tap into their own power as parents instead.

Although we offer what we can in the way of empowerment and advice, we also use this time to listen. Every parent we encounter has a unique parenting style and is making different choices about how they want to raise their children. But by sharing what works and doesn't work with each other, we soon find out how much everyone has in common. There's nothing more confidence building than the knowledge that the daily struggles of being a mom or dad aren't unique and that everyone comes up against similar difficulties. When you know that every four-year-old is going to be using bathroom words or that your three-and-a-half-year-old will be constantly testing limits, you're less likely to feel like you've done something wrong to make these behaviors happen. By exchanging ideas, parents learn from each other and can trust in their abilities to solve problems in their own way. They discover that there are many different ways to be effective, but the important thing is to find what works and to stick to it. Parents with older children can tell an anxious first-time parent, "Don't worry, I've been there; your child will grow out of it" and give practical suggestions for getting through the particular phase. In the communal environment of the meetings, parents begin to realize that this is about their children's development and not about their own ability or inability to do a good job as a parent. In this setting, everyone can laugh about their own failings. Time and again, we come back to the idea that parenthood is a humbling experience and that we have to give up the whole notion of parenting "perfectly."

By nurturing and supporting parents, we've seen that the whole family benefits. What's more, we can actually see results in the classrooms. We notice, for example, that children whose parents set clear limits are more able to accept direction from their teachers. Children who have regular bedtime routines and who are scheduled in fewer activities after school are happier and have more energy. When parents spend time teaching children to be more independent by showing them how to put on their own coats or put their toys away, these children are able to acclimate more successfully to classroom expectations.

In the ten years of holding these meetings, it's been a privilege to work with so many parents and to learn from them. Many suggestions from parents in our groups have found their way into this book—practical, useful, tried and tested tips from moms and dads who've been there. This advice is offered in the spirit of sharing rather than of expertise. What expertise we have comes purely from the experience of working with children, parents, and teachers. We aren't psychologists or doctors. Instead, we've seen firsthand what works for children and we've listened to the concerns of teachers and parents. We don't espouse a particular philosophy or theory, but our approach is practical and grounded in an understanding of what children really need and how the adults in their lives can best support those needs. From our fifty-nine years of combined experience of observing, listening, and learning from our own children and the teachers with whom we've worked, as well as the thousands of children and parents at school, there are a few things we know for sure.

The children we know who are confident and feel socially and intellectually competent are the children whose parents support them by:

- Loving them unconditionally.

- Setting limits and expectations for behavior.

- Establishing clear daily routines.

- Fostering healthy separation.

- Encouraging independence and age-appropriate self-help skills.

- Sharing regular family meals.

- Allowing children to experience frustration and to cope with disappointment.

- Helping children to problem solve and become resilient.

- Teaching respect for others, the difference between right and wrong, and the importance of taking responsibility for actions.

- Insisting on basic manners such as saying please and thank you.

- Thinking about the family as a team.

- Understanding that *all* of a child's developing skills are important, not just academic skills.

- Setting aside unstructured family time.

- Giving children the time and space to play.

- Limiting after-school activities.

- Understanding that although school is important, home is the most important of all.

- Accepting each child's unique qualities.

- Being a good role model.

- Having fun, maintaining a sense of humor, and knowing that there's no such thing as the perfect parent.

Everything you'll find in this book stems from this core of knowledge.

This book isn't meant to be read from cover to cover but to serve as a resource as and when you need it. We've organized this book into two sections, "School" and "Home," because we firmly believe that when parents and teachers work together—and when expectations are consistent at school and at home—children are given the best opportunity to grow and thrive. For clarity's sake, teachers and caregivers in this book are always referred to using the pronoun, "she." To be fair, children in this book are referred to as "he" and "she" in alternate chapters. The 92nd Street Y Nursery School is referred to as "the nursery school." Although we speak about many children in the nursery school in the course of the book, their names have been changed and many of the stories have been adapted in order to illustrate our points.

Our hope is that parents can read this book and benefit from the practical wisdom it contains. You may decide to use some of our advice and discard other elements of it. Feel free. You are your child's first teacher and her most influential role model. The ages from three to five are a magical time for establishing the foundation of intellectual, social, and emotional growth in a child. But there's no magic to understanding what children need and what parents can do to support this growth. You don't need any special training to do this. You don't need to enroll your children in extra classes in order to give them this advantage in life. You don't need your two-year-old to get into the "right" school. In truth, the two most important things you can do from the list above are *love your children unconditionally* and *set limits for them.* We believe every parent can do this, but you don't have to do this alone. Family, friends, teachers, and anyone you trust can be there with you in the ongoing, ever-changing adventure of parenting.

Part One

SCHOOL

Chapter One

CHOOSING AN EARLY CHILDHOOD PROGRAM

Frrom the moment your child began to walk or even before that time, you've probably been hearing playground chatter from parents about preschools in your area. If you're coming to this experience for the first time, it can feel as if you're being introduced to a whole new language: "sibling places," "traditional versus progressive approaches," "cutoff dates," "competition for places," "applications," and perhaps most perplexing of all, "child interviews." It's guaranteed that everyone you meet will have an opinion on this subject, usually based on something that they've heard from someone else. But even if other parents seem well informed, it's likely that they're feeling just as confused. As a new parent, you probably have very little knowledge about preschool, and it's only natural to ask questions: What exactly do you need to know about a school before considering sending your child there? How do schools differ? What are their educational philosophies and what do they mean? How do you identify a quality program?

It wasn't always this complicated. When we were growing up during the 1950s, it was rare for children to attend nursery school. In those days, many mothers (ours included) were stay-at-home moms, and, as a result, there simply wasn't the need or desire to send children to school at very young ages. In general, childhood was a much less hurried affair, without the pressure to "get ahead" that we've come to associate with modern family life. The assumption was that five years old was the appropriate age for children to have a first school experience and kindergarten would provide children with the skills they needed to transition from home to school.

By the time Ellen's eldest child, Alice, was nearing the age of three in the late 1970s, however, the situation had already begun to change. By then, it was much more common for families to send their children to school before kindergarten, beginning at age three. This shift had occurred for a number of reasons. Many more mothers were working outside the home, and parents wanted to know that their children would be spending time in a stimulating, sociable environment rather than staying at home all day with the babysitter. Research into children's early brain development had revealed the potential that exists for learning during the first five years of life, and parents felt they should capitalize on this if they wanted their children to develop to their full potential. Although a nursery school movement had been in existence since the early 1900s, by the late 1970s, many more early childhood programs were springing up, especially in urban areas. For Ellen, the process of enrolling Alice in school was remarkably easy: She looked around the neighborhood, identified a program that she liked, and had an informal meeting with the director. After a brief chat, the director asked Ellen if she wanted to enroll Alice for the mornings or the afternoons. It was as simple as that—no applications, school tours, or interviews needed.

Four years later, when Nancy's eldest child, Michael, was nearing the age of two, the situation had already begun to change. By then, many preschools in New York City had started toddler programs in response to pressure from families who wanted to send their children to school before the age of three. As a result, Michael would be able to attend school two months after his second birthday. The growing popularity of such programs also meant that there was now a formal application process, and Nancy's son would have to undergo an "interview" before being enrolled. Michael was eighteen months old when he went on his very first interview, the winter before he would attend school. Needless to say, the prospect made Nancy incredibly nervous. Even though it seemed absurd that a one-and-a-half-year-old was going to be judged in any way, Nancy still wanted the teachers and director to think that Michael was the perfect candidate for a school, in fact, that her child was perfect, period.

On the day of the interview, Nancy dutifully woke Michael from his nap in order to arrive at the school on time, thereby also ensuring that her son was cranky. When they got to the school, Nancy and Michael were escorted to a classroom where teachers and the school director were observing a group of children at play. The minute they walked into the classroom, Michael spotted a rabbit cage with a carrot sticking out of it. Michael, who loved carrots, immediately grabbed the half-gnawed vegetable and went to put it in his mouth. Nancy said, "No, sweetie, that's for the bunny." But when Michael started to whine, she panicked. Rather than have her son cry at his very first interview, Nancy let him have the carrot. She was actually more concerned about Michael doing well in the interview than she was about him catching a disease from a rabbit.

Choosing an Early Childhood Program

Each year, when Nancy tells this story to parents who are applying to send their children to the nursery school at the 92nd Street Y, there's always plenty of sympathetic laughter. Twenty-five years after Michael attended preschool, the competition for places at quality early childhood programs in New York City has increased tenfold. Demand has long since exceeded the number of spaces available, with the result that many popular schools have a ratio of ten applicants to every available place. Many parents no longer see preschool as a good opportunity for their children; they see it as an absolute necessity. And it's not just New York. In many urban areas, the high-pressure preschool admissions process has become legendary, with parents signing up for programs the minute a child is born. Preschool enrollment is no longer the straightforward affair it was when Ellen enrolled Alice after a chat with the director.

In the twenty-five years since we began working in early childhood education, this atmosphere of competitiveness is one of the most significant changes we've witnessed in the lives of families with young children. Since the days when our children were preschoolers, more and more emphasis has been placed on the brain development of infants and toddlers so that there's now an entire industry marketing educational products and programs to families. The positive side of all this emphasis on early learning has been the emergence of a wide range of high-quality educational programs that serve young children very well. Preschool teachers today tend to be highly trained, and there are national organizations that promote their professional development. The downside is that parents feel they must keep up if they are going to give their children the "best possible start in life" and fulfill their obligations as parents. It's not unusual for perfectly well-meaning parents to send us two-page résumés for their two-year-olds with a list of classes they've already taken. Although it's true that classes for infants and toddlers can be fun and stimulating, we believe that too many programmed activities without a balance of time to simply play and explore does not make a child better prepared for learning.

These days, so much importance gets placed on where your child goes to school that it's easy to lose perspective as to how your child is benefiting. For many parents, the whole process of applying to preschool can become agonizing. Competition for limited places can make you feel anxious, judged, frustrated, and unable to control the outcome when all you want is the best for your child. If you are already feeling a little overwhelmed, it can help to remember that your child will likely benefit from a school experience in many different settings. Core learning experiences such as socializing with other children and learning to follow a teacher's instructions will be the same wherever your child begins school. While it's very important that you look carefully and thoughtfully at the schools in your area, always remember that you are the most influential factor in your child's growth and development. A quality early childhood program can enhance your child's experience, but it can only do so much.

A quality early childhood program *can*:

- Provide your child with a safe and happy place to spend time in where everything is child sized, where the pace and tone is childcentered, and where there are stimulating and interesting things to learn, and friends to make.

- Help your child to take the first steps toward independence—learn how to separate from you, how to be part of a group, how to play cooperatively, how to listen, and how to take direction from a teacher.

- Help your child acquire the skills and confidence needed to be prepared for the next stages of learning.

A quality early childhood program *can't*:

- Guarantee your child success later in life.

- Replace the importance of your involvement in your child's life.

- Be a substitute for simply spending time with your child.

Beginning the Process

• When Should My Child Start School? •

If you are thinking about sending your child to preschool, you may be wondering at which age your child should start. Most early childhood programs offer parents a choice. With preschool, this is an important consideration. Of course, day care is another matter—many parents choose day care as child care for their children from infancy onward, and age doesn't need to be a factor in this decision. When it comes to preschool, however, we believe that parents should send a child only when that child is able to take full advantage of a school experience. The right age varies from child to child. Some two-year-olds are able to express themselves verbally, enjoy new experiences, and are comfortable with unfamiliar adults. Other children need more time to develop before they'll be ready. If a child isn't ready yet, this doesn't mean he's less advanced than other children or that he's going to fall behind. It simply means that he'll be ready to benefit from school when he's older.

For most children, three is the natural age of readiness. Children of this age are curious about their peers and the world around them and have enough facility with language to communicate with their teachers and classmates. In hindsight, Nancy can see that her son, Michael, really wasn't ready to attend school at the age of two. Although he had good language skills, he wasn't particularly interested in interacting with a group of children. By the time he was three, he was more intrigued by his classmates and more interested in experiencing what the school had to offer. At this age, children are also better able to understand the concept that parents come back at the end of the school day. A three-year-old will be able to imagine you at work or home, shopping, or being with the baby; he can retain a mental picture of you while you're away from him, and this will help him to handle the separation.

Although three is an ideal age for most children to begin school, the practical reality is that in areas where preschool places are limited, many parents feel the pressure to send a child to school at age two, rather than waiting until he's older when there may be fewer places available. If you do live in an area where there is competition for places, this is going to be a consideration. However, it's very important to balance considerations about your child's future against what he needs now. Remember that in order for him to have a positive first experience at school, he must have enough language to communicate his needs and feelings to teachers and he must be able to separate from you. If your child has difficulty making himself understood, if you've never left your child with a babysitter or relative, or if he regularly shows signs of distress when you leave him, you may decide to put off school for another year. Two-year-old programs are not a prerequisite for attending school at age three.

Practical Wisdom for Parents

In our years of working in early childhood education, we've observed that many children under the age of two and a half are not yet ready for a meaningful school experience. For example, Andrew, who began school at the age of two and three months, really wasn't ready and struggled throughout his first year. At this age, Andrew was too young to communicate his needs to the teacher. Instead, he either dissolved in tears or hit the other children in frustration. He was inconsolable when his mother left in the morning because his lack of language ability made it difficult for him to adequately express his needs to his teachers. This did not make for a happy beginning to school for Andrew, his parents, the teachers, or the other children in the class. Over time, with the teachers' support and his mother's help, Andrew's ability to cope with frustration and to communicate improved. He was able to tolerate being at school, but he wasn't able to enjoy the experience and neither was his mother. Andrew wasn't the only very young child we had watched struggle in this way. Since Andrew attended the nursery school, we've changed the age for the youngest children in the school to two years and six months.

Rather than sending a child to school before he's ready, you can always choose to wait a year and enroll him in other programs instead. Most communities have classes appropriate for two-year-old children. "Mommy and me" gym, music, art, and cooking classes are good alternatives. In this environment, your child can be introduced to social experiences with you or his caregiver in attendance, and you can meet other parents with children the same age. In truth, you shouldn't even feel compelled to sign your child up for classes. Two-year-old children thrive on one-on-one attention. Being at home with Mom, Dad, or a caregiver is just fine at this age. Informal playgroups with other parents and children are another good idea.

Above all, know your child and respond to his needs and the needs of your family. It may be hard to do this when all of your friends and neighbors are making other choices, and you feel the pressure to keep up. But if you keep your focus on your child, we're certain he'll benefit and so will you.

• When Should I Start Looking? •

While it's essential that you learn about the appropriate times to apply to the schools in your area so that you don't miss any deadlines, there's rarely a need to call the school minutes after your baby is born. In some cities, parents are encouraged to apply months before school begins; in other places, you can sign up the week before school starts. A good rule of thumb is that you should probably start finding out about schools a year before your child is old enough to attend. Before this, you are not going to have enough knowledge of your child and his needs to be able to make decisions about where he goes to school.

• How Do I Find Out About Schools? •

You know that you want the best for your child and instinctively feel that preschool is a good idea. But where do you begin? If you live in a big city, you'll have many early childhood programs to choose from. If you live in a small town, your choices will be more limited. When possible, location should be your first consideration. Start by looking at schools that are close to your home or place of work. There are good reasons to do this. A long commute by car or public transportation every morning adds an unnecessary burden for parents and children alike. If you have to rush to leave home early, you're only increasing your family's stress levels and creating a bumpy beginning to the day. If you have to travel forty-five minutes each way for a three-hour program, you'll end up in the car or on the bus almost as long as your child is in school. You'll want to arrange playdates, but other families may be reluctant to travel out of the neighborhood. In other words, location is key.

If you're a member of a religious or community organization, you may want to start by looking at its program if it has one. Some businesses offer day care or can refer you to local programs. In some states or cities, public schools offer an optional prekindergarten program for four-year-olds, and you may want to consider these. You can also check to see if the various schools in your area are accredited. Accreditation means a school has volunteered to be rigorously evaluated by an outside organization. The National Association for the Education of Young Children is the largest of these and offers a thorough accreditation process. You can check their Web site (www.naeyc.org) for accredited programs in your area.

Tuition fees will be another consideration. Most early childhood programs charge tuition. Costs will vary from school to school, so it's important to find out how much each school charges for tuition and if there are any additional fees. Some schools will offer financial aid to qualified families—usually a partial grant based on need. You'll have to furnish the school with some form of financial statement to be considered. Schools may also have payment plans that allow you to pay on a monthly basis.

Friends and family members whose children have recently attended a program can be good sources of information when you are beginning to look for schools. However, you must see the program for yourself and make your own judgments in each instance. Sometimes people will have strong opinions about a particular school, but if you question them further, you'll find they have no firsthand experience of that program. Perhaps the school wasn't a good fit for their family. This doesn't mean that the school isn't right for you. It's important to filter the information you receive from these "experts" and visit schools to see for yourself. The opinions of others, while heartfelt, can be confusing. Only you will know for certain what's the best environment for your child.

Looking for Schools

• How Schools Differ •

As you begin to look at the schools in your area, you'll hear many different terms and labels used to describe them. Programs may be referred to as nursery school, preschool, day care, or prekindergarten (pre-K). Many operate out of community centers or are affiliated with a religious organization. Just because a program is housed in a religious building, however, doesn't necessarily mean the school has a religious orientation. Many religious institutions simply provide the space for early childhood programs. Some public schools have programs for four-year-olds that are usually a half day, although this will vary from state to state.

Each school will have its own educational philosophy. Some schools will use a combination of philosophies—for example, some of a school's educational methods may be grounded in a "developmental" approach, but the way the children's day is structured may reflect a more "traditional" approach. Every school is unique. Even when a school has a specific label such as "Montessori," "progressive," or "traditional," practices can still vary between individual schools. The culture and atmosphere of each school is always going to be influenced by the current administration and the teaching staff.

We believe that early childhood programs come in many shapes and sizes and that there are many different ways to educate young children well. Different schools may suit different children. Alice, Ellen's eldest child, attended a smaller, more traditional school that suited her quiet nature and her comfort with order and structure. Charles, five years younger, was a very physical child and attended a school that was bigger, busier, with more outdoor space where he could enjoy the stimulation of the larger class sizes and greater number of activities. In our opinion, there is no "right" philosophy or type of school. The most important thing is that you see the program for yourself and assess whether or not it seems to be a comfortable fit for your child and family.

All of the elements that make for excellence can be found in all of these kinds of programs:

• Day care

Day-care programs are usually full day (from early morning to evening) and often have infant care as well. These programs generally run year-round. They may use a variety of teaching methods. Day-care programs may be nonprofit, proprietary, or run by a company as a service to employees.

• Head Start

Head Start is a federally funded comprehensive child development program that began in 1965 for preschool-age children and their families. The programs are child focused and have the overall goal of increasing school readiness for children of low-income families. Programs reflect the ethnic, cultural, and linguistic backgrounds of the families they serve.

• Montessori

Founded in 1907, Montessori schools are based on the educational philosophy of Dr. Maria Montessori, and teachers are trained in her methods. Dr. Montessori espoused that children learn best when they work at their own pace in multiage groups. Children challenge themselves through interactive experiences and become active learners in their own educational process. In a Montessori school, children choose from a variety of activities in a "prepared environment." Typically, you'll see children working on specific tasks using specially designed materials such as blocks or balance scales in a prescribed way.

Practical Wisdom for Parents

Children don't move on to a new activity until they have completed the task and a teacher has observed their work. In the most traditional Montessori schools, you may not see materials such as sand and water or dress-up clothes. Children work individually, with opportunities to socialize during meals and outdoor play. Children learn to take care of themselves and others by cooking, cleaning, gardening, or by participating in other community activities. Although Montessori programs can vary from school to school, most belong to one of the major Montessori organizations such as the Association Montessori Internationale (AMI) or the American Montessori Society (AMS).

• Cooperative

Cooperative schools require parents to participate in classrooms by assisting teachers, usually on a rotating basis. Parents may serve on school committees and have a strong voice in the running of the school. Educational philosophies differ from school to school.

• Developmental

Developmental schools are sometimes referred to as "progressive" or "Bank Street approach," named after the Bank Street College of Education. Established in 1916, Bank Street promoted innovative educational models of teaching using the theories of psychologists and educators such as Jean Piaget and John Dewey. In a progressive classroom, the approach is "child centered," and the children are generally grouped by age. Play and social interaction are emphasized, and the classroom is organized into different centers for learning. Open-ended materials such as sand, water, blocks, and art materials are used. Creativity is valued, and children are encouraged to explore materials and express their ideas and feelings through fantasy play and art. The teacher's role is more of a facilitator than an instructor, and the children's interests are the basis for the curriculum. Developmental classrooms are busy, noisy, and interactive environments with children's artwork displayed on the walls. The tone is usually informal, and teachers may be called by their first names.

• Traditional

Traditional schools have a more teacher-directed approach with programs that are clearly structured. The curriculum is planned for teaching basic skills such as shapes, colors, letters, and numbers. Many open-ended materials are used such as blocks, sand and water, and art materials, but worksheets and projects planned by the teacher may also be used. Teachers organize the day according to a specific schedule, and children meet with their teachers in groups to discuss the plans for the day or the curriculum themes. At a traditional school, there is usually group time, snack time, and outdoor time, as well as time scheduled for early academic skills such as writing and math. Children are encouraged to raise their hands at circle times, and the classroom tone is often quiet. Transitions from activity to activity are clearly defined, and teachers are usually addressed using last names.

All high-quality early childhood programs should have certain basic elements:

- A license from state or local agencies.

- A clean, safe, well-equipped environment.

- Teachers trained in early childhood education.

- Adequate indoor and outdoor space. Minimum standards set by the National Association for the Education of Young Children (NAEYC) are as follows: Indoor space thirty-five square feet per child and outdoor space seventy-five square feet per child.

- Staff with a high ratio of adults to children. The staff-child ratios recommended by the NAEYC are as follows: two-and-a-half-year-olds, 1:5; three-year-olds, 1:7; and four- and five-year-olds, 1:8.

• Choosing Which Schools to Visit •

As you begin to look around at the schools in your area, it's helpful to make some initial inquiries about how a school defines itself through its practices and policies before you arrange a visit. Many schools have brochures and written material, and many have Web sites. Although a school's educational philosophy will be an important consideration, there are also more practical matters to bear in mind. For example, if you have a busy work schedule, you may decide not to consider a school that requires you to participate in activities with children on fixed days. If you have an older child at another school, you may decide to send your younger child somewhere nearby in order to avoid a commute between the two schools.

When you're looking for a program, here are some things you can think about and observe of each school:

- What is the school's educational style?

- What is a typical day like?

- What are the hours? Is there an early drop-off or an extended day?

- How are the children grouped (by age, mixed ages, developmentally)? We believe there's no right or wrong grouping, just one that you and the school feel will be a good fit for your child.

- What is the school's separation policy? Is it gradual or more rapid? Are parents expected to stay or to leave quickly?

- How does the school handle discipline?

- Will your child be participating in group activities?

- How does the school deal with learning differences or special needs?

- Is there a religious component to the school?

- What kind of diversity does the school have?

- What is the length of the school year and vacation schedule?

- What is the geographical range of the children attending?

- Is there a bus service?

- Is there a sibling policy?

- Is there an option for children to have an additional prekindergarten year if necessary? (Many schools require children to be five or to turn five before the end of December to be able to enter kindergarten. If this is the case and your child has a fall birthday, you may find he doesn't meet the age cutoff and needs to stay for an additional pre-K year. It's good to know in advance if preschools can accommodate this.)

- Which schools do children go on to attend?*

*Many parents are concerned that if they don't get a child into a particular preschool it will diminish the child's chances of acceptance at a private school kindergarten. This may have been the case twenty years ago; however, schools have since changed their admission policies. These days, private schools are looking for a diverse student body, and there's no guarantee that one school automatically leads to another. In fact, we've heard admissions directors boast that students in their kindergarten come from as many as twenty-five preschools.

- How do parents involve themselves in the program?

- How are the schedules of working parents accommodated?

- What is the admissions process (first-come, interviews, affiliations to a religious or community organization)?

- What are the tuition fees? Are there additional fees? How do the fees change according to the length of the day?

- Does the school offer financial aid?

• Visiting Schools •

There's only one way to know if an early childhood program is of high quality—see it for yourself. Relatives, friends, park bench gossip, online chat groups, advertisements, or brochures will only tell you so much. You need to experience the school and speak to the people who work there before you can pass judgment. Most schools have special days when parents can tour. It's important to assess each school on its individual merits and to get a sense of its specific practices and policies. Remember that your background, values, expectations, and knowledge of your child are all going to influence your preferences (and prejudices).

When visiting schools, here are some questions you can ask yourself that will help you to define high quality:

Physical Space and Materials

- Are the classrooms clean and well lit with enough space for each child?

- Is the classroom well organized with furniture in good repair?

- Are the sinks and toilets easily accessible for children?

- Are the materials neatly organized and accessible to children?

- Do you see blocks, books, toys, and art materials? Are there science areas, areas for sand and water play, dramatic play areas, and soft elements as well as places for quiet activity?

- Is there a variety of children's artwork displayed on bulletin boards?

- Are there carpeted areas?

- Is there space for children to keep their personal belongings?

Practical Wisdom for Parents

- Does the outdoor area offer equipment for climbing, riding, balancing, and individual play?

- Are outdoor areas protected by fences?

- Is there a safety surface such as rubber matting or wood chips under the climbing equipment?

- Are there balls and other props for physical play?

Children and Activities

- Do the children in class look happy and involved?

- Do the children seem busy and purposeful?

- Is there a comfortable noise level in the classroom? Ideally, there should be a busy hum, but the levels shouldn't be so noisy that children can't converse quietly.

- Is there a balance of child- and teacher-directed activity?

- Are there alternating periods of quiet and active play?

- Are there times for individual, small-group, and large-group activities?

- Are routines well established with smooth transitions from one activity to another?

- Are there opportunities for children to use materials in ways that aren't teacher directed?

- Do children have a daily outdoor activity?

- Does the program offer music and movement enrichment activities?

- Do the activities offer children opportunities to develop language and social skills, math, science, physical movement, and drawing, and opportunities to work with manipulative toys such as puzzles, pegs, or Legos?

- Are children expected to respect the adults, the other children, and the school's property?

- Are children encouraged to express themselves creatively?

Teachers and Administrative Staff

- Do the teachers seem warm and friendly in their interactions with the children?

- Are the teachers smiling and speaking with children at eye level?

- Do the teachers listen and talk in an engaging tone with children?

- Does the director seem like a person with whom you would be comfortable communicating?

- Is the administrative staff helpful, organized, and responsive?

- What are the qualifications of the teachers? Are they certified in early childhood education?

- How long have the teachers been working in the school?

- Is there little or high staff turnover?

- Does the staff meet regularly to learn about and reflect on the program?

- Do the teachers communicate on a regular basis with parents? How often and in what form?

- Do teachers take into account the varying ages, levels, and abilities of individual children in planning their programs?

Parent Communication

- How does the school interact with families? How often are conferences scheduled and how do parents reach the teacher or director with questions or concerns?

- Is written information about the school given to new families?

- Does the school have a parent handbook defining its policies?

- Is there a written curriculum or description of what children do during the day with details of the program's educational philosophy?

- Is there a bulletin board with information for parents?

- Are parents welcome to visit and/or participate in class activities?

- Does the school refer parents to community resources (physical or mental health and social services) when necessary?

- Is the privacy of each family respected?

- Is the school respectful of cultural differences? Does the school welcome families of varied backgrounds? Does it celebrate different religious holidays? Do materials such as books, dolls, or posters reflect diverse cultures and ethnicities?

Health and Safety

- Does the school maintain medical records and emergency information for each child?

- Are the teachers aware of health and safety issues for the children in their class?

- Is there a plan for children with severe allergies?

- Is there a clearly defined emergency plan for medical emergencies, fire, and evacuation?

- Are emergency phone numbers prominently posted by telephones?

- Does the school have a clear policy for dealing with children's illnesses and attendance?

- Is there a system set up for daily arrivals and dismissals?

- Are children supervised at all times? How are field trips supervised?

- Who in the school is trained in pediatric first aid and emergency CPR?

- Are vehicles used by the program appropriately licensed and inspected?

- Are there signs posted in the bathrooms reminding children and adults to wash hands?

- Does the program require a change of clothes for each child?

- Are snack and meals nutritious and varied? How is food stored and refrigerated?

- Is there a rest time for children in full-day programs? Does each child have an individual cot or mat for resting?

A word to the wise: If you ask every one of these questions of a school administrator, you may run the risk of coming across as an overly aggressive parent. Instead, you can pick the issues and questions that are most relevant to you and your child.

The Application Process

The number of schools to which you decide to apply will depend on the availability of spaces in your area. Many schools give priority to siblings or, in the case of religious schools, to members of the congregation. If you already have an affiliation with a school, the chances are your child will be accepted and you may not need to apply to many schools. If you live in an area where there are many more applicants than there are spaces, you'll have to consider applying to a larger number of schools to ensure your child receives a place.

Once you have determined which schools you'd like to consider, you should inquire as to the specific admissions procedures for each program and whether your child's birthday meets their age requirements. These will vary from school to school. For example, a program might require that a child be two years old by March 31 of the year he's admitted.

Some schools send applications in the mail, some make appointments for you to visit, some have a lottery system, and some have applications available online. You'll need to fill out the application completely and send it back by the deadline. Only send what's asked for. A three-page résumé of your two-year-old's "accomplishments" will only be a turnoff to a school director. If a school requests references, these should only be from people who know your child and family well. It's helpful to be honest, sincere, and descriptive when writing about your child. Schools will use this information to better understand your child and family. If your child has any health issues or special needs, a school can best serve your family when these needs are known from the start, so don't be tempted to conceal them to give your child a "better chance" or expect that the school will be able to accommodate these needs later on.

• Parent "Interviews" •

During the application process, many schools will want to meet with parents either individually or in groups. If possible, it's best that both parents attend the meeting. This is an opportunity for the school to get to know you and for you to learn about the school's program and educational philosophy. Sometimes this "interview" is not an interview at all but an information session with an opportunity to see the school. Even if you do find yourself in a more formal question-and-answer session, this is the time for you to determine whether the school would be a good fit for your child and family. It's a chance to meet some of the school's administrators and to get a sense of the tone and atmosphere of the program.

Many parents feel nervous about these school visits, so it can help to know what to expect. Topics that will probably come up include separation, toilet training, and discipline. Some schools may want to know more about you, and others may put the focus on finding out about your child. If you have questions about the school, now is the time to ask. If you want to know about the school's policy on discipline, then ask. We always like it when parents are open and honest about their concerns. Your questions will help directors and teachers to know you and to have a better understanding of your family. We welcome questions about the teachers, their qualifications, and how long they've been at the school. Like most school directors, we're proud of the faculty and enjoy talking about the teachers. In general, we appreciate those parents who are curious about the school, as opposed to those who are so fearful of being judged that they forget to ask questions or voice their concerns.

Although it's good to be vocal, if you bring a clipboard with a laundry list of questions, this may be interpreted as over the top. It's also helpful to inquire about the school in a nonconfrontational tone. Be mindful not to ask questions that sound critical. Instead of saying, "Why don't you have the alphabet up in this classroom?" you could ask, "Do you introduce the children to letters?" Be aware of your body language. If you're worried about getting to a work meeting on time and you keep checking your watch, this may be interpreted as disinterest. Parents who smile, make eye contact, and show genuine interest always make a great impression.

• Child "Interviews" •

Many schools like to meet the children who are applying either individually or in small groups. When talking about children under the age of three, this could hardly be called an "interview," although the term is often used, especially by parents. We prefer the term "visit" or "playgroup." Although these visits are often a cause for anxiety on the part of parents, in fact, they will have been arranged so that your child will feel comfortable. The school will be looking for readiness and temperament, not to conduct an IQ test. The classroom will be set up to engage your child in play, and the teachers will be warm and encouraging. Parents often ask what they should tell their child before a visit in order to prepare them for the experience. We suggest that you find out the school's procedure beforehand so that you can let your child know what to expect. Then you can tell your child, "We are going to visit a school with fun toys and nice teachers who will play with you."

Most schools set up a thirty- to forty-minute playgroup where children interact with materials such as play dough, puzzles, cars, paper, and crayons. The children may have a snack or hear a story read by a teacher. With very young children, parents usually remain in the classroom. You may ask yourself what anyone could possibly learn about a two-year-old in a thirty-minute visit. In fact, there's a great deal that can be observed in a short time period. Teachers and directors know that they can't possibly learn everything about your child, but there are qualities that they look for that can help them determine whether a child seems ready for school.

During a visit, teachers and directors may look at your child's:

- Language development

- Large and small motor development

- Ability to follow directions

- Interaction with toys and materials

- Focus and attention span

- Interaction with teachers

- Interaction with other children

- Interaction with you

- Ability to transition from one activity to another

- Ability to sit at a table for snack or listen to a story

- Temperament (Is your child active or quiet? outgoing or reserved?)

Of course every parent wants his or her child to shine and be at his best during a school visit. As a parent, however, you know that on any given day or any given moment your two-year-old can go from being charming, cooperative, and talkative to whiny, cranky, and withdrawn. Often, there's little you can do to control your child's mood. However, if you appear relaxed and encouraging with a friendly demeanor, your child will take his cues from you and warm up after a short time. The teacher will help. Early childhood educators have seen every kind of behavior a child can demonstrate (crying, whining, grabbing, reluctance to enter the room) and know that most children's tears will turn to smiles with some distraction.

If a teacher is trying to engage your child in conversation and asks him, "What color are your shoes?" you should refrain from nervously providing the answer. When you ask your child to perform—"Can you spell your name for the nice lady?"—this interferes with the teacher's interaction and makes you look like an overbearing parent. The parent who can support and help a child become engaged in an activity makes a better impression.

It's true that many parents are so aware of being observed by the school that they forget to make some observations of their own. Remember, this is your opportunity to see firsthand the way in which teachers and administrators work with children and parents. Does the visit seem well planned? Are the teachers warm and welcoming? Is the focus on the children? All these factors can help you to make your final decisions about which school you would like your child to attend. If your child is not behaving in a typical manner and when you get home you discover he has a fever of 102 degrees, then you should let the school know.

Decisions

After you have visited all the schools on your list and completed the admissions process, all you can do is wait to hear if your child has been offered a place. This can make many parents extremely anxious. However, it's important to keep an open mind. If you've set your heart on a particular school, you may be overlooking some other wonderful options. Be aware that children thrive in lots of different settings and that there are many schools that would likely serve your child well.

A few months after the application process has been completed, schools will usually send out letters indicating if your child has been accepted or not, or if he's been placed on a wait list. If your child has been placed on a wait list, you should call the school to indicate your interest in remaining on the list should a spot open up. If your child has been offered a place at a school that you are not interested in, then it's important that you let the school know you are not accepting the place. This way other families waiting for that place can be considered.

For most parents, this is the first time that they feel their child—and by extension, their parenting—is being judged. If a school cannot accommodate your child, try not to take the decision too personally. It's only natural to be disappointed and even to feel as if you have somehow failed your child. Please reassure yourself that this isn't a rejection, even if it feels that way. Many factors have played into the decision. In most schools, spaces are limited, and it would be impossible to offer places to every eligible child and family. The school may have licensing requirements that restrict the number of children allowed in a classroom—these requirements are usually determined by the age of the child and the size of the available classroom space. Schools usually have admissions policies that give priority to siblings or to members of the religious organization with which they're affiliated. The school will want to create balanced classes made up of equal numbers of girls and boys, with children of different temperaments and appropriate ages. For example, the class dynamic would be affected if the classroom was only filled with exuberant, physically active children. When a school makes a decision, it's usually as much about the *whole group* as it is about the individual child. If your child isn't accepted by your favorite school, take heart. A year later, most parents find they are very satisfied with the school their child attends when they see that their child is thriving and happy there.

If you have the good fortune to be offered places at several schools, you may want to go back to visit them again. This is a time to ask more specific questions. There's usually no right or wrong decision in this situation, but you should trust your instincts and follow your gut feeling. If your child has not been accepted at the schools to which you applied, you can consider waiting until the following year. Schools often have places that become available if families move unexpectedly, so you should check with the school periodically. You can also call schools you haven't considered before. If you decide to wait a year, there are many art, gym, or music classes for young children that will allow your child to have a social experience and to learn in the process.

In any eventuality, remember there is no such thing as the perfect school. No matter where your child is accepted or when he attends, it's vital that you enthusiastically embrace the experience as your family becomes part of this new community. The most important thing is that your child senses that you are confident and excited for him to take this first step in a lifetime of learning.

Chapter Two

WHAT IS PRESCHOOL?
Orienting Yourself and Your Child

Once you've found an early childhood program that you're happy with and your child is enrolled, you can start to look forward to the beginning of the school year. As September nears, your child is standing on the cusp of a period of astonishing growth and development. When you send your child to a quality program, you're giving her daily opportunities to explore, play, create, and interact in a setting that's specifically designed for someone her age. In the environment of the classroom, your child's skills will be fostered and encouraged at every level, whether it's the emergence of greater social interaction, newfound independence, flourishing creativity, or the ability to master swinging on the overhead bars in the school playground.

The rapid progress a child makes in these first years of school is immensely gratifying to observe for parents and teachers alike. It's the reason we fell in love with this kind of work. After twenty-five years of working in early childhood education, we still experience the thrill of discovery along with the children. There's so much for them to learn at this stage in their young lives. One day a child can't cut paper with scissors, but the next day she can do it. Suddenly, a child understands the message contained in a book she's heard many times: "I know why Henry did that; it's because he didn't want to hurt his friend's feelings." The child who only wanted to play on her own looks around, sees the other children playing house, and joins in the game. The pride on the face of the child who finally pours juice from the pitcher by herself is reward enough for the teacher or parent who had to mop up the mess while she was learning to do this. Each and every school day brings new revelations and accomplishments for young children and for their teachers too.

Even on a day when a child has struggled at school, she continues to learn. We often tell parents that a child's worst day at school is often her greatest learning experience. If her friend didn't want to play with her on the playground, she may become upset, but she also learns that sometimes she'll have to relinquish control of the game if she wants to play with others. If she doesn't get to have a turn in the pretend rocket ship, she figures out that she can make a painting instead. If she had a hard time saying good-bye to Mommy, but Mommy comes back after story time, the next day she finds it's easier to say good-bye because she has the benefit of experience. In the safe, communal atmosphere of the classroom, children learn to work through conflict and difficulty, which lays a wonderful foundation for later learning and relationships.

Your first opportunity to find out more about your child's early school experiences will come at the start of the school year on your first parent night. Parent night is an opportunity for parents to meet the teachers, see the classroom, and hear about the school year. Teachers will talk about curriculum, routines, a typical day, goals for the year, enrichment activities (such as music and movement), the various things your child will need from home, what to expect from the first weeks at school, and the best ways and times to communicate with the teachers. This is a very important night for teachers since it's their one opportunity to convey their philosophy and goals for the year to parents as a group and to make a good first impression. Never underestimate the value of a friendly smile to a teacher on parent night. Although teachers are accustomed to talking to groups of children, a roomful of adults can often be intimidating, even for the most experienced teacher. In Ellen's early career, she remembers needing to sit behind a table during parent nights because her knees were knocking so badly. Many teachers have shared horror stories about the parent who fell asleep in the middle of the presentation or the cell phone that rang while an important point was being made. Nancy recalls the time a father's cell phone rang and he actually took the call. It's only respectful to teachers to give them your full attention. Your attentiveness will indicate that you have your child's best interests at heart.

On parent night—together with teachers—we always try our best to help demystify the world of school for parents. We believe the more parents understand what goes on in the classroom, the better they become at helping their children to adjust and thrive there. When you have an awareness of what actually happens at school, you'll be able to more confidently support your child during this transition and throughout her time at school. When your child comes home with a painting that looks like a brown blob, you'll be able to appreciate the skills and effort that were necessary to create it. When she recites a story she's heard many times, while turning the pages of the book, you'll understand that she has taken her first step toward reading. When she tells you that it was her turn to be the snack helper, you'll know what this means and expect her to help set the table at home. When you have an insight into the thoughtful and deliberate planning that goes into a preschool day, you'll be better able to share more fully in your child's experience during these years. The purpose of this chapter is to help you do this.

The Curriculum

"Curriculum" is a word you'll probably hear your child's teachers using to describe what goes on at school. When applied to an early childhood program, curriculum doesn't just mean academics. It means everything that the children do in the course of a school day, including arrival, story time, snack time, and dismissal. Every school will have its own curriculum, and the details will vary from school to school. Certain core elements will be the same whichever school your child attends.

• The Five Core Learning Experiences of School •

No matter where your child goes to school, there are five core experiences that all children learn there. Children learn to *separate* from their parents, they learn to *become part of a group*, they learn to *socialize* with other children, they learn to become more *independent*, and they learn to *follow a routine*.

1. Separation

When children are at school and away from their parents, they begin the process of becoming independent individuals. In the environment of the classroom, they can choose with whom to play, whether they want to paint a picture, do a puzzle, be alone, or play with a friend or teacher. The self-reliance your child learns from this experience leads to a greater awareness of herself as an individual, empowering her to feel independent and confident in her ability to manage in the world outside home.

2. Being part of a group

The classroom is the place where children learn that the world is bigger than "just me," or "me and my family." When a child becomes a member of the "Purple Room" or "Ms. Susie's Class," she forms an identity that fosters an expanded view of herself and her place in the world. Although the ratio of adults to children in early childhood programs is high, in the classroom, your child will start to become accustomed to being one child among many.

One of the first things children learn at school is that their individual needs may not be met immediately and that they must wait for the teacher's attention. This means they will have to adapt themselves to the teacher's expectations, listen while others speak, and wait for their turn. (If a child's parents allow constant interruption or respond immediately to every request or demand, this child will often have difficulty adjusting to the new expectations of school.)

By nature, groups demand rules. It would be impossible for a teacher to manage fifteen three-year-olds without consistent expectations. As any early childhood educator will tell you, children actually thrive on the clarity of these classroom rules and will often report their classmates' infractions to their teachers. This is not "tattling" exactly, but a young child's way of learning and reinforcing the rules. When teachers ask four-year-olds to develop a set of classroom rules, the list is usually lengthy. Often the children are naturally much stricter than the teacher would have been.

Some rules written by four-year-olds in the nursery school's classrooms:

- Play nicely with your friends. Fighting isn't nice.

- Running around playing monster is dangerous.

- Absolutely NO punching, pushing, hitting, kicking, choking, pinching, pulling hair, biting.

- Try to figure out a way for everyone to play.

- Always tell the truth even if you don't want to.

- Listen to your teachers ALL the time.

- Don't tattle—work it out.

- Don't laugh at someone's mistake.

- Speak in a medium-loud voice.

- No guns.

- Ask for things; don't grab.

- No teasing anyone.

- Don't knock down other people's buildings.

---

3. Socialization

This early school experience is a time of tremendous social development for children. In the environment of the classroom, children learn that their words and actions will have an impact on the other children and on their teachers. The classroom setting provides plenty of opportunities for children to learn to share and to take turns—after all, even if a classroom had fifteen blue trucks for fifteen three-year-olds, Sam and Joey would still be negotiating for the same blue truck. Basic communication skills are fostered as children learn to express their needs and feelings in a socially appropriate way instead of hitting, grabbing, or crying.

Teachers will require the children to accept adult authority and to use respectful language. When a child turns to a teacher and demands, "More juice!" a teacher will say she is waiting for a "please" before the juice is given. Imagine how helpful it is for children when these expectations are mirrored at home.

As children grow, their social abilities grow. They learn to cooperate and to work toward a common goal. They start to understand the reciprocal nature of friendship. They can help others in need, take responsibility for their own actions, and begin to show empathy. As language and social abilities improve, they learn to compromise and resolve conflicts independently using words.

4. Independence

As children begin school, they are in the process of mastering various self-help skills.

Skills that three- and four-year-olds in school should be doing for themselves include:

- Taking off their coat and putting it on their hook.
- Putting on their coat.
- Taking shoes and socks off and putting them on.
- Pouring from small pitchers.
- Helping set the table.
- Clearing their plates from a table.
- Sitting at a table to eat.
- Putting toys away.
- Washing hands.
- Managing their clothing when toileting.
- Learning to wipe themselves when toileting.

Children who are taught these skills at home are generally much more comfortable and confident at school. It always amazes us when parents send a child for violin or tennis lessons but haven't taken the time to teach her basic skills such as putting on her own coat and cleaning up her toys.

5. Routines

School days are specifically organized to allow for a balance of active and quiet times so that children will have the focus and energy they need to participate fully at all times. Throughout the day, children will have a chance to take part in large-group, small-group, and individual activities.

The daily schedule, structure, and routine of school are very important for young children. Children feel safe and secure when they can predict the sequence of the day and anticipate what comes next. Instead of saying, "We'll be having a snack at eleven-thirty," teachers tell children that snack time comes *after* outdoor time. (At this age, time on a clock means nothing to a young child.) Children will often become highly incensed if a teacher has the audacity to change the order of the day. If snack time is switched with outdoor time to accommodate a rainy-day schedule, children will protest, "You forgot! Snack is supposed to come before outdoor time!"

Children often become very absorbed in play and require advance notice to end an activity in order to prepare to move on to the next thing. Teachers may use a musical instrument, a song ("I looked at my watch, and what did it say? Five more minutes to play!"), a timer, or counting to signal that the activity is about to end.

• The School Day •

Every school will have its own schedule. A typical morning schedule may include:

8:45 to 9:00	Arrival
9:00 to 9:30	Free play
9:30 to 9:40	Cleanup
9:40 to 10:00	Circle time
10:00 to 10:15	Bathroom
10:15 to 10:45	Outdoor play

10:45 to 11:15	Washing hands/Snack time
11:15 to 11:30	Story time
11:30 to 12:00	Activities (art, music, games, puzzles, sand and water play, pretend play, block building, cooking)
12:00	Cleanup and dismissal

Most preschools offer a three-hour morning or afternoon program for three-year-olds. This is an optimum length of day for children this age. Often three-year-olds become very tired toward the end of a three-hour period as the demands of school sap their physical energy and emotional reserves. At the age of four, most children can enjoy a longer day that may include lunch, a rest time, outdoor time, and additional activities.

Arrival

During arrival time, teachers are at the classroom door, welcoming the children. When you arrive promptly, this teaches a good habit and lets the teacher and your child know that you value the school experience. If a child walks into the classroom late, the teacher may not be available to greet her individually, and the other children will already be involved in playing. As a result, she may feel uncomfortable and less able to connect with the other children.

During arrival time, your child learns to:

- Take off her jacket and place her belongings in her cubby.

- Greet the teacher politely (make eye contact, say hello).

- Separate from a parent. (A child who is hesitant may need a few minutes of special attention.)

- Transition to classroom activity.

`Free Play

During free play, children get to choose from a variety of toys and materials that can be used both cooperatively and independently. Activities and materials that promote cooperative play include building blocks, sand, dramatic play, art, and play dough. Activities that promote independent play include doing puzzles, drawing, cutting, painting, and using small building materials such as Lego or pegs.

Free play allows children the opportunity to make decisions about what they want to do and with whom they want to play, or to decide they wish to play alone. This allows them to experiment and take risks, which in turn builds confidence in their ability to make choices in the future. Playing with other children stimulates imagination and creativity and offers the opportunity to use language in conversation. Children need many social interactions in order to develop the skill of conversational communication.

Cleanup

After each activity, children are responsible for putting away the toys and materials that they've used. Teachers help by delegating jobs, directing the children as needed, and devising ways to make the cleanup more interesting. Most children do not want to clean up. We sometimes hear children say, "I'm too tired," or "I don't have to clean up at home. My mommy/babysitter does it for me," or "I didn't play with this." Teachers tell children: "Everyone cleans up; it's the rule."

Sometimes it's true that cleaning up is overwhelming for children. This is a less structured time and can seem chaotic to them.

In order to help children focus on the task of cleanup, teachers will:

- Give a warning shortly beforehand.

- Break down the job. ("First we will put the tops on the markers and then we will put the markers in the box. . . .")

- Delegate. ("Stevie can collect the cars, and Jake can collect the trains. . . .")

- Make it fun and cooperative. ("Can you find five square blocks to put in the bin? I'll pick up the red ones, and you can pick up the blue

ones. Can we put them away
before we count to twenty?")

• Have a designated and clearly
labeled place for each material.

When children clean up, they learn to respect and take responsibility for classroom materials. By putting everything in its proper place, they develop a sense of organization. They learn the value of cooperation and build a sense of community.

Circle Time or Group Time

Circle time or group time provides children with another opportunity to develop a sense of community. Often a special song is sung to welcome the children to the circle and help them to identify as a group. During circle time, children learn to share their ideas and listen to the ideas of others. This time also helps them to develop the confidence necessary to express themselves in front of a group.

Teachers use this time to introduce new concepts, to talk about the day's schedule, and to encourage the children to use each other's names when addressing one another. Some schools will use circle time to take attendance, assign classroom jobs, or talk about the calendar and the weather. Teachers may use songs, finger-plays, movement, and games that require listening and following directions.

Children also begin to develop the self-control to hold on to their ideas and wait their turn to speak. They learn that it's detrimental to the group when everyone speaks at once. The skill of waiting to speak is often very challenging for young children, who think that they will lose their idea if they don't vocalize it immediately. Teachers will tell children, "Hold the thought in your mind and save it until it's your turn to speak."

Outdoor Time

When you ask a child what she likes best about school, invariably she'll reply, "When we play outdoors." This is the time of day when children get to set the agenda, carry out ideas, acquire new skills, and rise to physical challenges. At this age, children are experiencing a period of rapid physical growth, so it's important for them to have many opportunities for physical play. Outside, children can learn to run, climb, jump, catch a ball, ride a tricycle, and balance. They also learn to cooperate and compromise about how a game will be played and how to incorporate themselves into play with others.

Different children behave differently when playing outdoors. Some will immediately take physical risks; others will watch cautiously from the sidelines before trying. Most know just how much they are capable of and will try when they're ready. At first, a child may ask for help from a teacher to swing from bar to bar on the playground equipment. Then she'll insist on doing it herself. Eventually, when she masters the entire length of the overhead ladder, she'll jump down and proudly exclaim, "I did it!" There are very few other opportunities during school time when she gets to challenge herself to this extent. Once she's accomplished her new skill, she'll probably swing across that ladder over and over again. The feeling of accomplishment and confidence that this gives her translates into everything else she does. A child will tolerate frustration more willingly, take more risks, and persevere more readily when she has mastered a new physical challenge.

Outdoor play is often a time when children experience social conflict. One child will say she doesn't want to play with another child. A group of children will exclude a child from their play. A child may come late to a particular play and won't be able to understand the game in progress. Teachers will help smooth over conflicts, helping children to acquire the language they need to resolve these situations. At this age, it really doesn't matter what the rules are when playing a game. The most important thing is that the children agree to play by the rules they have determined.

Snack/Lunch

At mealtimes, children participate in setting the table and washing their hands before eating. They're expected to sit at a table for a short period of time until the teacher tells them that the snack or lunch is over. This is a social time of the day when children can converse with their friends and teachers and learn to use table manners. Some age-appropriate expectations include saying please and thank you, sitting in a chair with feet on the floor, and chewing with mouths closed. It's helpful to the teacher and child if these expectations are consistent at home.

For some children, this is an opportunity to try new foods. Many times we hear parents say, "My child will never eat vegetables." When every other child at the table is eating cucumbers and red peppers, however, it's more likely that a vegetable-phobic child will give them a try.

One of the skills children love to master is pouring a drink. Small pitchers or partly filled measuring cups are provided so the children can learn how to pour. Spilling is expected. Teachers stay armed with paper towels and help the children learn to clean up the mess. Sometimes children will get upset when they spill, so it is important to let them know this is okay and that it takes practice to learn how to pour. The children need to know that they are capable of doing this.

At the end of snack or lunch, children are expected to clean up after themselves.

Story Time and Literacy Activities

Story time is often the most pleasurable part of the school day for both teachers and children. Children will sit wide-eyed and completely absorbed by the illustrations in a book and the sound of the teacher's voice as she reads. Young children never seem to tire of story time. They will ask for the same stories over and over again, deriving comfort and confidence from knowing something really well.

A lot is happening during story time. Children are learning to listen as part of a group, to share ideas, and to increase their attention span. Story time exposes children to new concepts, feelings, and values. Children learn that a story has a beginning, middle, and end. They learn that books are sources of information, imagination, and language. They learn to recall events and make predictions. Teachers will ask questions to stimulate memory, to encourage children to respond to details, and to promote the ability to hypothesize: "What do you think would happen if he stopped watering the carrot seed?"

Children find meaning in books and take pleasure in them long before they learn to decode words for themselves. By listening to stories and looking at books, they learn that print is a form of communication. Many children will remember a story they have heard many times and can recite it back verbatim. Sometimes we hear from parents that a child has been "pretending" to read a favorite book that she knows by heart. In fact, this child has taken the first step toward reading independently.

Reading aloud is just one of the ways that teachers encourage early literacy and promote readiness for later reading and writing. A typical preschool classroom will expose children to words in many ways. Cubbies are labeled with children's names, letters of the alphabet are on the walls, and words are posted around the room to designate things and areas in the room ("window," "block area," "sink"). Children are also introduced to letters and their sounds through word games, songs, and rhymes.

Activities

In most schools, activity time provides a balance of teacher-directed and child-initiated play. Children are encouraged to participate in a variety of activities designed to support their growing skills and abilities. Classrooms are divided into separate areas for each activity. Furniture is child sized and materials are organized and located near the area in which they will be used. A wide variety of interesting, stimulating, and age-appropriate materials are available for each age range. These materials are intended to stimulate creativity, encourage skill development, and promote problem solving.

• Block play

Blocks are one of the most important materials in any early childhood classroom. There's no right way to play with blocks—the children determine what they want to build and how to build it. Building with blocks helps develop the large and small muscles. By experimenting with blocks, children begin to learn mathematical concepts such as size, shape, quantity, symmetry, balance, sorting, categorizing, and spatial relationships. Blocks are also ideal for teaching problem solving and frustration tolerance. You can imagine the disappointment that occurs when a child has been working for a period of time and her building topples unexpectedly. She must then deal with the situation and start all over again. When the building topples repeatedly, she has many opportunities to become resilient and to learn to solve her own problems.

When children build together, they learn to cooperate and accommodate each other's ideas. If there are three children building with blocks, each one will have an idea about how to create the structure. In order to build successfully, they have to learn to negotiate with one another. Consensus and compromise become necessities.

Often children build what they see in the world around them: a house or a school, for example. If they have props such as animals, cars, or road signs, they'll extend the building to include a town, farm, zoo, or garage. This helps them to understand the places they've been or events they've experienced. After September 11, we saw many children building towers and knocking them down repeatedly. They were re-creating what they had witnessed on television and were trying to make sense of it in their own way.

• Dramatic play

In most early childhood classrooms, you'll notice a variety of props and furniture designed to support dramatic play. These may include pretend kitchens, food and cooking utensils, tables and chairs, pillows, baby dolls, house keys, dress-up clothing or pieces of fabric, tool boxes, briefcases, telephones, computer keyboards, doctor's instruments, and cash registers. These props reflect a child's world, allowing her to re-create her home life and experiences within the classroom. Children will often play at being Mommy, Daddy, big sister or baby brother, babysitter, or teacher.

This kind of play helps children understand the world around them while stimulating their creative thinking and imagination. Children often use dramatic play to help them understand the roles and relationships in their families and to cope with fears and new situations. It's not unusual to see a child who recently gained a new sibling feeding a baby doll with tender care before putting that doll in the oven. We've learned not to be alarmed at this kind of behavior. What this child is doing is expressing complicated feelings in a safe and appropriate way.

Through dramatic play, children learn the social and verbal skills needed to take turns, cooperate, compromise, solve problems, show empathy, and resolve conflict. For example: Two children in the pretend kitchen both want to feed the baby. There's only one bottle. Both children are desperately holding the bottle saying, "It's mine. I had it first!" One of several scenarios may ensue. One child may grab the bottle away; the other child may passively accept this or cry or walk away. The children may hit, pinch, or bite. Teachers will intervene by saying, "Robby, I see that you have the bottle. After you feed the baby, can you give your friend Abby a turn? Abby, can you ask Robby for a turn when he is finished feeding the baby?" Through these interactions, children learn the power of language and of compromise.

• Sand and water play

If you've ever spent time watching children playing on the beach, you already know how much they love experimenting with sand and water.

Letting wet sand slip through fingers provides children with a soothing, calming, and pleasurable way to play. Research shows that such sensory experiences can actually enhance the development of the brain's ability to take in and organize information about the environment.

In the classroom, sand and water tables are equipped with props such as different-sized cups and containers, scoops, funnels, sieves, and wheels. When playing with sand and water, children learn to be cooperative and play imaginatively. They experiment with cause and effect—when a child throws objects into water, she discovers which will sink and which will float; by pouring water on the water wheel, she learns it will turn, and if she pours water from a bucket into a cup, it will overflow. The act of pouring strengthens eye-hand coordination. While experimenting with sand and water, children can compare and contrast sizes. At home, bath time is a perfect opportunity for your child to experiment with materials that support similar play.

• Cooking

Cooking is a natural and enjoyable way to teach children about nutrition, math, science, and beginning reading concepts. Following a recipe takes patience and allows children to experience the satisfaction that comes from completing a real-life task. By baking a simple apple pie, children are involved in measuring, cutting, mixing, pouring, listening to directions, and following written instructions. Eye-hand coordination is developed, small muscles are strengthened, and all the senses are engaged. Cooking is also a great way to introduce children to holidays, cultures, and new foods. It's not unusual to hear a child who has just baked his first pie exclaim, "This is the best pie I ever ate. I never ate this before and I like it!"

• Art

We know that a child has had a good day when she leaves school splattered with paint. Art is one of the most important learning experiences a young child can have. Through art, children have a means of expressing their ideas and feelings. They feel empowered by the knowledge that they can create their own unique work. There's real joy for children in being creative. When a child makes something of her own and feels the pride of ownership, she's effectively building a strong sense of self. Children need to have opportunities to use all kinds of art materials and the freedom to experience these materials in ways that they can determine for themselves. Experimenting with a wide variety of materials allows them to learn from trial and error, solve problems, take risks, and make decisions. In the classroom, children's artwork is displayed so that the whole class learns that their work is important and valued by others.

The pleasure that children derive from the pure, tactile experience of art can be magical to witness. For children, art feels good: the sensation of squeezing a glue bottle while a puddle forms on the paper; the cool, smooth, malleable quality of clay; the silky texture of finger paint on wet paper. These experiences both soothe and inform children. If you watch a child's face as she paints at an easel, you'll see the concentration required—she's learning how to put the brush in the paint, figuring out how much paint is needed on the brush and what marks the brush will make on the paper, making decisions about how much of the paper she will cover and which colors to use, and finding out what happens when the colors mix. When a child discovers that mixing yellow and red will make orange, it's as if a whole new world has opened up to her. As her skills develop, the decisions that she makes become increasingly complex. If she wants to paint a picture of her family, she'll have to decide how to fit everyone on the paper, what size each person should be, which details to include, and what's going to be in the background.

If you give children paper, markers, crayons, chalk, paintbrushes, tape, scissors, clay, play dough, glue, beads, and string, there's no limit to what they'll do. We've seen preschool children create life-sized figures, make puppets, fold paper into envelopes and letters, build creative containers for magical worlds, or even design a new line of handbags. During art time, children are inspiring one another and learning from the creations of others. When children have the opportunity to use art materials, they strengthen the muscles needed to accomplish many basic skills, including the fine motor ability required to use a pencil to write words. Drawing is a precursor to writing—the muscles and control necessary to use pencils and markers are the same ones children will need when learning to write. The act of painting at a slanted easel builds the larger arm muscles that lead to the development of these small muscles.

Children can only truly experience using art materials if they are not hampered by their clothing or worrying about soiling a special outfit. We've heard children say to teachers, "I can't paint today. I'm wearing a new dress." If your child is wearing something that seems too special, she may be preoccupied by her clothing or resistant to participating for fear that her outfit might get ruined. Even when smocks are provided, art projects are messy and somehow the paint ends up in the place that the smock has not covered. We've often seen parents or caregivers greet a child at the end of a school day with the words, "What did you do to your shirt? It's brand new! I'll never get it clean." The child feels deflated and the message to the child is that keeping her clothes clean is more important than the wonderful, messy experience of creating art. Often, that child will tell the teacher that she doesn't want to paint the next time. Children should come to school dressed comfortably, knowing that grown-ups won't be upset if clothing gets paint or glue on it.

Sometimes your child will bring home a painting from school that looks like a brown blob. It can be hard for you to imagine the process that went into making the brown blob, but remember that your child worked very hard to create it. She had to place a red line over a blue line, then she made a yellow circle over that, and then she put the brush aside and began moving her hands across the smooth surface of the paper. It's important to remember that a child's artwork is an extension of her and how you respond can either encourage or discourage her creativity and willingness to try new things.

Imagine a child who has worked for days on a cardboard sculpture, thoughtfully adding piece upon piece as she develops her idea. Upon completion she's very proud of her hard work. Her teacher asks her if she's finished and wants to take the sculpture home. The child can't wait until the end of the day to show it to her mother. Her mother arrives at dismissal, and the teacher invites her into the classroom to see the masterpiece. The child is filled with excitement and anticipation. Meanwhile, the mother reacts by saying, "It's so big. What am I going to do with this?" The child feels crushed. By failing to acknowledge her child's artwork in a positive way, the mother sends a strong message that she doesn't appreciate her child's effort or respect her work.

When you take the time to talk to your child about her creation, you show her that you value and encourage her creativity. You can hang her latest painting on the refrigerator or put a clay sculpture in your office. This doesn't mean you have to turn your home or workplace into your child's personal art gallery. You can rotate her work from time to time or store her drawings and paintings in a portfolio. As time goes on, you can throw some of this artwork away so that it doesn't take over your closets. But do keep some of your child's work. Our grown children still enjoy looking at their early artwork and find it helps them to recall memories of their childhoods.

While it's essential that you show your child your appreciation, it's good to avoid going over the top with your praise. When you repeatedly say something is "amazing" and "beautiful," you're making a value judgment about your child's work. You're sending a message that your child needs to please you rather than pleasing herself. Be specific about what you appreciate: "I notice you made the sky purple." Your child will know when you're being sincere. It's also a good idea to avoid asking the question "What is it?" or suggesting what you think it is. The picture that you think is a small dog may in fact be a portrait of you. Instead, you can use what you see to stimulate discussion: "I wonder what you used to make that?"

There are several other ways that you can talk to your child about artwork she brings home:

- Tell me about your painting/sculpture/drawing/collage.

- I see you covered the whole paper.

- I noticed you left lots of white.

- What were you thinking about when you made this?

- I see you worked very hard on this.

- Did it take you a long time?

- I see you used a pattern here.

- I notice a triangle in the corner.

- You put lots of wavy lines in this picture.

Even so, there's no need to overwhelm your child with your ideas and words. Remember, for young children the process of creating art is much more important than the product.

• Music and movement

During music and movement, teachers use music, song, body movement, and finger-plays to promote learning, self-expression, listening, taking turns, following directions, and focusing.

Children love music and they love to move their bodies to music. Music is a wonderful way of promoting a sense of togetherness in a classroom. Songs can be used to smooth transitions from activity to activity, to set the mood, and to give directions. Music is also a very effective way of increasing children's attention span and listening skills. Children love to sing the same songs over and over again. They learn through repetition and feel secure when a song is predictable and known to them. Songs can also be an excellent means of conveying information. Everyone remembers the alphabet song from childhood and how "LMNOP" always sounded like one letter.

Movement is an activity that enhances physical awareness, coordination, balance, as well as strength and flexibility. Long before children can speak, they learn about the world through their bodies. Concepts such as fast and slow, big and little, and shapes can also be taught through movement. Think about how many concepts are learned when you place a hoop on the floor and ask a child to jump *inside* the hoop, *outside* the hoop, *around* the hoop, or *over* the hoop.

Dismissal

Most classrooms have some form of closing activity at the end of the school day. Children may meet on the rug to sing a good-bye song or talk about the day or plan for the next day. Before leaving school, children gather up their belongings. It's helpful for your child to have a backpack so that she learns to take responsibility for her possessions.

Home-School Communication: Playing Your Part

As a parent of a preschooler, it's true that you will be communicating with your child's teachers more frequently than at any other stage in her educational life. An early childhood school cannot effectively meet the needs of young children without good communication with parents. You know your child best, and you've been her first teacher. In order to fully understand your child, a teacher must learn from you and come to a shared understanding in the best interests of your child.

To begin with, teachers need to know basic information such as: Who's in your family? Who besides you cares for your child? What are your child's specific likes and dislikes? Is your child sensitive? Does she have health issues? For example, it's very helpful when a parent lets the teacher know that a child is frightened by the sound of fire truck sirens, that she is self-conscious when her name is sung before a group, or that she's comforted by sitting on a lap.

A good relationship with your child's school begins with mutual respect. You can help by maintaining a friendly tone, interacting politely, and listening to the school's point of view. You may not always see your child in the same way as the school. After all, home and school are different. The most important thing is that you and your child's teacher communicate and work together. If you are having difficulties talking with one of your child's teachers, of course, you should let the school's director know about this.

• Before School Starts •

Before school starts, you'll receive many forms and materials. Typically, schools require health forms, release forms, and emergency contact information. You may receive a school calendar and class list. It's important that you get into the habit of reading and responding to written communication from the school in a timely way.

Schools have different ways to learn about your child's developmental history, temperament, and personality. You may have a meeting with the director or fill out a profile with this information.

Some of the things that schools need to know about your child include:

- Language development (other languages?).

- Physical developmental milestones such as walking, talking, sleeping.

- Toilet training.

- Family profile.

- Caregiver information.

- Prior school or program experience. Did your child separate from you easily?

- Personality. Your child's likes and dislikes, favorite activities, typical response to new situations and people, things that comfort or upset her.

• Health Issues and Allergies •

It's very common for children in their first years of school to be sick quite often. A sick child is usually unhappy, listless, and unable to function well at school. She may also be contagious to others. Young children are unable to handle tissues properly or cover a cough effectively enough to protect their teachers and classmates from germs. When Billy sneezes on his hand, then touches the pretend pizza that next goes into Amy's mouth, the following day, Amy has a fever and a cold and needs to stay home. We urge parents to be very conservative when a child isn't feeling well. If you sense your child is unwell, you should keep your child at home in order to avoid infecting others. Call the school to let the teacher know your child is sick and if she has a communicable disease such as chicken pox, strep throat, or conjunctivitis. Children should return to school when they are symptom free and able to participate fully in all school activities.

Children need to stay home when they show any of these symptoms:

- Fever

- Runny nose

- Persistent cough

- Diarrhea

- Vomiting

- Reddened eyes with a discharge/crusty lashes

- Rashes with an unknown origin

- Fussy, cranky, atypical behavior

It's quite common for young children to have allergies that range from mild to life threatening. Of course, parents must fully inform the school regarding the specifics of a child's allergies prior to the start of school. In order to ensure your child's safety, you need to tell the school what your child is allergic to, what the symptoms of a reaction are, and what's the appropriate procedure for treatment. A plan must be in place so that the family and the school are both aware of the protocol in case of an emergency. As a parent of an allergic child, you can help by educating your child about her allergy and teaching her to be aware of the things that make her sick. Often, allergic children are very capable and mature in their ability to understand what they can and cannot have.

• Day-to-Day Communication •

One of the special things about being a parent of a preschooler is that you get to see and talk to your child's teachers on a regular basis. This communication can be in the form of a *brief* conversation at the classroom door, a note, an e-mail, or a phone call. When you do have an important piece of information to share with the teacher that needs more than a minute or two or that demands privacy, it's best to ask the teacher when she would be available to either meet with you individually or to talk on the phone. If you must impart information at the classroom door, keep the communication to a minimum and don't expect the teacher to automatically make time for you, especially at the beginning of the school day. When a teacher is busy greeting fifteen children, there's only one appropriate answer to a parent's question "How is Emily doing in school?"—and that's "Fine!" The teacher's priority is attending to the children, and she can speak with you at a greater length another time.

Other means of communication include the school's handbook, a parent bulletin board outside the classroom, and a newsletter home. These will help you to become familiar with the school's policies, procedures, personnel, and practical day-to-day information. Newsletters may report dates for upcoming class trips, holiday celebrations for you to attend, and requests for materials for special school projects, as well as information about things your child learned in school. It's a good idea to get into the habit of reading the school's newsletters and sharing them with your partner and caregiver if applicable. It's very frustrating for administrators and teachers when parents don't take the time to read the literature that the school sends home. We suggest that you have a place in your home (kitchen counter, desk, refrigerator door) where newsletters are left for everyone to read and refer to. Then, when your child answers the question, "What did you do in school today?" with a resounding, "Nothing!" you'll be able to use the information contained in newsletters as a conversation starter.

It's helpful to write a short note to your child's teacher regarding specific information, such as a change in who's picking up your child or if a child is going on a playdate after school without you. If eighteen different children have a change of plans, it's impossible for a teacher to remember everyone's details without a written note. It's also a good idea to let your child's teacher know when changes occur in your family. Children are easily affected by changes in their lives and households. Some things that may upset your child and affect her behavior at school include: a new baby, a new caregiver, a sick relative, marital difficulties, or a move to a new home. Teachers can be supportive, attentive, and understanding when they are kept informed. For example, a teacher will be able to give your child an extra bit of attention if she knows you're away on business.

If you need to discuss a problem your child is having with a teacher, or the teacher brings a difficulty to your attention, make sure you listen carefully to the teacher's observations. Ask yourself if what you've heard is consistent with what you know about your child. Your first reaction may be to disagree with the teacher, but remember that your child may be very different at school than she is at home. Try to work with the teacher to brainstorm ideas and strategies. We've found that when parents and teachers have consistent expectations and a planned goal for a child, the child almost always responds. Once a plan is developed, it's necessary to continue to touch base regularly with the teacher to check on your child's progress and to evaluate whether the plan is working or needs adjustment. If you are having any difficulty communicating with your child's teacher, don't hesitate to talk to the appropriate administrator at the school.

• Parent-Teacher Conferences •

Parent-teacher conferences generally take place twice a year: once in the fall and once in the spring. The first parent-teacher conference is often the cause of great trepidation on the part of parents. For most parents, this will be the first time that someone other than a family member is "reporting" on their child. Many parents have told us that they feel like this is their first "parenting report card." They feel, "If I've done a good job then my child will get a good report." We tell parents that this is an unrealistic starting point. There are so many variables regarding a child's development that a parent-teacher conference can never *only* be about your child's brilliance. It's the teacher's responsibility to describe your child's progress in school and to work with you to set goals in order to support her growth.

It can help to remember that parent-teacher conferences are often a cause of anxiety for teachers as well as parents. Teachers spend considerable time preparing for each conference. Schools will have set aside this day, and it's respectful to the teachers and other parents if you are punctual and end on time. If you don't feel that you've had enough time to talk with your child's teacher, you can always schedule a follow-up meeting.

Typical topics for discussion will include:

- Your child's adjustment to school.

- A description of a typical day and how your child

moves through the day.

- An overview of your child's social, emotional, physical, and intellectual development.

- An overview of the development of your child's self-help skills (toilet training, eating and drinking, putting on coats).

- Typical development at this age.

- Your child's learning style.

- Your child's favorite activities and special areas of interest (teachers may show samples of your child's work).

This is a chance for you to ask questions and to share relevant information about your child's home life and what your child tells you about school. You should think about any questions you may have before the conference and feel free to ask for clarification or examples of anything that is brought up during the conference.

Questions often asked by parents include:

- Who does my child play with?

- Does she talk in group time?

- Does she share?

- Does she follow directions?

- What happens when she gets frustrated or cries?

- What does she choose to do during free play?

- Is she eating her lunch?

- Do you have any suggestions for activities at home?

• How to Say Thank You •

Most early childhood teachers don't go into their profession for money or recognition but because they want to make a difference in the lives of young children and their families. When you say thank you to a teacher, this is a small but meaningful way to show your appreciation for the work that she does every day. Different schools have different policies about gift giving, but as any teacher will tell you, the best gift of all is an appreciative note or positive feedback.

Some simple ways to express your gratitude include:

- Telling the teacher when your child reports enthusiastically about something she did at school.

- Thanking the teacher for the Mother's Day card or the pumpkin bread the class baked for Thanksgiving.

- Wearing the beaded necklace that your child made at school when you drop her off in the morning.

- Writing a thank-you note at the end of the year telling the teacher how much you appreciated her caring and hard work.

- Making the teacher's job easier by teaching your child how to zip her own jacket, keeping her home if she's sick, labeling her clothing, and making sure she wears mittens, not gloves (mittens are quicker to put on).

- Smiling at your child's teacher even if you're ten minutes late for work.

• How to Participate •

As a parent of a preschooler, you'll regularly be offered the chance to participate in the life of the school. This is a great opportunity to observe your child in the classroom setting and for you to take an active role in her education. You may be asked to be a class parent: This involves helping out the teachers periodically and communicating with the other parents about classroom needs such as materials for projects or activities. You might be asked to come to the class to read a story. If you have a particular skill, profession, or hobby that the children would find interesting, you can offer to share it with the class. Most schools have a parent association, and your involvement in this may be in the form of organizing a book fair, a bake sale, or some other fund-raising event. From time to time, you'll be called on to help the teachers during class trips. You may also have the opportunity to attend talks at the school on parenting topics such as sibling rivalry, sleep issues, or discipline.

We always remind parents that preschool is a very short time in the life of a child. Don't miss out on these opportunities to participate when they come your way. When you have the chance to go digging for worms in the park with a class of fifteen three-year-olds or to go along on a school visit to a farm to pick apples or to bake bread with the children—say yes. As your child grows, you're unlikely to be welcomed to this extent by her teachers. The more involved you can be at this stage, the more you will gain from these preschool years, and your child will benefit too.

Chapter Three

SEPARATION:

Easing the Way

Each year, on the first day of school, we stand at the elevator greeting new parents and children as they step into the hallway of the nursery school for the first time. The expressions on the children's faces run the gamut of emotions, everything from anxious and confused to happy and excited. The faces of parents are just as expressive. It's not unusual to see parents with knitted brows, tears in their eyes, or encouraging smiles. When it comes time to go inside the classroom, there are those children who burst into tears and cling to a parent, those who walk right in without as much as a good-bye, and those who bravely grasp a toy and hold on to it for dear life, bottom lip trembling.

On the first day of school, we usually remain in the hallway for some time, not so that we can comfort the children (that's the job of the teachers) but so that we can comfort the *parents*. Even though most parents are excited about the prospect of school, many discover that they are experiencing surprisingly powerful feelings of anxiety or ambivalence when it comes time to leave. As your child begins school, he's also beginning the process of becoming an individual, apart from you and away from the family unit. For the first time, he's venturing into a noisy, busy classroom where you won't be able to completely control what happens to him. You may worry that your child won't be able to communicate his needs to the teachers, that he'll cry and no one will comfort him, or that the other children will find ways to upset him. It's only natural to feel uncomfortable at the prospect of this new stage in your child's life.

We can both remember our own feelings of unease when it came time to leave our children on their first days at school. Until Alice began school at the age of three, Ellen hadn't left her daughter with anyone but her parents. She'd anticipated that Alice—who was typically tentative in new situations—

would cry and cling to her. Instead, Alice walked right into the classroom with a big smile on her face and waved good-bye. As she watched her daughter leave, it was Ellen who began to cry. She had been so worried about her child that she hadn't thought about her own feelings. The realization that Alice's world was expanding beyond home and family was overwhelming, and the act of letting go brought up incredible sadness. Alice's teacher came over and started to comfort Ellen. Instead of consoling the child, the teacher had to console the parent! Ellen explained that she'd never been away from Alice before and that it was very hard to leave. The teacher told Ellen something she'll never forget: "Your tie to Alice is strong, but it's also long and can stretch." Then the teacher told Ellen that she would be okay and that she could leave, which Ellen did reluctantly. As the weeks progressed, Ellen saw that Alice had a natural enthusiasm and love of school, and her feelings of reluctance gradually dissipated.

When Nancy's first child, Michael, started school, she was working part-time, which allowed her to drop him off in the morning. He was a quiet child, and Nancy assumed it would take time for him to adjust to school. She was wrong. Michael walked right in. The school had a small purple bench outside the classroom where parents could sit while the children were getting accustomed to their new school life. After several days, the teacher poked her head out of the classroom and said, "You can go now." Nancy was horrified. Her plan had been to stay on that purple bench indefinitely in case Michael needed his mommy, even though he was clearly fine without her. Unlike Michael, Nancy's second child, Alissa, was outgoing and gregarious. Nancy assumed Alissa would have no trouble adjusting since she was familiar with the school, having accompanied her brother there many times. In fact, much to Nancy's surprise, Alissa took several weeks to acclimate and clung to her mother's leg each day until a teacher pried her off.

Over the years, we've witnessed hundreds of parents leave their children in our care. We watch as they unconsciously project their own expectations and discomfort onto their children, just as we did. It can take time for both children and parents to develop the trust needed for a successful transition from home to school. During this time, it's very important that you stay in touch with your own feelings about separation. Your reaction and your child's can be extremely unpredictable. Even parents who have done this before can find the experience confusing—it's often true that children in the same family will have very different separation styles. As a parent, there's a great deal that you can do to ease the separation and to allay your own fears in the process. With good support from your child's teacher and a little self-awareness, the early weeks of school can be a positive experience, enabling your child to move into a new phase of learning, independence, and growth.

Before School Starts

When a child starts school for the first time, every caring parent wants to prepare him for the experience ahead. You want to ease his transition from the familiarity of home into the unfamiliar world of school. As a parent, you come to this experience with some prior knowledge, so it's easy to forget that this isn't the case for your child. Unlike you, your child has no frame of reference for school. Nancy assumed that her younger daughter had an idea of school from going there with her brother. Young children, however, understand their world through firsthand experience, so until Alissa stepped into the classroom and was left there, she really couldn't appreciate what school was going to be like.

Here are some other things to bear in mind when preparing your child for school:

- It's worth waiting until a week or two before school starts to begin preparing your child. Children's sense of time is very limited. If you think about how long your child has been alive, the concept of a week or a month is well beyond his comprehension. Children don't define time in days or months, but according to the sequence of the routines of their day. A nap comes after lunch, a trip to the park is after nap time. Although you'll have anticipated your child's first school experience for many months, he really doesn't need to be told about it until close to the time he actually goes to school.

- A week or so before school starts, you can begin the conversation about school with your child. It's important to remember that children are very concrete and can only process what they have already experienced. The word "school," for example, has no real meaning for a three-year-old who has no previous experience of school. When a parent enthusiastically says, "You're going to school in September. Aren't you excited?" that parent might as well be speaking a foreign language. Don't assume anything. Break it down into its basic components. Talk about what the building will look like, how you will get there, who will be there, and what your child will do when he gets there:

    "We're going to school tomorrow. School is in a big building (church, the Y, synagogue) with a blue door near the park. We'll take the bus (stroller, car) there in the morning after breakfast."

"I'll take you to the classroom and we'll meet your teachers, Christy and Emma. Teachers are nice grown-ups who are like mommies and daddies and know how to take care of children. There will be other boys and girls there to play with you."

"There are special tables and chairs just the right size for you and lots of toys to play with and fun things to do. They have blocks, dolls, trucks, and books. You will even have a special place to keep your things from home. The school has a playground with slides and bikes just like in the park."

It's a good idea to review the teachers' names with your child so he will be more familiar with those too.

- Reading books about first days at school is a wonderful way of help-ing children process what's going to happen to them. Children feel comforted by stories, especially when they hear them over and over again. A story about going to school can give you and your child a way of understanding and talking about what's going to take place both before and while it's happening. A list of books about going to school is included at the end of this chapter. Some of our particular favorites include:

My First Day at Nursery School by Becky Edwards
This book starts at home on the first day of school. The engaging illustrations and simple language take the reader through a child's first day, beginning with breakfast and finishing at dismissal time. Readers learn what a typical classroom looks like, about activities such as painting and blocks, and how teachers and children interact. The expressions on the little girl's face communicate her initial feelings of reluctance about being at school. As she discovers new friends and fun activities, she quickly forgets to miss her mommy. By the time the book ends, she doesn't want to leave when Mommy comes to pick her up. This book is a great way of introducing the idea of school to children aged two and three and sends a positive message about how feelings can change in the course of a day.

The Kissing Hand by Audrey Penn
This book tells the story of a young raccoon, Chester, who doesn't want to go to school. His mother reassures him by telling him about all the

fun things he'll do there. She explains to him that sometimes you have to do things you don't want to, even if they are scary. Chester learns a secret from his mother that she learned from her mother, called the "kissing hand." The mother kisses Chester in the middle of his palm, and he gets a wonderful, warm feeling. She tells him, whenever he feels lonely, he should press his hand to his cheek and think, "Mommy loves you. Mommy loves you." Chester reciprocates and kisses his mother's hand, saying, "Now you have a kissing hand too." This book sends the message to children aged three to five that it's possible to cope with scary feelings. It also gives them a very helpful tool for comforting themselves.

Will I Have a Friend? by Miriam Cohen
First published in 1967, this book is a wonderful story about a father taking his son to school for the first time. The child, Jim, worries about whether he will have a friend at school. He says good-bye to his dad reluctantly and at first he isn't happy. Everyone has a friend but him. At rest time, a child called Paul shows Jim his toy car, and the two boys become friends. This story is easy for four- and five-year-old children to relate to as they begin a new school experience. It opens the door for discussion with parents about concerns and fears that children often have, such as whether or not they'll make a friend.

Starting School: The Transition

As the school year begins, parents, children, and teachers are all going through a transition time. It can take everyone a while to adjust. Be patient with your child, your child's teacher, and yourself. After a little less than a month, most families have adapted, and the teacher will be more accustomed to your child and to his classmates.

• Parents' Feelings •

It's natural for parents to have various concerns as their child begins school: Will the teacher like my child? Will they think I'm a good parent? Will they understand my child? Will they know my child's special bathroom words? Or that my child only likes the color red? Or that "appaju" means apple juice? Will they know how to comfort him when he cries? What if my child misbehaves? What if he bites or hits? What if the teacher discovers that my child isn't perfect or isn't a creative genius?

These feelings are typical for any parent whose child is starting school for the first time. You need to recognize that this new step in your child's life may create a conflict for you. As much as you are excited about the prospect of school, you may feel uncomfortable about your child becoming less dependent on you. You may even be experiencing feelings of jealousy and ambivalence: Why should I trust the teacher? Will my child love the teacher more than me? Will my child not need me in the same way anymore?

It's not unusual for parents' reactions to be shaped by their own experiences of early separation. Memories of childhood can have a powerful impact during this time. This was true for the two of us. Unlike the outgoing adults we've become, we were both very reserved and quiet as children. We both remember loving school, but at the same time, we can vividly recall the pain of saying good-bye to our parents. No wonder we were anxious when it came time for our children to go through the same experience. It can be helpful to try to recall your own earliest memories of separation so that you can be aware of them when guiding your child through this transition. You may remember the newness or strangeness of your first school experience. You may have been excited, frightened, or sad. The smell of a fresh box of crayons or the feel of a new notebook can trigger powerful memories. Whether these memories are happy or painful, it's important to be aware that these are *your* experiences and that your child may react or feel quite differently from you. When you are aware of your own feelings and memories, you'll be less likely to project them onto your child. Having these feelings and memories is perfectly normal. It's how you manage them and how you communicate with your child that can make the difference in creating a positive separation experience.

Remember that the school your child is about to attend is probably a very different place from the school you attended when you were young. Twenty or thirty years ago, the expectation was that children would just begin school, and not much thought was put into the process of transitioning to school. Neither parents nor teachers were particularly attuned to the psychology or developmental needs of preschoolers. Today, most early childhood educators have thoughtful plans in place for acclimating children and gradually phasing them into a full day. Prior to school, children often visit the classroom to meet the teacher; teachers sometimes visit children at home;

and schools sometimes begin with a shorter day and groups are kept small at the start so that teachers can give the children extra attention. Teachers understand how overwhelming this first separation can be for parents and children. They can help to ease the way and set the tone for your child's ability to deal well with new experiences in the future.

Bear in mind that children are very alert to their parents' facial expressions and body language. If you have a worried expression on your face, you're communicating to your child that something is terribly wrong. We often see parents who look as if they were taking their child to the guillotine rather than a wonderful, fun classroom. When this happens, the child may get the impression that there's really something to worry about. In the first weeks of school, we always walk the hallways on "smile patrol" reminding parents to be aware of how they appear. Don't underestimate the power of a smile and a warm, friendly greeting to the teachers. Even if you're wracked with anxiety on the inside, when you do something as simple as pointing out your child's coat hook and cubby to him, he'll feel more at ease. When you give the appearance of calmness and confidence, you communicate this to your child and he gets the message that he's capable of doing this.

If you're the kind of person who's always embraced new experiences and jumped right in, you may expect your child to behave in a similar way. Your enthusiasm might be overwhelming for your child, especially if he tends to be slow to warm up in new situations. You may become frustrated if he's not as quick to adapt as you. Observe your child. Notice how he copes with new situations in general. He may be timid and cautious. Respect your child's style. Slow down and follow his lead.

• Children's Feelings •

Until the beginning of school, your child's life revolves around the expectations and reactions of his parents or caregivers. Your child defines the adult world in terms of parents' and caregivers' behavior. When he comes to school, he's required to learn a new set of expectations in a new environment. Teachers may have some of the same expectations as at home and many that are different. At school a child may be allowed to play with water or sand inside, whereas at home that might never happen. At home a child may eat on request, while at school there may be a designated snack time. At school the child is part of a group and needs to wait to have his needs met, while at home it may be possible to have an adult respond to his needs immediately. It takes time for children to learn exactly how school and home are different.

In the beginning, everything is new. Children may unconsciously feel, "No one here knows me, and I don't know them. No one knows that I don't like juice. I only like water. I don't like to get my hands dirty. Loud noises scare me. My favorite song is 'Old MacDonald.' I don't know anyone's name or when my mommy is coming back." The early days of school are all about learning new names, new faces, and new routines, as well as navigating the physical space of the classroom and school.

The most important thing you can tell your child during this period of adjustment is that the teachers will look after him. Ellen remembers overhearing one child say to a crying child: "Don't feel sad. The teachers know how to make you feel better." When your child expresses anxiety about school, you can do the same. Tell him, "It's okay. Your teacher will help you. That's what teachers do." Recently we heard Sean, a child in the three-year-old classroom, tell his teacher, "I'm worried. I can't remember. There are so many things." The teacher responded, "Don't worry, Sean. That's why we have a schedule. I'll remind you."

Often parents expect instant results from children. Have confidence that your child will adjust, if not immediately, then soon. Gradually, day by day, familiarity will replace the unfamiliar, and your child will begin to feel safe and secure in the classroom.

• Teachers' Feelings •

As a good parent, you'll probably be so focused on your child during this transition period, that you may forget that the beginning of a new school year is a difficult time for teachers too. On the teachers' first day back at school after summer vacation, we always ask, "Who didn't sleep last night?" Every single hand in the room goes up.

Teachers, like children and parents, are excited and anxious about the beginning of school. They need time to build relationships with children and parents. You'll probably enter the classroom thinking only about your child. For you, it's as if no other child exists in that classroom. You can't help yourself. The teacher, meanwhile, must meet the needs of the group, not just your child. In the first few weeks of school, teachers are laying the groundwork for the entire year. They must establish clear routines and a sense of belonging and community. This can't be done quickly or without repetition.

Some schools have a "phase-in" schedule so that children can gradually learn the routines of each day. Children begin by coming for shorter periods and in smaller groups and the day gradually lengthens until the whole class stays for the full day. Parents often say, "My child is ready to stay for a longer day. Why are they still coming for such a short time?" We tell parents that until each of the children in the group is ready for a full school day, the class isn't ready.

• Separation Styles •

Every child is a unique individual and will respond to separation in his own way. There's no wrong or right way to separate. Different children will adapt to new experiences differently. As your child begins school, you'll start to learn his unique separation style and what you can do to ease his adjustment. Often the parent whose child is the last to separate may feel embarrassed or as if he or she has failed in the process. There are no prizes awarded for the fastest separation. No matter how your child reacts, the most important thing is to remain calm and to trust that your child will be able to cope.

Over the years, we've watched hundreds of children adjusting to school for the first time. We've observed a number of different styles of behavior and learned how parents can help smooth the transition:

• The Child Who Doesn't Look Back
Child response: This child is eager to jump right in and embrace the new experience. He may hardly look back at his parent or say good-bye, leaving his parent feeling bereft and rejected.
Parent response: Say good-bye but don't insist on your child saying good-bye as you may interfere with his momentum. Try to take pleasure in your child's excitement about this new experience. Look forward to spending time alone together later in the day, and don't be surprised if your child has a delayed reaction somewhere down the road. Make certain to check in with the teacher to find out how he's been doing during the day.

• The Child Who Cries
Child response: This child bursts into tears when a parent tries to leave. There are usually two types of criers—loud and quiet. The loud-crying

child lets everyone know how he's feeling, but this doesn't mean he's in greater discomfort than the child who is crying softly in the corner. Some children cry at the moment of saying good-bye and quickly move on while others may cry intermittently throughout the day.

Parent response: Try not to look worried or you'll communicate your anxiety to your child. Remember that young children don't have the language or emotional maturity to understand their own feelings. Crying is their way of expressing sadness or fear. Many parents are uncomfortable about leaving a crying child, but it's important to understand that this is a normal expression of a child's feelings. Remind your child about the fun activities, children, and teachers at school. Acknowledge that it's hard to say good-bye and remind him that you'll be back later. Tell your child that the teacher is there to take care of him and that she'll help make him feel better. Don't prolong the good-bye. After you leave, the teacher will be able to comfort and distract your child, and it's important that your child begins to trust her to comfort him. It's very likely that he'll stop crying soon after you leave, but you can always ask someone at school to call you later to reassure you.

• The Brave One

Child response: This child has his shoulders back and head down. He won't be able to make eye contact and will engage in a ritualistic activity each morning (kneading the play dough or playing imaginatively with his favorite truck). Often he'll be unable to muster a good-bye to his parent as it demands too much of him.

Parent response: Many children won't respond to you when you say good-bye. Some parents find this upsetting. It doesn't mean that your child didn't hear you; it's just that he's working very hard to hold himself together, and it's probably too difficult at that moment to respond. Make sure you say good-bye to your child, but don't pressure him to say good-bye. Expect that he may fall apart as soon as he sees you at the end of the day. Make sure you give him some undivided attention, and plan some relaxing and calm time together after school.

• The Delayed Reactor

Child response: This child walks into school and seems fine for days or weeks. One day he looks around the room and begins to wail, "Where's my mommy?" This child was so interested in all the new experiences that he didn't realize that his parent had left.

Parent response: Don't panic. Nothing is wrong, and your child didn't suddenly decide that he doesn't like school. He's simply having a delayed reaction to the separation from you. Talk to him about his friends, his teachers, and the things he likes to do. Speak to the teacher so that she can give him some extra attention, and work with her to develop a good-bye ritual. These rituals need to be kept simple and short, however.

• The Solitary Child

Child response: This child prefers to spend time alone rather than playing with the other children. He adapts by exploring independently and sends a strong hands-off message to the teachers. He needs time to acclimate and to connect with teachers and children. He'll form relationships in his own time.

Parent response: Be patient. It will take time for the teacher and the other children to get to know your child. You can help by communicating with the teacher about your child's likes and dislikes and by setting up one-on-one playdates with children in his class. Respect your child's need to take things slowly as he establishes relationships with teachers and children.

• The Observer

Child response: This child may not participate in activities but needs to observe and take it all in before feeling comfortable enough to engage with teachers, children, and activities.

Parent response: Read books about school with your child. Play "school" with him when at home. Mention the names of the teachers and children often. Learn about what's going on in the classroom so that you can talk about school in meaningful ways. Talk to the teacher about what makes your child comfortable. Remember that your child is learning as he's observing.

• More Tactics for Good Good-byes •

- Leave the cameras and video cameras at home on the first day. Turn off your cell phone. Focus on your child. Your child needs you to give him your full attention.

- Keep it brief. Ultimately, it's much easier for parents and children alike when good-byes are brief. By prolonging the good-bye when your child is upset, you're actually prolonging his agony.

Practical Wisdom for Parents

- Don't ask permission to leave. When we hear a parent say to a child, "I'm leaving now, okay? okay? okay?" we know for a fact that the child will respond that it's "not okay."

- Develop a good-bye ritual. Children often benefit from a special good-bye ritual. Again, this should be kept brief. You and your child may decide one hug and three kisses is your special ritual, but if you are negotiating for the fifteenth kiss or hug, it's too long.

- Bring something from home. Some children are comforted by bringing something from home to help them transition. Schools have limited storage space, so it needs to be something that can be kept in a small cubby. It should not be so precious that if lost, your child would be inconsolable or so small that it could be easily lost (or swallowed).

- Be on time for arrival. This way the teacher will be able to give your child the attention he needs as he arrives. If your child is late, the classroom activity will already be under way, which can be disconcerting for children, especially during this period of adjustment.

- Try not to carry your child into school. When you do this, you're sending him the message that he's still a baby and isn't ready for this new experience. Your child is much more likely to cling to you if you're holding him. By age two and a half, all children are old enough to walk into school.

- Avoid coming to school with both parents. It can be overwhelming for your child to have to say good-bye to not just one but two of you.

- Let your child know where you're going to be. It's helpful for your child to have a mental picture of where you'll be or what you'll be doing while he's at school. If you say you're going to be sitting on the bench outside the classroom, don't go down the hall to speak to another parent. The teacher may bring the child to find you, and you won't be there. If you are wearing workout clothes, don't say you are going to the office. One parent we know told her child she was going for coffee, and her child responded by saying, "But Mommy, you don't drink coffee; you only drink tea." Be clear and reliable so that you don't cause your child additional worry.

- Be aware that your child is listening to everything you're saying and the tone in which you're saying it. On a day when you might be feeling rushed or stressed, you may be relieved when you drop your child off and jokingly say to the teacher, "Oh boy, you're going to have your hands full today." It's a virtual guarantee that your child will fulfill that expectation. Children don't understand the subtleties of sarcasm and will take your comments to heart.

- Give your child a mantra. One mother we know would always say to her three-year-old, Phoebe, "Good-bye. I'm leaving now and I'll be back at pickup time." Phoebe would go tentatively with her teacher to the play dough table, without making eye contact or conversation with anyone else. She would start to intensely knead the play dough. Under her breath she would chant repeatedly, "Mommy always comes back." This child was using a soothing mantra to reassure herself while adjusting to separation. When you give your child something to repeat after you leave, this can be a source of great comfort. "I'll see Mommy after story time" is another good phrase to use.

- Trust your child. Remember that children will find their own way of comforting themselves when they're dealing with newness. Don't feel guilty. School is fun, and your child will enjoy his time there. Be confident. Know that he can do this.

• To Stay or Not to Stay •

When we first started working together at the nursery school, we would allow parents to remain in the classroom for extended periods of time during the first weeks of school. Soon, it became clear to us that extending the good-bye period was actually detrimental to the whole class. Although it worked for some children and parents, for other children, it also set up an impossible conflict. In one class, three-year-old Josh was sitting with the other children at story time. The teacher was reading Eric Carle's *The Very Hungry Caterpillar*, which was Josh's favorite story. Even so, Josh couldn't keep his eyes on the book because he was preoccupied with looking over at his mother. Her presence was actually hampering his ability to attach to a teacher since Josh could always go to his mother instead. In general, we have observed that it's much more difficult for children to participate fully in school when there's a parent in the classroom.

Practical Wisdom for Parents

We decided that it was time to rethink the process. The teachers communicated a clear plan so that parents could understand what was expected of them. On day one, parents and children stayed in the classroom for a short period of time. On day two, parents said good-bye at the door and sat on a bench outside the classroom where the teacher would bring the child if needed. After a few more days, parents would go to another part of the school, and after that, the teacher would tell them when it was time to go. The children quickly learned that the classroom was a place for teachers and children, not for parents. The separation period started to go much more smoothly.

Every school will have different separation policies. Some schools will have parents stay in the classroom for a period of time. If this is the case, you need to stay quietly in the background so that your child can learn to rely on the teacher to meet his needs. This means making yourself "invisible." Bring a book or newspaper and read or pretend to read. When you engage your child in any way, this will only distract him. Once, we saw a parent giving her child candy while in the classroom—not advisable. If your child asks you to take him to the bathroom or to get a drink of water, you can tell him to go to the teacher. If your child refuses to go with the teacher, you can go together, but try to let the teacher do as much as she can. Your child needs to learn to put his trust in her. If other parents are sitting with you, limit your conversation and wait until you are outside the classroom to socialize. Never keep your cell phone on in the classroom.

Some classrooms have windows in the door or a one-way observation window through which parents can look. This can be a helpful way to watch your child as he adjusts to school, although we know some parents who can't keep themselves from standing with their noses pressed to the window all morning. Remember that it's easy to misinterpret what you see through a window when you can't hear. Sometimes you may think a teacher isn't being attentive to your child, while, in fact, the teacher may be responding to your child's need for some space. When looking through a regular classroom window, remember that you can be seen. It's inevitable that one of the children will announce, "There's Liza's mommy." Everyone stops playing and points to the window, and Liza, who's been fine all morning, starts to cry.

Occasionally, a parent will designate themselves the class "reporter" for those parents who have already left that day. When you call another mother at work to tell her that you saw her child sitting alone looking sad, this will only serve to upset her. Most of the time, it may not be an accurate or complete picture of that child's experience at school.

The Adjustment Period

As your child begins to adapt to school, it's often true that he'll behave in unexpected ways. This is to be expected. At school, your child is being called upon to learn so many new things each day that he may begin acting in ways you haven't seen before. Sometimes a child who is very talkative at home becomes extremely quiet at school. Another child may love to play with friends on the playground but prefers the company of the teacher in the classroom. A child who's comfortable trying new things with a parent may hesitate to try something new with the teacher. These differences may continue or may change with time. They aren't a cause for concern and don't mean that your child isn't comfortable at school. It's just that he's in the process of discovering who he is when apart from you and beyond the context of home.

An adjustment period for children of this age typically lasts two to three weeks. Here are some things to bear in mind during this time:

- During the first weeks of school, children commonly exhibit "babylike" or regressive behavior. Your child may have more sleep disturbances or toilet accidents. He may become more clingy, whiny, or argumentative. He may be more fragile and tire more easily. Nothing is wrong. Remember, it takes tremendous physical and emotional energy to adjust to school.

- Well-established meals, bedtime, and other family routines can help a child enormously during the transition period. Make sure that routines are clear, unhurried, and calm so that children can enter school in a relaxed manner. On nights before school, bedtime should be as consistent as possible so that children are getting the ten to twelve hours of sleep they require. During the mornings when everyone is feeling rushed and pressured to be on time for work and school, it helps to keep routines the same each day. Pick out clothes the night before, eat breakfast together in the same room each day, and turn off the TV. This way, everyone knows what to expect.

- Minimize any other changes. If at all possible, don't get a new bed, hire a new caregiver, or require your child to give up bottles, pacifiers, or regular naps during the adjustment period.

Practical Wisdom for Parents

- Set your usual limits about health, safety, and routines, but pick your battles, especially in the mornings. By staying flexible about issues that don't involve health or safety, you can help set the tone for the morning ahead. The child who enters school upset from battling over Cheerios versus Frosted Flakes is guaranteed to have a rocky start to the day. You wouldn't let your child wear shorts in January, but if he insists on wearing his shirt inside out, you can let this one go.

- This is a period when you need to make fewer demands on your child's time in general. While a child is in the process of learning to separate, it's important to simplify expectations at home. If you can, spend more one-on-one time with your child and limit your evenings out. Playdates and after-school activities should be kept to a minimum, and weekends should be as relaxed and unhurried as possible.

• What to Do When Your Child Is Having Difficulty Separating •

After two or three weeks, most children acclimate to the routines of school and are comfortable saying good-bye. For some children, it can take longer. If your child is still struggling after a month, then it's important to communicate with the school. Teachers can work with parents to develop a plan if a child is having continued difficulty.

It's very unusual for a child to be unable to separate at all; therefore, it's important to try a number of strategies over a period of time before you assume a child isn't ready for school. Anna was just turning three when she began at the nursery school. At the time, her mother was about to give birth to her third child. Each day, when Anna said good-bye to her mother, her ear-piercing screams resonated down the hallways and into every classroom. Ellen would have to take Anna to the outdoor playground so her crying wouldn't upset the other children. After half an hour, Anna would calm down and then she would have a great day, playing with her friends in the classroom, and we always called her mother to reassure her that the screaming had subsided. What we observed of Anna was that she really enjoyed school; she just hated saying good-bye to her mother. After trying a number of different strategies over a period of a month—such as making the good-bye very brief, giving Anna something from home to hold on to, trying to distract her—we finally found the key to helping this child deal with separation. We discovered she loved music and singing. We began singing songs to her from a particular book that she liked, and this became her morning ritual. Anna is now nine years old and still loves music. We recently learned from her mother that Anna spent four weeks at a summer music camp, without a single scream.

Often children who cry at the moment of saying good-bye recover quickly and engage in happy play for the rest of the day while the parent goes away with a heavy heart, imagining a crying, unhappy child. Make plans to call the school or have someone call you to let you know how your child is doing. This way you won't be imagining the worst.

Some other ideas to try if your child is having difficulties:

• It can help if you tell the teacher about your child's favorite toy, color, song, or book. This allows the teacher to have a greater familiarity with your child. For example, the teacher may greet your child with his favorite Thomas the Tank Engine book, and the child feels that the teacher knows him. A bond is formed that can help your child trust his teacher.

• You can try leaving a family photograph at school or something that belongs to you so that your child will have a visual connection to you. You may want to take a picture of the teachers to have at home so that your child can become more familiar with their faces and names.

• Some children like to know what to expect. Ask the teacher to outline the routine of the school day and find out what your child has enjoyed so far. Is there anything new or different coming up that could help you to prepare your child? Then you can talk in a very specific and positive way about the day ahead.

• It may be necessary to develop a different separation routine. There's no magic way of accomplishing this. Work with your child's teacher to come up with a plan that can be implemented for several days and then adjusted if necessary. Sometimes it works if another relative or your caregiver drops off the child at school instead of you. This can help break the pattern of difficult good-byes.

- If there's a new baby at home, if possible, come without the baby. This means you can be more focused on your older child.

- If your child says, "I hate school and don't want to go," don't take his words to heart. It's natural for a young child to have a strong reaction to new circumstances. When children say that they hate school, it usually means something else: "I miss you." "I'm worried." "I'm not comfortable yet." When this happens, you can acknowledge your child's feelings ("I know you feel this way now, but remember how much fun you had with the trains/painting/singing?"). Try not to overreact. Your child is looking for your reaction and will take his cues from you. This is a time to remain calm and appear confident even if you're feeling unsure.

Reunions

Most parents anticipate that saying good-bye will be difficult, but not everyone expects the end of the school day to be challenging as well. Reunions frequently cause children to become upset and parents to feel rejected when a child refuses to give a hug or hello. Don't be surprised if your child, who has been happy all day, suddenly bursts into tears when he sees you or is angry with you for leaving him. Your child may refuse to leave the classroom. He may be feeling hungry or overstimulated to the point of exhaustion. While you've been away, your child has expended so much energy on integrating new feelings and experiences that it's natural for him to feel tired and cranky.

It's very important that you or your caregiver are always on time for dismissal. Children worry needlessly when adults are late for pickup. This is a time of day when children need a calm transition. As you greet your child, meet him at eye level and give him your undivided attention. Smile warmly. If he's crying, then calmly and quickly take him home with little discussion. A quiet time with a snack or lunch and a story can help your child make the transition back into the world of home.

Parents often tell us that their children don't want to talk about school at the end of the day. This can be frustrating for the parent who wants to be able to participate in a child's school life. If your child doesn't want to answer your questions, remember that children tend to be overwhelmed by general questions and are much more able to answer specific ones. If you ask a question like, "What did you do at school today?" it's likely that your child will respond, "Nothing." More specific questions are best.

Some suggestions for stimulating conversation include:

- What did you have for snack today?

- Did you paint (draw, build with blocks, play a game)?

- Who did you sit next to at lunch?

- Did you go outside to play?

- What color was the play dough?

- Did you hear a story?

- What was the story about?

A quick perusal of the classroom or the bulletin board or most recent newsletter can also help get the conversation going. At the same time, don't inundate your child with questions. You'll only overwhelm him. Many children have difficulty recounting the day and like to keep school separate from home. This is quite typical although parents often find it hard to accept a child's need to keep the details of the day private.

Letting Go

Never underestimate what is taking place during these first days of school. As you and your child learn to separate from each other, you're setting the tone for an experience that will recur at various stages in your relationship as time goes on. Now that our own children are in their twenties and thirties, we can look back and remember the separations that occurred at each stage of their development. Whether it was the first day at school, going on the bus to day camp, going to sleepaway camp, or even leaving for college, we can see how accomplishing each of these transitions—even if they were initially difficult—helped to define our children, to make them independent and confident people. If you want your child to feel strong and capable when you're not there, it's very important that he learns to become comfortable leaving you.

Even those children who initially struggle with separation often go on to

Practical Wisdom for Parents

become surprisingly independent in a short time. Nancy's daughter, Alissa, had clung to her mother on the first day of school, so when it came time for Alissa to attend day camp, Nancy remembers having a lump in her throat as she watched her daughter board the bus. But as the bus pulled away, Alissa smushed her nose against the window and made a face at her mother, thereby curing Nancy of any separation worries. Ellen's children were both naturally cautious in nature and would send her long, sad letters from sleep-away camp pleading to come home, while in reality they loved camp. Both Alice and Charles have grown up to become adults who aren't afraid to take on new challenges with confidence.

As a parent, the ways in which you handle each separation will help your child to feel more competent and capable of achieving the next phase of independence. Through the years, we have seen so many children who struggled with separation leave preschool secure in the knowledge that they can do it. Every parent and child must experience separation in their own way. It may take time, and it may be stressful for a while, but it will happen. When it does happen, this achievement needs to be celebrated and enjoyed. It's a time to be proud of your child's accomplishment and growth, and your own as a parent.

Recommended Books for Children About Beginning School

Oh My Baby, Little One	Kathi Appelt
Clifford's First School Day	Norman Bridwell
D.W.'s Guide to Preschool	Marc Brown
Going to School	Anne Civardi
Will I Have a Friend	Miriam Cohen
You Go Away	Dorothy Corey
My First Day at Nursery School	Becky Edwards
Corduroy Goes to School	Don Freeman
Curious Kids Go to Preschool	Ingrid Godon
Bernard Goes to School	Joan Elizabeth Goodman
I Am Not Going to School Today	Robie H. Harris
Wemberly Worried	Kevin Henkes
Spot Goes to School	Eric Hill
Froggy Goes to School	Jonathan London
Sumi's First Day of School Ever	Soyung Pak
The Kissing Hand	Audrey Penn

Separation: Easing the Way

Chapter Four

THE SOCIAL LIVES OF CHILDREN

The ability to socialize is the most important skill a child learns in her first years at school and one of the most compelling reasons for sending your child to an early childhood program. When you expose her to a classroom of children—under the careful watch of her teachers—you're ensuring that her social abilities will develop at a pace that simply wouldn't be possible if she stayed at home with an adult or her siblings.

Each year, we watch as the very youngest children in the nursery school begin to interact with their peers in ways that go beyond the simple grabbing or watching that often constitutes play between very young children. In the course of the preschool years, friendship becomes a key factor in the children's happiness. The child who has difficulties separating from her mother in the morning soon forgets her tears when she discovers that she enjoys playing house with another child. In the mornings, the children's faces light up when they see a favorite playmate or drop with disappointment when they're told a friend is absent that day. A child who has friends feels secure and enjoys her time at school.

Not every child will acquire friendship skills at the same age, however. Some children don't want to participate and need encouragement before they'll join in, especially when faced with a large group. Other children quickly make friends with everyone in the class. Your child may be happiest playing with one friend at a time, or she may enjoy playing alone at first. A child who is very reluctant may take many months to fully adjust to the classroom. It can take all her energy to separate from her parents and to get to know her teachers before she becomes comfortable interacting with the other children. Every child learns to socialize at her own pace. A child who is more outgoing may seem to be "ahead," but the reserved and cautious child will make strong connections with the other children, just in her own time.

As a parent, if you can step back and observe your child's unique social style, then you'll be better able to support her growth. Remember that your child's temperament may be very different from yours. If you had one best friend throughout school, it may be difficult for you to accept that your child always chooses to be part of a group. If you were outgoing and enjoyed being one of the gang, then it may be hard for you to watch your child playing alone. This was true for Nancy. When her son, Michael, was preschool age, he preferred to be off to one side on the playground, playing with his imaginary friends, while all the other children interacted on the playground equipment. Nancy was someone who always preferred playing with others as a child. She was concerned, so she talked to Michael's teacher, who reassured her that Michael was happy playing alone, that he was a naturally curious and imaginative child with a rich fantasy life. The teacher pointed out that Michael often played with other children inside the classroom. Nancy recognized that her discomfort had more to do with her own expectations and experiences than with Michael himself.

Alice, Ellen's daughter, preferred playing with three special friends at school, rather than interacting with lots of children in the class. At home, she was content to play alone, drawing pictures, making up stories, and playing with her toys. Charles, on the other hand, had a built-in playmate with Alice, who was five years older. She would direct their play, and Charles would happily follow. If Alice told Charles he was her pet dog, Charles would willingly lap up Cheerios from a bowl on the kitchen floor. When Charles began school, he engaged easily with his classmates. Even at a young age, he didn't especially enjoy solitary play. He required the company of other children to play happily. Ellen recognized that Charles needed to be more self-sufficient and encouraged him by balancing playdates with time spent alone with her. It's often the case that children in the same family will have very different social styles, and you may have to adjust your expectations accordingly.

While your child's social skills are developing in the communal environment of the classroom, her social life outside school will also be taking off. Playdates are a preschool staple, and after a few weeks of school, you'll probably hear your child asking if she can play with a friend after class. Other children will need a parent to initiate playdates for them. In either instance, your social life will begin to change alongside your child's. Sometimes you'll meet other parents and get along with them immediately. Other times, your child may be attracted to a certain child, but you find you have little in common with the parents. Although there's no need to become close friends, you'll need to be cordial and pleasant for the sake of your child. If you don't make friends easily or are uncomfortable meeting new people, try to overcome some of your hesitancy so that your child can benefit from these social interactions. You may benefit from this too. Parents with children this age often make strong connections that last for many years. Both of us are still in touch with mothers whose children were at nursery school with our sons and daughters.

Your Child's Developing Social Life

Although every child develops at her own pace, there are typical stages of development for acquiring social skills.

Until now, your child has probably been happiest playing alone or with an adult. As an infant or toddler, she's been almost completely focused on her own needs; she lives for the moment and demands to be instantly gratified. She may notice other children but she's usually absorbed in her own play.

At the same time, her social skills are growing. As she nears school age, although her play is still mostly solitary, she's becoming more aware of and interested in other children. She remains egocentric, and her communication is minimal, but she's probably beginning to interact with other children, even if it's only by touching them, grabbing at their toys, or imitating them. She may enjoy playing close to another child, but without cooperating or reciprocating. (Developmental psychologists call this kind of play "parallel play.")

At this point, she's still learning how to express herself with words, and she needs help understanding the concepts of taking turns and sharing with others. You can understand why playing with another child of the same age and level of development is so demanding. Both children want to have their needs gratified immediately, and compromise is an enormous challenge. Occasionally, a parent whose child is having difficulty playing with the other children tells us that this child plays beautifully with her older cousins and that maybe she needs to be with more mature children. We explain that older children often accommodate the demands of a younger child or may dominate the play. It takes greater social skill to play with a child of the same age.

For a two-year-old starting school, her first social relationship will be with her teacher. Your child could be sitting at the play dough table with three other children, but she'll only have eyes for the teacher. Once she begins to adjust to school, she'll start to notice the other children around her. After several weeks, she may look up from the play dough table and say with surprise, "Who *are* all these children?" After a few months, she'll notice the child sitting next to her and say, "Can I use the rolling pin?" or "What are you making?" By the end of the year, the children are having conversations back and forth: "Can I put candles in the birthday cake you're making?" "Let's sing 'Happy Birthday.' "

The three-year-old classroom is a much noisier place, where the children's voices dominate. Initially, the children's friendships are still defined by proximity. A friend can be someone your child happened to sit next to at the snack table, or that she met in the sandbox, or the one who was also playing with blocks today. As adults, we wouldn't walk into a party and tell the first stranger we met that she was our "new friend." But that's what friendship is like for young children. At this age, a child will simply play with the child sitting next to her.

Soon children within the group begin to get a better idea of who likes to play with what. They start to choose playmates based on common tastes and interests. A child who likes building with blocks will naturally make a friend with another block builder. If your child loves to play house, it's likely that she'll spend time with other children who enjoy imaginative play. When a child repeats the same activity with the same friend, this is how young relationships begin to form.

As your child matures and her language ability improves, she can start to communicate enough to interact in more meaningful ways. She begins to understand that a friend is someone she likes and that she's known for a period of time. She may say, "When I first came to school, I didn't know Ella; now she's my friend." Although children are still drawn by common interests, friendship takes on new meaning. Children may be attracted to one another because they are fun, funny, silly, nice, or powerful. They can sustain play for longer periods and include other children and their ideas. Two children may begin a firefighter game where they're putting on their clothing, getting in the fire truck, driving to the scene, and putting out the fire in the pretend house. Then they may recruit another child to pretend to be a dog that they can rescue. They may repeat this game day after day.

Through interacting with their classmates, the children gradually acquire the essential skills of sharing and compromising. They learn to accommodate to others and to delay their need for immediate gratification. They find new ways of communicating. They can play together imaginatively and try on roles of leader and follower. They learn to handle aggression and impulsivity. In the safe environment of the classroom, the children experience a sense of belonging and caring. They learn new skills and their relationships give them a sense of identity and self-confidence. Children begin to understand that coming to school means you get to be with your friends. This is the time when the joy and fun of playing with other children becomes central to children's lives.

• What to Do When Your Child Feels Left Out •

Inevitably, when children in a classroom become better accustomed to one another, they also begin to discover the power of banding together and excluding another child. At some point in your child's school life, you're probably going to hear her say the words, "No one wanted to play with me today." Of course you'll feel sad for your child and possibly angry at the other children who hurt her feelings. Although it's only natural to feel upset, it's your job as a parent to understand what actually happened and to help your child cope with these experiences when they arise.

Try not to overreact. We promise you that nine times out of ten, when a child says, "No one wanted to play with me today," this usually means that for five minutes out of a five-hour day, another child did not want to play with her. It could be that your child asked to be the little sister in the pretend house but the children playing had already chosen someone else to be the little sister and didn't want another little sister. It could mean that your child said, "Could I play?" but the game was already in progress and someone said, "No." Or it could mean that she asked to play with a friend, but the friend wanted to be alone and was not interested in playing for that moment. Exclusion of this kind is perfectly normal. It's part of social development.

Instead of expressing your concern and giving your child the impression that she really has something to worry about, try to stay positive and problem solve with your child. Acknowledge your child's feelings ("I bet that made you feel sad"), and then tell her that you're going to help her solve the problem ("Let's figure out what you can do tomorrow when you want to play with Jack and Sara"). You can practice responses with your child so she'll know what to say if this happens to her again:

If Sara says: "I don't want to play house again with you."
You can say: "Okay, let's go on the tricycles."

If Jack says: "This game only has two Power Rangers."
You can say: "That's okay; I'll be the bad guy."

Here are some other ways to help your child when she's feeling left out:

- Teach your child how to jump right into the game. Tell her to ask, "What are you playing?" instead of asking permission to play. When a child asks, "Can I play with you?" she's automatically setting herself up for a negative response.

- Tell your child that she can ask a teacher or adult for help if she has problems playing with the other children. Early childhood educators are experts in getting children to interact with one another. A teacher might say to the children:
  "Can you think of something that both of you would like to do?"
  "Why don't you play Oliver's way first and then Will's way."
  "Kate can have the ball for five minutes, and then Jessica can have it when the timer says five minutes are up."
  "Look at Lucy's face. She looks sad. Can we all think of a way to play that will make everyone feel better?"
  "Why don't you both sit on the bench for a few minutes and try to think of a new way to play that game."

  At the nursery school we also teach the children the rhyme "You can't say you can't play" (quoting the title of Vivian Gussin Paley's excellent book on the social lives of children).

- The next day, if your child doesn't bring up this problem again, then put the previous day's troubles out of your mind. Whatever you do, *don't* ask with a worried look on your face, "Did anyone play with you today?" We once heard Michael Thompson describe this kind of questioning as "investigation for pain." When you investigate for pain, your child will sense that this is something you're concerned about and will try to get your attention by bringing up negative situations in the future. She may also become anxious at the possibility of children not playing with her. In general, it's best not to overreact to your child's hurt feelings but to help her to deal positively with the situation instead. This doesn't mean you're brushing her feelings aside; it simply means you're giving her the tools to better handle her relationships.

- If your child tells you: "I don't like Zoe," try not to take this complaint too seriously. Sometimes, children just don't get along. Tomorrow, Zoe could be your child's favorite friend again. It's not unusual to hear one child say to another: "I'm not your friend anymore." What that child is really saying is: "I don't like your game. You didn't do what I said. I don't like that you let Alex be the firefighter." Children who say they don't like each other may play happily with one another within minutes.

- If your child tells you that someone doesn't want to be her friend anymore, you can say, "Sometimes children like to play with someone else. Maybe tomorrow you can play with your friend again." You can suggest that she find another friend or activity when this happens, or she can tell her friend, "It hurts my feelings when you say that to me." If your child is continually hurt or upset by another child, and you have tried to help resolve the issue, you can tell her that she can walk away and find another friend.

• Best Friends and Other Problems •

As in adult relationships, sometimes an unexplained chemistry forms between two children. They just like each other. This can be wonderful or problematic. Or both. You may find that your child is drawn to another child. At first, the play proceeds happily. But after a while, things start to go wrong. It's amazing how quickly children learn to push each other's buttons. In one of the nursery school's four-year-old classrooms, a teacher observed that "best friends" Beth and Caroline were having a lot of conflicts. Beth knew that Caroline loved the blue teddy bear more than any other toy and didn't like to share it, so Beth persistently taunted Caroline by taking the toy. Caroline knew that Beth liked to sit next to her at the snack table, so she deliberately began to save a seat for another child. When the teacher spoke to the girls' parents, she discovered that Beth and Caroline were seeing each other every day after school, and the families were getting together on the weekends as well. The girls' parents were friends and were delighted that their daughters seemed to enjoy playing together. But after a while, Beth and Caroline had had too much of a good thing. They simply knew each other too well. After taking a break from playing together for a while and after the number of playdates was reduced, Beth and Caroline could enjoy their friendship again.

We believe that at this age it's not helpful to encourage your child to have a "best friend." When you schedule a playdate with the same child each week or always ask your child about "your best friend Caroline," this promotes exclusivity at a time when children benefit greatly from exploring play with children of both sexes with many different personality styles and varied interests. Your very active child may play with Legos in a calm, focused way with a less active child. A child who doesn't like to challenge herself physically might discover a love of climbing when paired with a child who loves outdoor play. A boy who's obsessed with superhero play may sit and draw a picture or play a board game with a girl who enjoys these activities. Another drawback of best friendships is that the other children in the classroom will avoid approaching two children who are "best friends" because they assume they'll be excluded. It's often the case that when one child is absent, then the other child feels at a loss during the school day without her friend.

It's very important to be aware of the language you use when talking to your child about her friendships. Just as it's best not to use the phrase "best friend," you should also avoid describing your daughter's male friend as her "boyfriend" or your son's female friend as his "girlfriend." When a boy and a girl form a close relationship, we'll often hear parents say, "Oh, those two are so cute. Maybe they'll get married." This can actually be upsetting for young children and can send the message that a boy and girl can't just be friends. Children take the things their parents say literally. We know children who have said to their parents, "But I don't want to be married." A child may spend the day worrying that she must play with her "boyfriend" instead of playing with the other children. By all means encourage your child to have friends of both genders; just don't bring adult concepts of love and marriage into it.

• What to Do If Your Child Is Having Problems Socializing •

Not every child is a social being. Some children may need adult support in order to play with other children. Rebecca, a little girl in one of the nursery school's three-year-old classrooms, always sat quietly as all the children chatted during snack time. She never joined in the conversation. The teacher mentioned this to her parents and suggested that they help Rebecca with her conversational skills by practicing at the dinner table. Each family member would take turns telling about the best thing that happened to them that day. In a short time, Rebecca became more comfortable talking at snack time.

Sometimes a child simply needs to learn how to use social cues, such as a friendly tone of voice or facial expression. Ryan, a four-year-old at the nursery school with very expressive features, often scowled and put his hand on his hips when his friends did something he didn't like. The other children began to avoid playing with him as they didn't like his angry facial expression or aggressive posture. Ryan's teacher took him to one side and showed him what he looked like when he was scowling with his hands on his hips. She explained to him that this was upsetting to his friends. The teacher demonstrated a "friendly face" and talked about what Ryan could say when he was angry. The teacher made sure to remind Ryan about his facial expressions, and after a couple of reminders, he stopped making his angry face. As soon as he stopped, the other children wanted to play with him again.

If your child is struggling socially or having difficulty making friends, it's helpful to talk to his teacher so you can share your concerns. The teacher can tell you what she's observed and can strategize with you to help improve the situation. Sometimes your child will tell you about a specific issue, and you can relate this to the teacher so she can keep an eye out for the situation in the future. If a teacher tells you about a social problem that your child is having, try not to react defensively. Parents aren't always the first to observe their children's social difficulties. As a parent, you're usually seeing your child at home or during one-on-one playdates. You're unlikely to have observed how she interacts in the context of the classroom, where the social dynamic is more complex.

Playdates

Playdates are a great way for young children to develop their newly emerging social skills. During playdates, children learn about each other's likes and dislikes and about one another's families and homes. They discover different toys and hopefully share them. We always encourage parents to make playdates for their children, especially if a child is having difficulties socializing in a larger group. If a child is reluctant to interact with others, playing with just one child is much less intimidating than trying to play with the whole class.

Here are some good rules of thumb you can follow to ensure happy playdates:

- Make sure playdates are one-on-one. Playdates work best when limited to two children. We tell parents, "Three's a crowd." With three, one child usually gets left out. One-on-one play allows your child to experience the give and take necessary for friendship. It also gives her a chance to really get to know the other child.

- Ask a teacher for suggestions. Who does your child like to play with at school? Often parents arrange playdates based on adult relationships. While it's nice to socialize with parents whose company you enjoy, playdates are for the children, not the adults, and should be guided by your child and her interests.

- Don't schedule too many playdates. If your child is at an age where she attends school every day, a playdate once or twice a week is enough. More than this is simply too exhausting for a young child. Some children will ask for a playdate every day, especially if they see another child going on a playdate. As a parent, you need to exercise your judgment and curtail your child's social life if necessary. At the end of a school day, when your child asks to play with Rachel and you look at your calendar and see that the first available date is in three weeks, you know you've overdone it.

- Vary your child's playdates. It's a good idea to schedule playdates with different children so that you introduce your child to different styles of play and more than one other family. We do not recommend "steady" playdates. If you have booked your child for a playdate every Thursday with the same child, the two "friends" may quickly tire of each other and develop negative patterns that then carry over into the classroom.

- Don't tell your child about the playdate too far in advance. If you tell your child in the morning that she has a playdate later in the day, she may become preoccupied with this information. Parents don't always realize that if a child knows she has a playdate after school, she will often think that she's supposed to play with that child exclusively during class time. In most cases, it's okay to wait until the end of the day to tell your child about a playdate. Some children are more concerned with knowing what their plans are after school and need to be told earlier in the day. You may want to check with your child's teacher if either one of these issues comes up.

- Cancel a playdate if your child is tired or unwell. Sometimes your child will either be too tired or not feel well enough after school to have a playdate that you've previously scheduled. When your child cries because you've canceled her playdate and her friend is disappointed, the best thing you can do is to reassure both children that you'll reschedule some other time. You could also suggest that your child take a short rest at home before seeing if she's able to play later in the day. Even though this is uncomfortable for everyone involved, it's in both children's interests to postpone a playdate if a child is tired and irritable.

- Limit the length of the playdates. An hour and a half is a sensible amount of time for a playdate. After an hour and a half, most children at this age will lose interest and become tired and irritable. Whining, fighting, and tears will ensue. For the same reason, you should avoid making a playdate on a day when your child has an after-school activity or a birthday party, as this will simply be too much for her.

- Be there to supervise. Young children must be watched closely when they're playing. A perfectly good interaction can quickly turn to fighting and tears without adult supervision. If the children hit, grab, or push you can remind them: "Your hands need to stay on your own bodies." If you're not in the room, you need to be listening close by so that you can anticipate and intervene when you hear the tone change or escalate. If you hear nothing for a long period, it may mean that your child and her friend have taken off all their clothes or are painting your walls.

- Be prepared to participate. Some children will jump right into playing together, but others may need your direction to get things started. It usually helps to have a plan for the visit. Some suggestions for fun playdate activities are outlined on page 94.

- Don't turn on the TV, video, or computer during a playdate. It defeats the object of inviting another child to your home since these activities are solitary, not sociable.

- Keep your child's siblings otherwise engaged. If you have another sibling at home while your child is having a playdate, it's helpful to try and engage the sibling in a separate activity. Younger siblings can be disruptive to the playdate, and an older sibling can be an enticement to your child's friend. If it isn't possible to separate the siblings, you need to supervise so your child can enjoy herself and not feel responsible for her little brother or distracted by her older sister.

- Tell your child that she needs to follow the rules of the house, wherever she goes. Every family has different rules about what is and isn't acceptable. You can tell your child that when she visits someone's home, she needs to follow *that* family's rules. In your house, you can have your child's friends follow *your* rules. All children should clean up toys in everyone's home.

- Give a warning before it's time to leave. Children will be reluctant to end their play when they are having fun, and you'll be tempted to let them continue until they tire of playing. But when children of this age grow tired, they fall apart quickly. It's better to give the children plenty of warning that a playdate is going to end so that they have time to clean up and make a gradual transition toward leaving. It will be a more positive experience for all involved if the playdate ends on a happy note.

- End a playdate if it starts to fall apart. It's perfectly fine to end a playdate early and suggest that you plan another visit when the children are not so tired. You can tell your child: "I can see that you are both very tired right now. I'm going to help you clean up and we'll play again soon."

• Getting Your Child to Share •

Some children have difficulty sharing their toys and are reluctant to have another child come to their home and play with their things. If this is the case with your child, it's helpful to talk to her ahead of time about which toys she would like to share with her friend and which special toys she would like to put away. This can help eliminate some of the conflicts associated with sharing.

If two children want to play with the same toy and begin fighting, you have a few courses of action:

- You can encourage them to take turns. Use a timer so that each child knows when time's up.

- You can figure out how to change the play. If two children are fighting over a toy horse, you can say, "Okay, here's a cow. Let's build a farm."

- If two children are stuck fighting over a toy, it's always best to distract them. Move on to a snack or a story. Get them out of the moment. Parents of young children quickly learn to be masters of redirection.

- When the play dissolves into tears, you can help resolve the conflict by offering solutions and suggestions (see above). Or you can ask the children what *they* think might be a good solution. When children reach the age of four and five, they're better able to figure out how to solve problems for themselves. At this age, you can move the children away from the scene of the conflict and into another room, then ask for their suggestions by saying, "Is there another way you can play this game so you'll both have fun?" "Can you think of another game to play?" "Let's take a five-minute break and see if you have any ideas of what you can do."

- When the play has broken down, avoid asking what happened. If you ask very young children, "What happened?" you can be sure each child will give you a different story. While it may be helpful to hear what each child has to say, and you should always acknowledge the children's feelings, this may not help resolve the issue.

- If all else fails, take the toy away.

• Ideas for Fun Playdates •

When you invite another child for a playdate, it's always a good idea to have a few fun activities planned. Sometimes children need something to get the play going, and it can be a more pleasurable experience for adults and children alike when the playdate is structured with some organized activities.

• Arts and craft projects
Materials include paper of all kinds, crayons, markers, colored pencils, chalk, watercolors, tape, glue, scissors, popsicle sticks, play dough. Projects include collage, cardboard tube or box sculpture, sock or paper bag puppets, stringing macaroni or Cheerios on pipe cleaners.

• Cooking
Recipes should be simple, with only a few steps. Children can cut with plastic knives (with supervision), help to measure ingredients, pour, and mix. Good things to make include English muffin pizzas, fruit salad, muffins, cupcakes, and cookies.

• Reading and music
Read books aloud, listen to stories or music on CD, play instruments, sing, and dance.

- **Dress up**

  Give the children hats, scarves, gloves, sunglasses, briefcases, pocketbooks, ties, vests, and shoes, and see where their imaginations take them.

- **Out and about**

  A playdate doesn't necessarily need to be in your home. Children can play outdoors or in the park. You can go out for a snack or meal. You can also visit a local place like the firehouse, zoo, library, or museum.

Birthdays

When your child is old enough to go to school, she's also beginning to be old enough to understand what it means to have a birthday. Whereas in previous years, she was too young to appreciate the fun, now she'll begin counting down the days. The anticipation of the next big number is magical for children. They sense that "being three" or "being four" is very grown-up and important. We've seen five-year-olds who hold up five fingers and say: "Now I'm a whole hand!"

For parents, each birthday feels like a milestone too. You remember the time of your child's birth and marvel at how the years are flying by. Birthdays are for celebrating, and it's natural to want to include your child's friends and family in her big day. But what's special for an adult can be very different from a child's idea of what's special. When Alissa was turning three, Nancy, like all good parents, was wracking her brain to come up with a fun and exciting idea for a party. Now that Alissa was in school, Nancy had observed that other parents were inviting the whole class and arranging for entertainment. Alissa had already been invited to gym parties and parties with magicians and puppet shows. When Nancy asked Alissa whether she would like a gym party, magician, or puppet show, Alissa replied, "Can't we just have Alice and Charles over for pizza and cake?" That's exactly what happened, and Alissa's third birthday was everything she wanted it to be.

When we were growing up, a birthday party meant that a few friends and relatives came to your home for hamburgers, hot dogs, and cake. You wore fancy party clothes and a pointy hat and played pin the tail on the donkey. Everyone watched while you opened your birthday presents. You had a great time. Nowadays, we regularly hear about parties for forty or more guests with elaborate entertainment and catered food. Parents tell us they feel pressured to keep up with other families and obligated to reciprocate every invitation their child has received. Like Alissa, however, most children would prefer something small scale.

In reality, birthday parties can be overwhelming, overstimulating, and difficult for young children. From a child's perspective, parties are noisy, busy, and chaotic. Your child may feel as if she's out of control, and often she will be. If she's the birthday child, she may be uncomfortable being the center of attention. The guests may want to open the gifts, blow out the candles on the cake, and steal the spotlight from her. Many children are afraid of clowns. They're not used to eating so many snacks and cakes. They don't like the sound of the balloons popping, and they cry when the helium balloon they've been given floats away.

A small celebration with family and a few close friends, a birthday cake and candles, and of course, a few presents—this is really all a preschool child needs to feel special.

It's true that the birthday party guest list can sometimes become a sensitive issue for families. If you decide that you want to have a small family party with only a few friends, you mustn't worry about excluding the rest of the class. You can always celebrate with cupcakes in school as well. Most schools have policies regarding birthdays, and you need to find out what these are, such as inviting the whole class or just one or two special friends. If you follow your school's guidelines, this will help ensure that children aren't excluded and don't end up with hurt feelings. It's a good idea to mail the invitations rather than dropping them off at school to help avoid this issue. Besides, children enjoy opening an invitation that comes to them in the mail, and invites often get lost at school.

In the same way, don't feel as if your child must attend every party she's invited to. If your child really doesn't like birthday parties, it's fine to politely decline some invitations. If the party is for a very close friend, you can encourage your child to go to the party by explaining that the birthday child's feelings might be hurt.

Some other helpful hints for happy birthdays:

- Keep it small. Try to limit numbers as much as possible.

- Keep it short. One and a half to two hours is long enough.

- Schedule a party on a weekend rather than after a long day at school.

- Allow your child to help pick out the invitations and decorations.

- Have a theme for the party that's personal to your child. Choose a favorite animal or character and decorate the table and cake in ways that reflect this.

- Keep the food simple: pizza, chicken nuggets, sandwiches cut in fun shapes.

- Come up with some simple but fun activities: decorating cupcakes or cookies, making sundaes, decorating hats, decorating placemats or tablecloths with stickers.

- Play simple, fun games like pin the tail on the donkey and musical chairs, or plan activities such as going on a treasure hunt or hitting a piñata for treats.

- Goody bags are fun and children enjoy getting them, but there's no need to go overboard.

- If children are at the party without their parents and a child misbehaves, remove the child from the activity for a short time and remind her of what's expected.

- Teach your child to say thank you when she receives a gift.

- Plan for a quiet time after the party since your child may feel exhausted and let down.

Overscheduling

In the past fifteen years, so much has been studied and written about overscheduling and its negative effects on children. This is an issue where psychologists, pediatricians, and educators are in agreement. Overscheduling is detrimental to young children. Despite all this conclusive evidence, however, in recent years, we've observed a marked increase in the amount of hours children are spending in programmed activities.

Teachers have received letters from parents like the following example:

Dear Ms. Summers,

I'll be away on business for a few days and I just wanted you to know about Justin's schedule for the week. Mary, his usual sitter, will pick him up on Monday a half hour early so that he can get to his dentist appointment, and after that he will have a sleepover with his grandparents. On

Tuesday, he will go directly to his pottery class and will go home with Leo for a playdate and dinner. Wednesday he has his weekly violin lesson and will play with Luke and Jeremy, the twins who live upstairs. Grammy and Poppy will pick him up on Thursday and take him to the Museum of Natural History and then out for dinner. I'll be home on Friday and will pick him up to bring him to Samantha's gym party. Justin loves school and can't wait to come every day. If he seems a little tired, please let him have some extra rest time. Have a great week. I'll see you Friday.

    Jill Adams

It's hard to blame this parent, who only wants the best for her child. From the moment her child was born, she's been told about the importance of early brain development and that "early exposure" to a variety of activities can increase a child's capacity for learning. She's been informed that it's important for young children to have social experiences in order for them to develop their ability to play with others. Now that he's in school, and she hears that his classmates are going to soccer and pottery classes, she feels she should give him the same opportunities. Besides, she's busy with work these days and feels badly that her son spends so much time with the babysitter and would rather he was in a programmed activity instead. She worries, above all, that if she doesn't expose her child to as many educational and social experiences as everyone else in the class, he'll fall behind.

In a world where we can take our laptops and cell phones wherever we go and productivity is prized, it follows that we think that our children need to be productive as well. Many well-meaning parents have fallen into the trap of imagining that by signing their children up for multiple activities they are being better parents and therefore will "produce" better children. It may feel like you're doing your job as a parent by taking your child from class to class—it may even assuage any guilt you have about not spending enough time with your child—but in fact, the parent who overschedules a very young child can cause problems for that child.

We cannot stress this strongly enough: It is counterproductive for your preschool-age child to be doing too much. Children who do too much too soon tend to be stressed, anxious, and susceptible to feelings of low self-esteem. At the nursery school, we have seen how overscheduling effectively inhibits children from fully participating in and getting the most they can from school. Natasha, a little girl in one of the four-year-old classrooms, had started school with plenty of interest and enthusiasm for classroom life. She always had her hand up at circle time and would work for extended periods on art activities. After a month or so of school, however, she'd become listless and unable to concentrate when playing alone or with others. Often, at the end of the school day, she'd cry and say she didn't want to leave. The teacher told her parents about this behavior and discovered that Natasha was attending four after-school classes each week. On the teacher's advice, the parents wisely withdrew Natasha from two of her classes. The mother told the teacher that her daughter actually thanked her for not making her go to a class each day. Natasha's energy and enjoyment of school soon returned.

Teachers always know when a child is doing too much outside of school. There are some very clear signs. Overscheduled children tend to be:

- Tired or hyperactive and have difficulty focusing and holding on to basic information.

- Preoccupied and distracted because they are thinking about the next activity.

- Anxious for acceptance, unable to trust their own judgment, and in need of approval for everything they do.

- Unable to create games without an adult directing them.

- In conflict when they don't want to go to an after-school activity but feel they need to please their parents.

- More likely to say they are "bored" when they mean, "I don't know what to do."

- More likely to lose their sense of spontaneity and excitement at doing something new, saying, "I already did this."

- Unable to spend valuable time alone, when being alone stimulates creativity.

- More fragile and less resilient.

We recommend: For three-year-olds, no more than one activity a week; for four- and five-year-olds, no more than two.

There's nothing wrong with giving your child an opportunity to explore a range of activities outside of school. But you don't have to cram all these activities into a single week or even a single year. A young child has all the time in the world to learn tennis or guitar or French. She doesn't need to do all this before she's five. If your child is mastering these skills at the expense of more basic tasks such as putting on a coat, going to the toilet alone, or holding a cup, then it's time to scale back and reassess the situation. If you begin to feel like you're acting as your child's personal assistant—arranging and facilitating her schedule—as opposed to actually participating in her life, then you've overdone it. If you find yourself feeding your child dinner in the car coming home from an activity rather than sitting down at the table for a meal together, then you need to reprioritize family time.

In our parent groups, we ask parents to think back to their own childhoods, to remember the things that enriched their lives then and made them happy. Time and again, parents acknowledge that the things they enjoyed most were simple activities such as playing with others or spending time alone. Their happiest memories have little to do with classes or lessons, and neither did they discover their interests and passions in the first five years of life. It's important to keep this truth in mind and reassure yourself that you're helping, not harming, your child by limiting her after-school activities.

• Is It Fun? •

If you decide to enroll your child in one (or at the most two) activities a week, then you'll have plenty of choices. In any local newspaper, you'll see many advertisements for classes and activities geared to very young children. Many of these can be fun and enriching, but keep in mind their appropriateness when you're contemplating enrolling your child. Children learn best in a stimulating environment that's warm and supportive and allows them to set the pace. In a nonpressured atmosphere, children acquire confidence and the enthusiasm for lifelong learning. For this age, you should chose activities based on whether your child will enjoy them, not because you think she *should* accomplish them. Classes involving lots of drills, waiting time, or too many directions can be stressful and frustrating for young children. Look for programs that are creative and playful and allow for a large range of skills and ability levels. It's best to choose activities such as a music-making class where the children play rhythm instruments together, rather than traditional instrumental lessons. You need to keep in mind your child's energy levels and typical attention span. When classes are geared to the age and stage of your child's development, they'll better meet her growing needs and be more pleasurable for her.

Before you enroll your child, it's important to take note of your own expectations and how these are affecting the selections you make:

- Is the activity interesting to your child or is it more about what you wish you'd done as a child?

- Does the activity reflect your own interests or your child's?

- Do you feel your child will enjoy the activity or do you think she "ought" to do it?

- Are you targeting your child's interests or do you have a preconceived need to "enhance" her skills?

- Is your child physically or emotionally ready to meet the expectations of the class?

- Does your child have the attention span for a teacher-directed activity such as cello or ballet?

Above all, ask yourself, "Is it fun?"

Sometimes, children will ask to participate in a specific activity. This doesn't mean that they understand what's involved. When Ellen's son, Charles, was four years old, he loved banging on the keys of the piano in their living room and often asked to learn how to play. Although he enjoyed messing around on the piano and listening to music, Ellen knew that he didn't have the attention span required for lessons. Postponing formal lessons until he was eight years old gave Charles the time to acquire the discipline needed to succeed with less frustration and more enjoyment. By starting too soon, he may have later lost interest and the desire to learn when he was actually ready to do so. Charles continued to take lessons until he was eighteen and still enjoys playing piano.

It's helpful to remember that young children often do not fully understand what you have "signed them up" to do. One mother came to us with the following dilemma. Simon, her four-year-old, had asked to "go to" karate. She responded by signing him up for the class and buying the outfit. Simon excitedly put on the white pants, top, and belt and went happily to the class. The next week, as he was getting ready to go to the class, he said, "I don't want to go. I already went to karate." Simon didn't realize that "going to" karate meant going once a week for twelve weeks. He wanted to go to karate. He went. Now he didn't want to go anymore. His mother insisted that he go again, but after the next class, Simon had the same response. The mother wanted to know what to do. Should she keep encouraging Simon to go? She didn't want her son to abandon something before he'd started, but neither did she want to turn him off karate by forcing him to continue. We advised her to problem solve with Simon by asking what exactly he didn't enjoy about the class. He may have been hungry and needed a small snack before going; he may have been worried about where the bathroom was; he may have been concerned about another child not being nice to him; he may have been worried about who was picking him up from the class. We told her that if Simon couldn't verbalize the problem, she should observe the class or talk to the instructor. We also said that while it was a good idea to encourage Simon to go back to the class at least once or twice, it was just as important not to force the issue. Parents are often reluctant to stop an activity if a child is resistant or unhappy as they don't want to send the message that "quitting" is okay. We think that it's perfectly acceptable to withdraw an unhappy child from an activity at this age. We always tell parents that although going to school isn't optional, other activities are.

If your child is enjoying a particular activity, this doesn't mean that you should sign her up for another similar one. If she shows an aptitude for ballet, for example, there's no need to enroll her in a jazz dance class. When you push a very young child to succeed in a single activity, it rarely pays off. Your child may love ballet at three; however, you run the risk of turning her off that activity altogether if you pressure her to excel at dance at such a young age. Although she may have a natural flair, she could lose interest and fail to realize her talent when she's older. If you want to encourage her potential, the best thing you can do is to play music at home and let her dance around the room with you.

• Downtime •

Our lives these days are busy and complicated. We're all guilty of overscheduling ourselves, keeping our calendars filled to the brim with appointments, meetings, and social engagements. Often, parents assume that children need to be busy too. If you ask a five-year-old what makes her happy, however, she's unlikely to say gymnastics class or horse-riding lessons. She's more likely to say: "when my mommy brings me to school" or "when Daddy reads me a story" or "when my family goes to the park." It's the everyday, ordinary things that children appreciate the most. The actual needs of under-fives are remarkably simple.

We tell parents that if they want to give their children the "best possible start in life," then they need to cut back on the scheduled activities and set aside regular time to do "nothing" instead. Give yourself conscious permission to spend downtime with your child each week. Don't feel badly because you are doing "nothing" or "being unproductive." By doing nothing, you are doing something very important. You're letting your child know that you value time together and you're discovering who your child is in the process.

Once you have set aside this time for your child, you need to slow down and adjust to her pace. Put aside the stack of mail on the counter and wait to check your phone messages and e-mails. Come down to her level and make eye contact. Tell her about your day, your work, the experiences you've had. Ask her about her day and the things that she's done. In this space you've set aside for her, you can listen without interruption and show her you value what she has to say. You can observe the world around you and talk about any changes you've noticed in nature or the weather. Encourage her to ask questions, explore how she's feeling about her life, and tell her how you feel about yours. Put on a favorite piece of music and talk about how it makes you feel. If your child has brought artwork home, you can sit together and look at what she's created, then decide where to hang it on the wall. Sometimes, just being together in the same room is enough. Your child can sit and look at a picture book while you read the newspaper, and you'll both experience a feeling of togetherness. This space you've made in the day is also a good time to nurture self-help skills such as undressing herself to get ready for bed, brushing her own teeth, and putting her clothes in the hamper and her toys away.

Even if you do need to run around doing chores because you only have a limited amount of time to accomplish them, you can still be with your child as you do them. Encourage her to participate: Folding laundry, putting away the groceries, setting the table, and helping prepare the evening meal are all age-appropriate tasks for under-fives. This will give you the chance to talk with your child about what you're doing: "What do we need to set the table?" "Let's put all the fruit away and then the vegetables." "Will you please help me pour the detergent into the machine?" When you do these things together, you make your child feel she has a responsibility to the family.

In our years of working as educators, we've observed that children who spend regular unstructured time with their parents are more likely to be intellectually curious, less fearful of risks, and better decision makers. They're often the children in a class who initiate ideas and lead creative play, who are enthusiastic about learning, and who are good problem solvers. When you give your child the gift of unstructured time, you are giving her a hundred and one opportunities to create, imagine, discover, and experiment.

And it's not just children who benefit from downtime. Busy parents need it too. When you slow down and go at your child's pace, you're giving yourself a break from the demands and pressures of adult life. When you meet your child at her level, she can help you to see the world from another perspective. One mother told us that after a rough day with her boss her four-year-old told her, "Mom, I'm going to yell at that mean man!" Time with your child will afford you the opportunity to remember the things that made you happy in your childhood, to be silly and playful, to laugh and express yourself, and to find pleasure in her discoveries and experiences. You spend so much of your day working to ensure the best for your child. In this time that you've set aside to spend together, you're not only doing something for your child, you're allowing your child to do something very special for you.

Recommended Children's Books About Friendship

We Are Best Friends	Aliki
Being Friends	Karen Beaumont
How to Be a Friend	Laurie Krasny Brown and Marc Brown
Mike Mulligan and His Steam Shovel	Virginia Lee Burton
That's What Friends Do	Kathryn Cave
Chester's Way	Kevin Henkes
Frederick	Leo Lionni
It's Mine!	Leo Lionni
Frog and Toad Together	Arnold Lobel
George and Martha	James Marshall
Elmer and Wilbur	David McKee
Rainbow Fish	Marcus Pfister
Making Friends	Fred Rogers
The Little Mouse, the Red Ripe Strawberry, and the Big Hungry Bear	Don and Audrey Wood

Chapter Five

UNDERSTANDING YOUR CHILD'S DEVELOPMENT:
What to Look for and When to Intervene

As a parent, your child's unfolding development is one of the most fascinating things you'll ever experience. By the age of three, your child will have already passed so many astonishing milestones—first attempts at crawling, first steps, first words. Now that he's preschool age, he'll continue to develop in leaps and bounds. His vocabulary will increase, his physical abilities will strengthen, and his social skills will flourish. When you send a child to a quality early childhood program, you're ensuring that all this inherent aptitude will be nurtured and encouraged on every level. Research has shown that children learn more rapidly during these years than at any other stage in their lives. As educators we get to see firsthand the extraordinary progress that preschool children make when they're given the right support and guidance.

This doesn't mean that we believe that young children should be reading and writing from the age of three. Academic skills are acquired over time. We tell parents that a child needs to know how to crawl before he can walk. Before a child can put pencil to paper, he needs to develop the muscles in his arms and hands that enable him to do this. In a preschool classroom, he gets to paint at an easel, knead the play dough, and draw with crayons, all of which help build the motor skills that will be necessary for later writing. Although vocabulary and letter recognition are important for young children, the ability to hop or to share a toy with another child is just as challenging and of equal importance. At this age, all your child's skills are interdependent. We've seen time and again that when a child lacks confidence in any of the areas of his development—physical, emotional, or intellectual—it's likely to impede his enjoyment of school and ability to learn in general. If a child doesn't feel physically able on the outdoor equipment, for example, this may effect his emotional development because he lacks confidence when playing outside. If his confidence is lacking, then this can affect his social skills because he may avoid playing with other children on the playground, which then may carry over to the classroom.

For parents, it can often be difficult to know exactly what constitutes "typical" development. Children change so quickly, and especially if this is your first child, you're unlikely to have a frame of reference for the many steps in his growth. At what age should a child begin to recognize his own name? When will he be able to dress himself before coming to school in the morning? Does the average child learn to hop and skip at three or at four? Even with a second child, it can be difficult to judge if your children are simply different or if there's a genuine lag. At eighteen months, Ellen's eldest, Alice, was already speaking in sentences. Ellen assumed this was normal development until Charles came along and still didn't speak in full sentences at the age of two and a half. Ellen was initially concerned, but after speaking to her pediatrician, she learned that Charles's language skills were fine. He was just developing along his own path. Instead of beginning by naming things, as Alice had, Charles went straight to full sentences in his own time.

Although there are typical ranges of development at each of the preschool ages, your child will grow according to his own unique pattern, temperament, gender, or physical type. What's "normal" for each age is wide ranging and the younger the child, the wider the parameters. Most children do not progress on an even continuum—they're more likely to develop rapidly in one area and lag behind in another. Nancy's youngest, Alissa, had excellent early physical coordination. She could climb to the top of the monkey bars, and she could catch and hit a baseball easily. Her letter recognition came much later, as opposed to her older brother, Michael, who knew the alphabet and started reading early, but to this day can't catch a ball very well. Throughout her youth, Alissa loved sports, while her brother was happier at home in his room with a book. Like most parents, Nancy wanted to encourage her children to do the things they were naturally good at and already enjoyed. But as an educator, she knew how important it was to encourage all aspects of Michael's and Alissa's development. Children will naturally be drawn to activities in their areas of strength but will avoid activities where they don't feel confident in their abilities. Nancy helped to promote her son's physical development by often taking him to a pool to swim since he enjoyed that activity. Alissa was a reluctant reader, so Nancy encouraged her by frequently reading out loud to her throughout elementary school. In the same way, when you find fun and relaxed ways of helping your child to do the things he finds frustrating as well as the things he loves, you're building his confidence and his willingness to try new things.

On the other hand, it's important not to push your child to achieve something before he's ready. It's possible that he's struggling with a certain skill because he's not yet old enough to do it and that if you continue to push him, he'll become overly frustrated. How do you know if a child is ready? Teachers can be a great resource for you in this respect. Early childhood educators are trained in child development and can tell you if a child is developing typically or if he needs some extra support. Over the years, an experienced teacher will have witnessed hundreds of children of the same age pass through her classroom and can let you know how your child is doing in relation to his peers. If you're at all concerned about your child's abilities, a teacher will be able to inform you when it's time to stretch your child in a certain area or reassure you if there's no reason to worry.

When there is some unevenness in a child's development, it's likely that it will be noted first at school. Unlike parents, teachers observe children in the context of their age group, rather than alone or in relation to their siblings. Sometimes, there will be situations where a child needs some extra help. This doesn't necessarily mean your child needs to work with a specialist. It can mean that you should strategize with your child's teachers to find ways to encourage a skill or change a behavior.

The purpose of this chapter is to help demystify the development of preschool-age children so that you can better understand your child and have appropriate expectations for him. When you understand what constitutes typical development and a teacher comes to you with a developmental issue, then you will have some context for this information and will find it easier to work with the school to support your child.

Developmental Benchmarks

In our parent groups, we often begin by giving parents a sense of what constitutes typical benchmarks for physical, emotional, and language development. Generally, the reaction of parents when they have this information is one of relief: "Oh, that's why my child isn't doing that; he isn't ready yet." "That explains why he's doing that. It's just that he's a three-year-old."

We find that when parents have a better understanding of development, they're more likely to set reasonable expectations for a child. It's often the case that parents will push a child to do something before he's ready. Other times, parents won't realize that a child is ready to learn a new skill. If you're expecting your three-year-old to put on his own socks and you're becoming frustrated because he can't do it, you're expecting too much of him and need to give him more time. However, if your four-year-old is still not putting on his own socks, you'll have to show him how to do it and practice with him. Before long, you'll see that he was ready to dress himself.

We don't, however, intend for parents to run down a checklist of expectations or to always compare their child to others of the same age. Benchmarks can be useful, but only if you're aware that all children develop differently in different areas, sometimes in big leaps, sometimes in small steps, and sometimes with one step forward and two steps backward. Instead of thinking of these benchmarks in terms of what your child *should* be doing, think of them in terms of what you *can* be doing to support your child's development at different ages. This is how teachers see their role, as the facilitators of the individual child's naturally evolving skills, rather than as some kind of development drill sergeant. The potential is there; it's up to all of us to encourage it.

• Physical Development •

During the school day, almost everything the children do involves some kind of physical activity, whether it's running and jumping outside, holding a crayon to draw a picture, pouring from the pitcher at snack time, or putting on a coat at the end of the day. A child who struggles with physical skills may find it harder to take care of himself, which in turn limits his independence. A child with good physical skills can set his own goals, challenge himself, and will continue to push himself when left to his own devices. These skills give him the confidence to take on his world.

Gross Motor Skills

From ages three to five, children are still developing the large muscles of their bodies that control the gross motor skills. At this age, children need many opportunities to strengthen these muscles so that they can develop coordination and acquire new abilities. It's very important to encourage a child to use his large muscles. He can play outdoors on playground equipment or create artwork at a slanted easel. You can play at "wheelbarrow walking" with him or have him lie on his stomach on a scooter board and push forward with his arms. When your child dips a paintbrush in water and "paints" the side of your house, this is another fun way to get him to use his large arm muscles.

Here are some other activities that children take part in at school to help promote gross motor skills that you can encourage your child to try at home:

For three- to four-year-olds:

- Running and galloping
- Jumping in place
- Walking up and down stairs
- Marching in place
- Throwing and catching a large ball with arms extended

- Climbing
- Kicking a large ball
- Walking up stairs with alternating feet
- Walking down stairs one step at a time (not alternating feet)

For four- to five-year-olds:

- Walking up and down stairs with alternating feet
- Skipping
- Hopping
- Balancing on one foot
- Jumping over objects
- Riding and steering a tricycle
- Going hand over hand on the overhead ladder

- Catching a ball or beanbag with hands
- Somersaulting
- Zigzagging when running
- Being aware of the physical proximity of other people and things around him

Practical Wisdom for Parents

At school, your child will be exposed to different materials and equipment designed to support gross motor development. You can choose to have some of these at home if you have the space:

- Large rubber balls
- Beanbags
- Slides
- Climbing equipment
- Tricycles, scooters
- Hoops
- Cones

- Balance beam
- Soccer goal
- Music for dancing
- Scarves and streamers
- Exercise mats
- Hollow wooden blocks

Fine Motor Skills

During the period between three and five years of age, fine motor skills involving the small muscles of the hand are also being developed. These small muscles are necessary for later writing skills. Before a child can write or draw figuratively, his hand muscles must be ready to grasp and manipulate writing utensils. One of the reasons you see so much play dough in preschool classrooms is that it helps develop these muscles (and is fun too). Three-year-olds will flatten, squish, pound, and roll the play dough. Five-year-olds, whose muscles are more developed, can make a person, an animal, a bird's nest, or a bowl. A child won't be ready to do this, however, until his larger arm muscles are developed.

Here are some other activities that children take part in at school to help promote fine motor skills that you can encourage your child to try at home:

For three- to four-year-olds:

- Turning single pages in a book
- Manipulating and completing simple puzzles

- Stringing large beads
- Building towers with blocks
- Tearing paper

- Cutting paper
- Painting with a brush
- Pouring from a pitcher
- Drawing lines
- Drawing a circle

- Drawing a person with two or three parts (a head with sticks for limbs or body)
- Using fingers to pick up small objects

For four- to five-year-olds:

- Buttoning and unbuttoning
- Zipping and unzipping
- Completing puzzle with eight pieces or more
- Cutting on a line with scissors

- Drawing a person with six parts (body, head, arms, and legs)
- Copying most letters (uppercase)
- Drawing simple objects
- Writing his first name in uppercase letters

At school, your child will be exposed to different materials and equipment designed to support fine motor development. You can choose to have some of these at home:

- Puzzles
- Legos, Duplo, pegboards, Tinkertoys, magnetic boards, lacing cards
- Play dough and clay, rolling pins and cookie cutters
- Blocks
- Easel
- Chalkboard
- Scissors
- Paintbrushes

- Thick and thin markers
- Crayons
- Fat chalk
- Squeeze bottles
- Spray bottles
- Tweezers
- Clothespins
- Finger paint
- Stencils
- Sand and water tables

Practical Wisdom for Parents

- Books
- Dress-up clothes
- Pipe cleaners and beads
- Hole punchers
- Tape

- Stamps and stamp pad
- Stickers
- Sewing materials
- Small pitchers
- Eye droppers

• Language Development •

Children's ability to acquire language is one of the greatest miracles of human development. By the age of three to four, your child will most likely have a vocabulary of around a thousand words. By five, he will have acquired approximately fifteen hundred words. (No. Don't start counting.) The ability to communicate effectively is critical for young children. When a child can communicate, he can make himself understood, he can engage in play with his friends, and he can express his needs and ideas. Words give children autonomy and allow them to begin to master their environment. A child who struggles with language has difficulties resolving differences with the other children and with forming relationships. It's much harder for him to communicate his ideas and to understand the ideas of others. As your child's ability to talk about his observations and experiences improves, his world naturally expands.

Parents often confuse language with speech. Nancy recently told one father that his daughter, Jennifer, had excellent language skills. The parent replied, "What do you mean? She mispronounces things all the time." Nancy explained that although Jennifer had problems with speech (articulating words), she had no trouble with language (expressing her thoughts). She may have said "psketti" instead of "spaghetti" but she was able to tell an elaborate story about going out for a pasta dinner. Young children are often unable to speak in a clear and understandable way. They may substitute sounds, blend words together, or have trouble producing specific sounds. They may stutter or have difficulty with the flow of language. This dysfluency is usually part of normal speech development—it simply means the brain is working faster than the muscles of the mouth. Children will usually outgrow these typical patterns by age five.

It's also true that the ability to comprehend language is a very different skill from simply having a large vocabulary. Occasionally, we come across a child who can talk and talk, but doesn't always understand the meaning behind the words. Max was a talkative four-year-old who already knew the names for countries of the world and of the major classical composers when we first met him. But if you asked Max why a character in a story had done something, he couldn't tell you because he didn't comprehend the meaning of the story. He would often become inattentive during story time and ask to leave the rug area to go to the bathroom because he couldn't follow the story.

Speech and language specialists describe the ways in which children communicate as "expressive language" and "receptive language." Expressive language involves using words to express ideas and feelings in a clear, organized manner using appropriate syntax (the correct order of words in a sentence); it also involves answering questions, relating events, and participating in a two-way conversation. Receptive language refers to the skills involved in comprehending and processing language: the ability to follow simple directions, as well as to understand stories and questions. For example, Jennifer had good expressive language skills but typical dysfluency for her age. Max had a good vocabulary but poor receptive language skills.

At three to four years old, a child's developing language skills are likely to include:

- Speaking in four- to five-word sentences.

- Telling a coherent story.

- Asking questions in sentence form.

- Saying his full name.

- Beginning to use words to express feelings.

- Engaging in give-and-take conversation.

- Following two- or three-step directions.

- Understanding yesterday, today, and tomorrow.

- Understanding concepts of relative size (bigger, smaller) and proximity (next to, between, behind).

- Being understood by most people outside the family.

Practical Wisdom for Parents

At four to five years old, a child's developing language skills are likely to include:

- Speaking in sentences of six to eight words.
- Asking "why?" questions.
- Describing what things are for.
- Asking meanings of words.
- Retelling simple stories.
- Telling a story and staying on topic.
- Relating an event in sequence.
- Repeating phrases of four words or more.
- Understanding opposites.
- Rhyming simple words.
- Counting to ten.
- Listing the days of the week.
- Sitting for longer periods of time listening to more complex stories.

Your child's teacher will help support your child's language development in the following ways. You can do the same by:

- Modeling good language by talking slowly to your child using clear articulation and expressive tones.
- Responding to your child's questions and ideas by listening actively (making eye contact, nodding or smiling, and expanding on his ideas).
- Reading to your child every day using a variety of books (fiction, nonfiction, and poetry).
- Playing with language: rhyming, singing, telling jokes.
- Playing listening games like Simon Says.
- Being sure not to "baby talk" to your preschooler.
- Waiting for your child to make requests—not responding to pointing.
- Asking open-ended questions.
- Getting your child to make predictions. When reading a story you can ask, "What do you think is going to happen?"
- Comparing and contrasting items (a banana and an apple).
- Helping him to learn new words to express his feelings.
- Waiting for your child to respond—it may take a few minutes for him to formulate his response.
- Being sure not to speak for your child if someone is talking to him.

- Being sure not to correct mispronunciations—simply model the correct pronunciation instead.

- Introducing more complex stories and vocabulary as your child grows.

- Encouraging your child to make up and tell his own stories or retell stories he's heard.

A note on bilingual children: Just because a child is bilingual doesn't automatically mean that this will affect his language development in ways that are either beneficial or detrimental. We have seen children who come to school speaking three languages who have no difficulty communicating. We have seen children whose acquisition of two languages is more uneven, who mix up words between the languages, who don't always keep their languages separate, or who are acquiring one language faster than the other. As with all early childhood development, children go at their own pace. If a bilingual child mixes up words or lags behind in one language, this should not be interpreted as a delay—it's simply how young children acquire more than one language.

As a parent of a bilingual child, it's important that you give your child many rich and varied experiences in both languages. If you read, sing, tell stories, and have conversations in one language, you should do the same in the other. This is usually easier to achieve when both languages are part of the culture of the family. When parents decide that a child should be introduced to a language simply so that he can gain a useful skill but the parents don't speak that language, it becomes much harder for the child. A second language will be much more meaningful if it has real applications in his day-to-day life.

Sometimes bilingual children come to school and haven't yet acquired enough vocabulary in either language to be proficient socially. These children will need more support and time to adapt to the language of the classroom. If you are worried that your child is having difficulties comprehending either language or is struggling socially because he's having trouble communicating, you may want to work with his teacher before deciding if it's appropriate to contact a language specialist.

• Social and Emotional Development •

Your child's social and emotional development takes place first in the context of her relationships within the family and then with friends, teachers, and other adults outside the home. Children derive so much pleasure from their friendships with their classmates and their teachers. When a child struggles socially, it affects every aspect of his ability to enjoy school—he simply won't be so happy or eager to learn. Your child's social and emotional skills also include the ability to perform tasks for himself, such as cleaning up his toys, feeding himself, and dressing himself. When children aren't encouraged to learn these skills at home, it impedes their ability to participate fully in classroom life. Equally, if you don't set limits for your child at home, it will be more difficult for him to accept the rules of the classroom, to learn self-control, and to take responsibility for himself and his actions.

At three to four years old, a child's developing social and emotional skills will include:

- Separating from a parent.
- Communicating his needs to adults.
- Learning to share.
- Learning to take turns.
- Listening to directions.
- Conversing with children and adults.
- Following the rules.
- Beginning to take responsibility for his actions.
- Treating property with respect.
- Helping with routine tasks.
- Sitting at a table for short periods during meals.
- Responding to adult authority.
- Learning to tolerate frustration.
- Beginning to use words to express feelings.
- Using "please" and "thank you" when making requests.

At four to five years old, a child's developing social skills will include:

- Making eye contact when conversing.
- Using courteous and polite behavior.
- Being able to have a reciprocal conversation.
- Listening when others speak without interrupting.

- Participating in cooperative activities and working toward a common goal.

- Respecting and standing up for the rights of others.

- Helping others in need.

- Using compromise and discussion to resolve conflicts.

- Understanding and respecting differences in others.

- Beginning to have a few special friends.

- Beginning to understand right from wrong.

- Exhibiting empathy.

- Being able to postpone gratification.

Just as your child's teachers will help him to develop socially and emotionally, you can support these aspects of your child's development by:

- Setting clear limits.

- Having consequences for negative behavior.

- Complimenting good behavior.

- Giving your child responsibilities in your home (putting toys away, setting the table, placing clothes in the hamper).

- Helping your child to acquire self-help skills (dressing and undressing, brushing teeth, toileting).

- Teaching your child polite behavior.

- Modeling respectful behavior in front of your child.

- Not automatically replacing a broken toy.

- Encouraging your child to make decisions for himself by providing either/or choices.

- Avoiding the use of sarcasm or deliberately embarrassing your child.

- Being sure not to talk about your child in front of him as if he's invisible.

- Expecting him to complete a task.

- Allowing him to learn from his mistakes.

- Teaching him new words to express his feelings.

- Sending a "can do" message to your child by letting him do things for himself.

- Complimenting your child for attempts, not just for accomplishments.

- Refusing to tolerate physical aggression or hurtful language.

- Involving your child in activities that help others (bringing food to a shelter or toys to a children's hospital, calling a sick friend).

Problem Behaviors

As your child grows, it's inevitable that you're going to have to deal with some form of challenging behavior: tantrums, whining, stubborness, defiance, anxiety, impulsivity, shyness, refusal to share, inattentiveness, or aggressiveness. Many of these behaviors, such as the tantrums, will be outgrown between the ages of three and four. Other behaviors, like the refusal to share, may change when you set clear limits and have consequences for behavior. In fact, there are various approaches you can try to help alleviate these problems. Parents tell us that they have benefited greatly from learning about techniques that teachers use in a classroom.

- Defiant and oppositional behavior: These children may have frequent tantrums, whine or cry at the drop of a hat, are loud and call negative attention to themselves, refuse to listen, and are stubborn and insist on doing things their way. They may have sleeping, eating, or toileting issues. A teacher would: Give your child clear expectations and consistency. Give a warning before a transition. Ignore whining and crying. Be firm but be calm and neutral. Use humor and create challenges and games to encourage cooperation. Notice and reward good behavior.

- Anxious or fearful behavior: These children may be slow to warm up. They may stand back and assess things first before becoming involved. They may refuse to participate in activities that other children find pleasurable. They may worry and ask a lot of questions. They may cry and refuse to leave their parent or teacher.
  A teacher would: Give children lots of support and praise. Look reassuring and send a message that they can do it. Model confident behavior ("Oh, the lights went out! Let's go find a flashlight"). Encourage independence and give children responsibility. Prepare them in advance for what to expect. Role-play to help them deal with anxiety. Remind children that the grown-ups will always keep children safe. Reassure with a hug or a hand to hold. Encourage children to confront their fears, little by little.

- Highly active and impulsive behavior: These children are often physically active, always touching, jumping, or bumping into people and things. They talk incessantly and constantly interrupt. They have difficulty listening. They're easily overstimulated. They move from thing to thing and are unable to sustain an activity for more than a very short period. They have difficulties in large group situations. They find it hard to make friends and move easily through transitions.
  A teacher would: Establish routines and good structure. Lessen distractions by providing smaller group experiences. Give lots of outlets for physical activity. Give warnings before transitions. Take a break when children become overstimulated. Encourage relaxing tactile activities such as water play and play dough. Instead of saying no, use positive redirection: "Let's do jumping jacks instead of jumping on the couch." Suggest that parents eliminate TV with aggressive themes. Try not to overwhelm children with too many choices or too much language.

- Inattentive and disorganized behavior: These children have difficulty listening and sustaining attention. They may not join the group. They have trouble following routines. They can seem a little disconnected and in their own world. They may be forgetful and have a hard time sustaining play with other children.
  A teacher would: Help children complete tasks they have already begun. Use a chart to show the routines of the day. Stick to the routines. Give children simple jobs. Have children repeat what's just been said. Make eye contact and teach children not to interrupt. Organize toys with places and labels for specific things. Suggest parents limit the number of toys on children's shelves and make their rooms visually calm.

- Shy or withdrawn behavior: These children are somewhat inactive or less inclined to participate. They tend not to ask for adult assistance. They're very slow to warm up. They're reluctant to speak to people outside the family. They avoid eye contact and lack animation.
  A teacher would: Slowly introduce children to new experiences. Stay close to them but without hovering or pushing too hard. Develop confidence by following children's interests and encouraging special skills: If a child is shy but physically adept, a teacher would applaud his physical accomplishments. Model friendly behavior, and role-play situations that are difficult. Have him say hello to familiar people he sees every day. Suggest playdates with one other child to develop friendship. Read stories about characters overcoming difficulties.

• What to Do When There's a Delay •

In recent years, early childhood educators have been noticing more and more children beginning school with a variety of issues and delays in development. We hear this all the time from our colleagues, not just in urban areas like New York, but across the country. Everyone is asking the same question: Why is this happening? There's plenty of speculation surrounding this subject, but part of the reason seems to be that teachers' observational skills have become much more sophisticated. Today, early childhood educators receive ongoing training in understanding atypical development and are becoming more able to identify children with issues and delays. At the same time, pediatricians are now much more likely to look at a child's needs overall, rather than his physical and medical well-being alone, and are more proactive in recommending early intervention by specialists.

If you've tried encouraging your child and carefully observed him over a period of time, but you don't see any improvement in a certain behavior and he's becoming increasingly frustrated, you can ask yourself some of the following questions:

- Are there specific circumstances that trigger the difficult behavior?

- Does his language affect your child's ability to socialize or make himself understood?

- Is your child's voice very high pitched or hoarse?

- Does your child have a persistent stutter?

- Does your child have difficulty understanding simple directions?

- Is it necessary for your family to always accommodate your child to avoid conflicts or confrontations?

- Is your child unable to sit for short periods in a chair?

- Is your child unable to sustain interest and play productively with toys?

- Does your child overreact to noise or stimulating environments?

- Does your child have difficulty controlling his impulses or responding to clear limits?

- Does physical aggression dominate his interaction with other children?

- Does your child avoid large or small motor activities?

If you just answered yes to some of these questions, and your child's difficulty has persisted over a period of time, you may decide to look into this further by talking to your child's teacher, nursery school director, or pediatrician, who can refer you to a specialist if necessary.

Sometimes, despite parents' best efforts, there are real problems in the way a child is developing. If you've observed that your child is struggling, the first thing you must do is talk to his teacher. Ask if she's observed similar behaviors and delays and if these are developmentally typical. Teachers can help you to determine whether your concern is valid or whether you just need to give your child time to grow. For example, if your four-year-old doesn't recognize the letters of the alphabet, even though he sees them every day on the schoolroom wall, this may be typical. Many four-year-olds don't recognize all the letters of the alphabet. However, if your child sees his name in print over and over again and still doesn't recognize "David," a teacher may decide to give his letter recognition skills some special attention during classroom time while suggesting you do the same at home. Teachers are often very experienced at coming up with strategies to help your child learn the things that he finds challenging.

When parents and teachers work constructively together in a child's best interests, so much can be achieved. A parent with a daughter at the nursery school raised a concern about her four-and-a-half-year-old, Ali, who didn't seem to use logical strategies to figure out puzzles. She couldn't match colors or shapes or use the picture to help her put the right piece in the right place. Ali's teacher remarked that she'd noticed the same problem. The teacher also observed that Ali had trouble finding her cubby and was often one of the last children to find a seat at the snack table. It seemed that there was a difficulty with Ali's visual perceptual skills. The teacher helped Ali by putting a special sticker on her cubby and taught her how to talk about the picture on the puzzle before she took it apart so that Ali could use her strong verbal abilities to compensate for her less-developed visual skills. At home, the mother gave Ali the same simple puzzles to do and talked about the images on the puzzles, so that Ali could have fun and gain confidence in her abilities. Over a short period of time, Ali began to take on more challenging puzzles.

In other instances, it will be important to speak to your pediatrician. If your child's problem is speech related, for example, your pediatrician may recommend a hearing test, especially if your child has had frequent ear infections. Sometimes a teacher will observe that a child is inattentive during group times, doesn't notice when his name is being called, and isn't following directions well. If parents have made the same observations, we usually recommend that they consult their pediatrician. It may be the case that the child has fluid in the ears from ear infections. Once this condition is dealt with, the child is then able to make great progress with his language development.

• Working with Your Child's Teacher •

Often, a teacher will inform a parent about a child's difficulties, and often, that parent will initially become upset or defensive. While it's only natural to feel anxious when someone suggests that your child is struggling in school, it won't help anyone if you try to deny the behavior. Stay calm and try not to overreact. If you don't understand or agree with what you've been told, repeat it back to the teacher in order to clarify what's been said. Give yourself the time to process and think about what the teacher has described. Wait and see if you observe any of the behaviors at home; you might not have noticed some of them before. Don't let your first reaction stand in the way of doing what's best for your child. When you think of your child's teacher as your ally, you can both work together in his best interests.

In some cases, parents may have good cause to be wary of what teachers are telling them. If a teacher states a problem but doesn't fully describe the behavior, you should ask her to give you examples and then work with her to create step-by-step solutions. If a teacher immediately labels the problem—"I think your child has attention deficit disorder"—you need to ask questions. Teachers should *never* diagnose or label a child. That's the job of specialists. It's the teacher's job to describe the behavior and make practical suggestions for home and school improvement. She may recommend an evaluation, but she should not give one. If you do feel conflicted about the information you've heard from a teacher, it's a good idea to discuss it with your spouse, your pediatrician, the school director, or a specialist before taking further action.

When to Seek Professional Intervention

Even the most effective parents and teachers who have tried every possible strategy sometimes need the support and expertise of professionals. If you have collaborated with your child's teachers over time and consulted your pediatrician, but your child is still not responding, then you may decide it's time to confer with an outside specialist. We view this type of intervention as normal. We would never want parents to feel that their child is being stigmatized or labeled. For this reason, we describe a child's developmental difficulties as being uneven or delayed. Most children don't develop on an even continuum and many will have particular strengths and weaknesses. When uneven development or a delay does affect a child socially, emotionally, or cognitively, we have seen that early intervention can be very helpful.

The preschool years present parents, educators, and specialists with a golden window of opportunity to help a child with developmental issues. The early timing of intervention effectively contributes to the success of the treatment—children learn faster during the preschool years than at any other time in their lives. Not only can early intervention enhance a child's development, it may also prevent the low self-esteem and frustration that often affects children who aren't succeeding. Parents are sometimes reluctant to seek out professional help because they're fearful their child will be labeled. However, it's our experience that if parents avoid dealing with problem behaviors at this early age, the problems become more difficult to deal with as the child grows and the demands of school increase.

Some parents seek special services privately through referrals from their school or pediatrician. Others receive services through federally mandated, state-run intervention programs. To receive these services, a child must have a confirmed disability or established developmental delay, as defined by the state he resides in, in one or more of the following areas: physical, cognitive, communication, social-emotional, and/or adaptive. Criteria can vary from state to state, however. To find out about Early Intervention (ages zero to three) or Preschool Intervention (ages three to five) programs in your state, you can talk to your pediatrician, local school district, or hospital.

Once you have made the decision to consult a professional, it's essential that you stay involved in order to maximize the effects of the intervention. Parents often expect specialists to solve their child's problems. You have to be your child's advocate, you have to facilitate communication between specialists and school, and you have to follow the specialist's recommendations for your child at home. If for some reason you don't feel comfortable with the psychologist or other specialist, or if your child isn't making progress after a period of time, don't give up; try to find someone who is more in tune with your child and family. We have seen that when families find specialists who are a good fit, the parents feel supported and the child becomes much happier and more successful at school as a result.

This was true of Lauren and her family. Although Lauren had been very happy in the three-year-old classroom, when she joined the four-year-old classroom she became highly anxious about many aspects of school. She had great difficulty saying good-bye to her mother in the mornings and cried each time they had to separate. Although Lauren was very attached to one of her teachers, she continued to whimper throughout the day and didn't participate fully in activities with the other children. When it was time to go to gym class, Lauren clung fearfully to her favorite teacher and refused to join in. At home, her parents observed that she was often anxious when they would go out, even though she loved her babysitter. Sometimes children have difficulties transitioning into a new classroom, but when this behavior persisted after a typical adjustment period, we became concerned. We recommended that the parents consult a psychologist. Through play therapy, the therapist learned that the recent death of a grandparent was very much on Lauren's mind and that she was worried about her parents dying also. The psychologist developed a behavioral plan that was carried out at home and at school. With the help of her therapist, her parents, and her teachers, Lauren was able to work through her anxieties. She became less worried and much happier. Eventually she was able to separate from her mother without tears. She relaxed and began to enjoy her time at school again.

• Working with Special Educators and Therapists •

If you're already working with specialists when your child begins school, you'll need to inform the school from the outset so that your child's teachers can understand your child's needs and maintain a consistent approach. This was true of Sam, a boy who came to the nursery school at age three. A year before he began school, Sam's parents noticed that his language was not nearly as well developed as his brother's was at the same age. Sam was frequently frustrated, had tantrums, and often bit and hit others. He cried when he heard loud noises and was unable to tolerate crowded or noisy places. Sam's parents consulted their pediatrician, who advised them to have him evaluated.

After a comprehensive evaluation through the Early Intervention Program, Sam's family was given an Individualized Family Service Plan (IFSP). The IFSP recommended and mandated that Sam receive speech therapy and occupational therapy twice a week for forty-five minutes per session. A speech therapist was assigned to work with Sam on his expressive and receptive language skills. An occupational therapist worked to help Sam learn how to regulate his body. Sam's parents were shown how to implement these techniques at home so that there was a consistent approach. Over time, Sam's physical impulsivity improved, he became more attentive and focused in group activities, and he could tolerate other children being close to him.

Before Sam started school, his parents notified us that he was receiving special services. In order for Sam to continue his therapies, he needed to be reevaluated by the Committee on Preschool Special Education (CPSE), which is responsible for making recommendations for children ages three to five. After his reevaluation, Sam's family was given an Individual Education Plan (IEP) which approved them for a variety of services. In addition to his speech and occupational therapies, Sam would be provided with a Special Education Itinerant Teacher (SEIT) to support him in the classroom for ten hours each week. The SEIT's role was to use his IEP to work on specific goals for Sam in the classroom setting.

Before the school year began, we set up a meeting with Sam's parents, his teachers, and his SEIT, Stacey. Stacey outlined Sam's needs, described his IEP and the other therapies he was receiving, and explained how she was going to support him in the classroom. The teachers described their classroom routines and the curriculum so that Stacey would be familiar with them. Sam's parents voiced their concerns about what other parents would think or say about having a SEIT in the classroom. We reassured them that we viewed SEITs as a welcome support and that we would be writing a letter to the other parents introducing Stacey as a support teacher. We also reassured Sam's parents that it was the school's policy to leave out the name of the child being helped by the SEIT in the letter.

Initially, Sam struggled in the new environment of the classroom. His difficulties with impulse control and his language delay interfered with his ability to play with the other children. He insisted that he only play firefighter every day and needed to have the fire hat with him at all times. With the help of Stacey and his teachers, however, Sam gradually began to incorporate others into his play. Stacey and the teachers made a cardboard fire truck, obtained several fire hats for the classroom, and made sure to regularly read stories about firefighters so that Sam could feel he was part of the group. When Sam's social interaction was encouraged in this way, he was gradually able to expand his play to include other children and different games. Stacey always gave Sam warnings before transitions were about to occur, she reinforced the routines and expectations of the teachers, and when Sam became overstimulated, she took him for a short walk outside the classroom to calm his body. Periodic meetings were set up with the parents, teachers, and specialists to review what was being done, what was working, and what adjustments needed to be made.

Throughout the year, Sam's behavior continued to improve, but it was clear he would need the help of his specialists and SEIT for the following school year. In Sam's second year of school, Stacey was able to step back somewhat as he had already internalized many of the self-control techniques she had taught him. She created a "body check" chart so that Sam could use this independently when he needed to gain self-control, and he would look for her when he needed additional support. One of the major changes in behavior occurred when Sam developed enough language to express his feelings of anger and frustration and no longer needed to cry or have a tantrum in order to have his needs met. Over time, Sam relied on Stacey less and less, and by the end of the year, he was able to participate in school fully and independently. By age five, Sam no longer needed these services and was able to thrive in a stimulating and challenging kindergarten class.

We have so much respect for parents like Sam's who cooperate with teachers and specialists in the best interests of their child. When everyone works together, it is an ideal situation for a young child with learning delays or behavioral difficulties. With consistent expectations and good communication between parents, the school, and the specialists, dramatic progress can be made. Children at this age have a tremendous capacity for adapting and learning. It's extremely heartening to see how much happier and more confident they can become when they're helped in this way.

Recommended Source Books for Parents

Raising a Sensory Smart Child	Lindsey Biel and Nancy Peske
The Child with Special Needs	Stanley I. Greenspan and Serena Wieder
When You Worry About the Child You Love: Emotional and Learning Problems in Children	Edward M. Hallowell
It's Nobody's Fault	Harold Koplewicz
The Out-of-Sync Child	Carol Stock Kranowitz
A Mind at a Time	Mel Levine
Is My Child OK?	Henry A. Paul
The Difficult Child	Stanley Turecki
Yardsticks	Chip Wood

Recommended Books for Children

FEELINGS

Hands Are Not for Hitting	Martine Agassi
What Makes Me Happy?	Catherine and Laurence Anholt
When Sophie Gets Angry—	
Really, Really Angry . . .	Molly Bang
Let's Talk About Feeling Sad	Joy Berry
The Way I Feel	Janan Cain
Go Away, Big Green Monster!	Ed Emberley
Mean Soup	Betsy Everitt
How Are You Peeling?	
Foods with Moods	Saxton Freymann and Joost Elffers
Sheila Rae, the Brave	Kevin Henkes
Now It's Your Turn	Denise M. Jordan
On Monday When It Rained	Cherryl Kachenmeister
Me First	Helen Lester
I'm Sorry	Sam McBratney
There's an Alligator under My Bed	Mercer Mayer
There's Something in My Attic	Mercer Mayer
I Was So Mad	Mercer Mayer
Glad Monster/Sad Monster:	
A Book About Feelings	Ed Emberley and Anne Miranda
Brave, Brave Mouse	Michaela Morgan and Michelle Cartlidge
The Feel Good Book	Todd Parr
It's Okay to Be Different	Todd Parr
When I Care about Others	Cornelia Maude Spelman
When I Feel Angry	Cornelia Maude Spelman
When I Feel Good about Myself	Cornelia Maude Spelman
When I Feel Sad	Cornelia Maude Spelman
When I Feel Scared	Cornelia Maude Spelman

SELF-ESTEEM

I Like Myself!	Karen Beaumont
Olivia	Ian Falconer
Elmer	David McKee
The Little Engine That Could	Wally Piper

Chapter Six

THE TRANSITION TO KINDERGARTEN:
Getting Ready

By the time your child is about to begin her final year at preschool (generally called pre-K), both of you will have come a long way since you left her at the classroom door on her first day at school. You watched as she learned to separate from you. You learned that she was able to thrive independently in a busy classroom and develop strong relationships with her classmates and teachers. You took pride in every new skill and development as she progressed to this point. Now, just as you've become more comfortable with your role as the parents of a preschooler, it's time to begin thinking about kindergarten. Around the time your child is beginning her pre-K year this is an ideal time to look at the schools in your area so you'll be fully informed of your options for kindergarten and beyond.

When trying to identify the school where your child will continue her education, you should bear in mind that kindergartens today may be very different from the one you attended as a child. In the past, kindergarten was the place where children acquired readiness for school. Kindergarten classrooms were very similar to the ones you see in preschools today, with areas for block play, dress up, and painting. Children weren't expected to begin academics such as math or reading and writing until they started first grade. When Ellen's daughter, Alice, was ready for kindergarten twenty-five years ago, this was very much the case. Although Alice's new school was different from her preschool in many respects—it was all girls, uniforms were required, and it was a rather formal place where the headmistress greeted the children each morning with a handshake—her transition to kindergarten was very gentle. She was already accustomed to separating from Ellen, she was used to being in a classroom, and she loved playing with different materials, creating artwork, and interacting with her classmates. She was happy to put on her uniform and go to school. And she still has a very good handshake.

The Transition to Kindergarten: Getting Ready

Nowadays, kindergarten expectations have changed enormously. As pressure has increased on schools to show measurable standards for academic achievement at earlier ages and with parents anxious for young children to "get ahead," kindergartens have become much more like first grade. Playtime has been sacrificed for more time spent on reading and math lessons and the expectation is that children come to kindergarten ready to learn. Today, it's the responsibility of preschool programs, not kindergartens, to prepare children for school, to teach preacademic skills and emotional and social readiness.

For most children, this means that the transition from preschool to kindergarten will mean acclimating to many new experiences. Your child may be moving to a new and bigger school where she'll be among the youngest children. She may have to go on a school bus for the first time. The classes are often larger in size, your child may not know many other children, and kindergartens usually have a longer day. She might be eating in a cafeteria where she'll need to make choices and try foods that are unfamiliar. The bathroom may be down the hall, and she may have to go there independently. She may have to change her shoes for gym by herself. In the classroom, she'll need to listen for longer periods of time and work independently following a teacher's directions to the group.

This is the kind of kindergarten that Nancy's youngest child, Alissa, attended, and Nancy was initially concerned that her daughter would have difficulty with so many changes. It was a big leap. Alissa was used to going to school with a parent or caregiver. Now she would have to take a half-hour ride on the school bus there and back. Instead of bringing lunch from home, the school provided lunch. What's more, Alissa was going to be taught beginning reading for the first time, and Nancy knew her daughter wasn't yet interested or ready. Although Nancy anticipated that kindergarten might be a difficult transition for Alissa, in fact, the opposite was true. Alissa's exposure to letters and numbers at preschool helped prepare her for the more academic focus of kindergarten. Most importantly her independence and good social skills enabled her to adapt easily, and taking the school bus soon became her favorite part of the day.

By the time your child reaches the end of her pre-K year, her teachers will have already exposed her to letters and numbers, and she'll probably be learning to write her name. Often, parents put great emphasis on these beginning academic skills. But this isn't the most important aspect of a child's readiness for kindergarten. Readiness is reflected in your child's interest in learning, her ability to be a responsible member of a group, and to adapt to the routines and expectations of a school day.

Practical Wisdom for Parents

We've seen that children who make the smoothest transition to kindergarten:

- Are able to comfortably separate from you.
- Are confident about their ability to perform age-appropriate self-help skills.
- Are able to effectively communicate their needs and thoughts to others.
- Are able to wait their turn and can listen in a group.
- Are able to tolerate some frustration.
- Are developing empathy for others.
- Are able to listen to others.
- Are able to respect other children and adults.
- Value acceptance and approval from peers and teachers.
- Are often able to resolve conflicts with their peers.
- Know how to ask for help from a teacher when they need it.
- Are usually comfortable and confident about learning new things and mastering new skills.
- View school as an important place in their life.
- Have grown intellectually, socially, and emotionally over the course of the pre-K year.

You can help foster readiness by:

- Establishing daily routines and setting clear limits.
- Listening to the problems your child expresses and helping her to work out solutions.
- Reading aloud everyday.
- Limiting TV and computer time.
- Limiting after-school activities.
- Observing and having conversations about everyday life with your child.
- Sharing stories, songs, poems, and word games.
- Encouraging her to make eye contact when speaking and to respond to others when greeted.

- Having puzzles, markers, pencils, scissors, and paper available for your child.

- Giving your child time to think and play.

Choosing the Next School for Your Child

As your child begins her pre-K year, it's time to start inquiring about the schools in your area. The first thing you need to find out is the various cutoff ages. Unlike preschool—where there's a choice of ages when your child can begin—most kindergartens require children to be a specific age in order to start. This varies from school to school and by district, city, or state. Some schools require that children are five years old by the start date of school; others require children to turn five by December 31.

In some communities, the next school is your local elementary school where all the children in your area attend. In other areas, you may have a range of options to consider. These options include other public schools, religious schools, and independent or private schools. It's a good idea to visit your local school as well as investigating the other options that are available to you.

• Public Schools •

Most children in this country attend public schools, usually the one in their neighborhood. The very best public schools share three common criteria: an excellent principal with a clearly articulated vision for the school, highly qualified and committed teachers, and an actively involved parent body. Although different public schools will have different philosophies, the basic foundations for learning and educational success can be laid if the school has these important elements.

Most public schools are required to have programs for children with special needs and often serve children with physical or learning issues extremely well. If your child has been diagnosed with special needs and has an Individual Education Plan (IEP), your local school is mandated to meet your child's needs.

Some communities have a variety of public schools and may offer parents a choice. Some of these types of schools include:

- **Gifted and talented programs (G&T, TAG)**
  Your child will need to be evaluated in order to be considered for one of these programs. This might include standardized testing and/or an interview. The classes may be homogeneous (with all the children at the same level) or offer pullout programs (where mixed-ability levels are in a group together, and children are pulled out for special classes such as math, science, or reading).

- **Magnet schools**
  Magnet schools receive federal funds that are targeted to special programs or to the school in general. These schools are often trying to attract a diverse range of students.

- **Alternative schools**
  These schools are usually smaller in size and may be housed within a larger public school building. They can be organized around a specific philosophy, and parents are often very involved in the school.

- **Charter schools**
  These nonsectarian publicly funded schools operate without many of the regulations that apply to traditional public schools and are currently authorized in forty states. Charter schools must establish a "charter" detailing their mission, program, and goals, and outlining how they will be assessed to determine if they are meeting their aims. Charter schools are open to all students. These schools need to demonstrate academic success and must adhere to their performance contract.

• Religious Schools •

Many religious schools are connected both philosophically and financially to religious institutions, or they may operate independently from them. With some schools, you'll need to be affiliated with the religious institution in order to enroll. With others, you'll need to go through an application process.

Parents usually consider religious schools for a variety of reasons. They may have strong religious beliefs and want to impart them to their children. They may appreciate the quality of the education and smaller class size at a particular school. They may approve of the school's emphasis on moral and ethical teachings. When considering sending your child to a religious school, however, it's important to examine your own personal beliefs and lifestyle.

Often parents will choose to send a child to a religious school to compensate for the fact that they're not particularly religiously observant at home. This can be confusing for children and can set up a conflict for them if the school's teachings are inconsistent with their home life. If the practices of the school are reflected in the culture of your family, then a religious school can be a more meaningful experience for your child.

• Independent Schools •

The terms "independent" and "private" are often used interchangeably. Although both types of schools charge tuition and have an admissions process for students, there are some differences. Independent schools are nonprofit, governed by an elected board of trustees, and financed by tuition, fees, and contributions. Private schools may be for-profit institutions.

Independent/private schools are free to develop their own philosophy and curriculum. They can determine teacher qualifications and admit students based on their own criteria. Generally, such schools have smaller class sizes and higher student-teacher ratios. They may offer a wide variety of extracurricular classes and activities. Some schools have very homogeneous student bodies, and others are quite diverse. In many parts of the country, schools are highly selective of candidates, often attracting many more applicants than there are openings. In other areas, however, independent schools are not the preferred choice to public schools.

Most independent schools offer financial aid so that cost doesn't deter qualified applicants. The amount of aid is based on the family's need and the availability of financial aid funds that year. Schools require families to submit confidential financial aid forms and copies of tax returns. Generally, grants are partial, with parents paying a portion of the tuition.

Many independent schools are accredited by state, regional, or national independent school organizations such as the National Association of Independent Schools (NAIS) or your state's association of independent schools. Accreditation is a rigorous process of formal evaluation that takes approximately six months. If you wish to know if a particular school is accredited, you can find out this information on the NAIS Web site (nais.org).

Practical Wisdom for Parents

• What to Look for in Any School •

Whether you're sending your child to your neighborhood school or choosing between different public schools or between different independent schools, it's important to visit each institution and, if possible, meet the principal. There's a great deal you can learn about a school in a short visit if you know what to look for:

- What's the class size?
- What's the student-teacher ratio? Are aides hired if enrollment expands?
- What's the school's teaching philosophy?
- What's the role of the principal?
- What kind of extracurricular/ enrichment activities are there and how often do they take place? Are there provisions for art, music, computer studies, physical education, science, and foreign languages? Are there adequate spaces, materials, and equipment for these?
- Is there a library? Is there a special area set aside for younger students in the library?
- Are there early drop-off or after-school options?
- What are the school's test scores for reading and math?
- How are parents involved?
- How do budget cuts affect the program?

- Does the physical space appear safe, clean, inviting, neat, well organized, and well lit?
- How does the school sound? Too noisy, too quiet, or a good balance of teachers' and children's voices?
- Do the teachers seem caring, engaging, creative, happy, and energetic?
- Do the children seem happy, purposeful, involved, courteous, and relaxed?
- Is the children's work displayed? What does it look like?
- What's the degree of formality/ informality in the school and how would it suit your child and family?
- Is there a dress code?
- What kind of diversity does the school have?
- How does the location of the school impact the program? Is it in a pleasant neighborhood; is it accessible to transportation; does it have adequate outdoor playground space?

How to Apply to Independent Schools

Most major cities in this country will have a large number of independent schools from which you can choose. The reality is, however, that the number of applicants often exceeds the number of available spaces at these schools, and you may feel as if the choice is being taken out of your hands. Competition for these coveted spaces can cause even the most laid-back parents a few sleepless nights during the application process. We advise nervous parents to take a leap of faith and trust that admissions directors know their schools and want to admit children who can do well there. If your child isn't accepted by a school, it's likely that she may not thrive in that environment.

During the admissions process, the objective of the admissions director is to get to know you and your child in order to make a good match of school, child, and family. Directors are looking to form a community of students and parents that will fit well in the school's environment and support the school's educational goals. Parents often feel very uncomfortable about being "judged" in this way. It can help to turn the tables and to remember that it's your job as a parent to look critically at the school and assess whether it's a good fit for your child and family.

• Define What You Are Looking For •

As a parent, you need to define what you are looking for in a school. The first and most important thing to think about is your child. What are her intellectual, social, and emotional needs? You can assess these needs by asking your child's teachers about her learning style and how she socializes in group situations.

You might start by asking your child's pre-K teacher:

- What kind of learning environment suits my child best?
- What kind of guidance does my child need from a teacher?
- Does my child take the initiative or does she need encouragement from a teacher?

- Under which circumstances is my child most attentive?
- Does my child prefer working alone or in a group?
- Does my child need to have new information repeated several times before understanding it?
- Does she work better with more stimulation or need a quieter environment?
- How much structure does my child need throughout the day?

Other things you should consider:

- What do you expect from a school?
- Are you looking for a school that encourages parent involvement?
- Do you expect the school to take a role in the life of the family or do you think that the school's role should be solely academic?
- Are you looking for a coed or single-sex school?
- What about school size and class size?
- Geographical location? Campus? City?
- Are you looking for an elementary school with kindergarten through eighth grade (K–8) or through twelfth grade (K–12)?

• Gathering Information •

As you begin looking for schools that will suit your child and family, it's a good idea to ask your child's preschool director for suggestions. She'll be familiar with schools in your area that children who have attended her program have gone on to attend. She knows your child well and will be able to suggest which schools might be a good fit.

Some communities have independent school directories that can give you the basic information. Most schools have Web sites, catalogs, and written curricula available upon request. It's helpful to research and read about schools to determine if the school's philosophy and program match your expectations before visiting.

Friends or relatives with older children at school can be a useful source of information, but be aware that they may be biased. They are only seeing the school through their own experience, and their child may be very different from yours. Schools may have a reputation in your area that doesn't accurately or fully describe the school. If you hear that a school is a "pressure cooker," "too loose," "snobby and elite," or "second tier," you shouldn't take these labels at face value. No school is so one-dimensional that it can be summed up in a few words. Often these stereotypes were established years ago and are no longer relevant or true. Schools change and sometimes reputations are slow to follow.

Always consider the source of information carefully. Is your source a disgruntled, unrealistic parent whose child had problems academically or socially? Is it an overly enthusiastic alumnus? Is it someone whose child was rejected by that school? Has your source even visited the school in question? Someone else's negative impressions shouldn't prevent you from seeing a school for yourself. This school might end up being an excellent choice for your child.

• Applications •

Generally, you may begin requesting school application forms from September through November of the year prior to entry. If you live in an area where you have a number of choices, you may want to apply to multiple schools. In Manhattan, we know of families who have applied to a dozen schools. We usually recommend no more than six to eight. Any more than this won't necessarily increase your chance of getting into a good school, but it's guaranteed to completely exhaust your child who will have to go on multiple school visits.

Applications need to be filled out completely, accurately, and neatly, and should be sent off in a timely manner. Don't send more information than the school requires. Lengthy essays, unsolicited letters of recommendation, a parent's curriculum vitae, or anything that seems excessive will not be looked at favorably. If a school asks you to write about your child, it's helpful to be honest about her strengths and weaknesses (although not brutally so). This is the school's opportunity to learn something about your child from your perspective and to find out what you value about her. It can help to show your description of your child to a colleague, friend, or family member to get feedback on tone and content. If the school requests references, they should be from someone who knows you and your child well: a teacher, family friend, camp counselor, clergyman, or family doctor.

• Visiting a School •

The best way to learn about a school is to visit it during school hours. You may be invited to take a tour individually or as part of a group. What's essential is that you see the school during the course of a regular day when the children and teachers will be interacting with one another. Before you go, familiarize yourself with the school's written materials so you can determine whether the literature is consistent with what you observe.

Trust your instincts about what you see and how you feel when you visit a school, but keep an open mind. Although the admissions director may be the representative of the school with whom you spend the most time, he or she ultimately is not as influential as the head of the school or the division head. You may love a school because you bonded with the admissions person, or you may be turned off because the admissions director was dull. Try to assess each school based on what you observe as much as what you hear.

• Parent Interviews •

A parent interview is almost always part of the admissions process for independent schools. An interview can take the form of a meeting with an individual family or with a small group of families. Usually the parents meet with an admissions officer and may also meet the head of the school or division head. This is a chance to share information and let the school get a sense of who you are and to see if your goals for your child are compatible with the school. You may be asked questions about your child and family, and you should be prepared to ask questions about aspects of the school you're particularly interested in. Read the school's literature beforehand so that you aren't asking about information that's addressed in the written material. Your questions will be an indication to the school of your degree of interest.

Some of the kinds of questions you may want to ask are:

- How many openings does the school anticipate this year?

- What's the length of day for kindergarten?
- What constitutes a typical day?

- How does the school evaluate students?
- How does the school handle children who are academically advanced or may need additional support?
- How is discipline handled?
- What's the homework policy? How much, how long, and what kind?
- How do parents and teacher communicate? How often do they meet?
- Are meetings scheduled to accommodate working parents?

- Does the school have the enrichment activities my child is particularly interested in?
- Are there any religious observances?
- How do families apply for financial aid?
- Are there any expenses that aren't covered by tuition?
- Is there bus transportation?
- What's the geographical range within which most students live?

Schools are anticipating a long-term relationship with you, and the parent interview is your chance to make a positive impression. Many deserving, well-qualified children have been denied a place at a school because of the way their parents conducted themselves during the admissions process. Of course, in most cases, parents mean well and aren't deliberately sabotaging their child's chances, but an unaware parent can inadvertently do something inappropriate or rude.

Throughout the interview and tour, it's important to be conscious of the tone of your questions. One mother we know was appalled when her husband, on a tour of a girls' school, asked, "Don't you think you're missing something by not having boys here?" This mother assumed his challenging question ruined their daughter's chances, and she wasn't surprised when her daughter wasn't accepted at the school. The same question could have been appropriately phrased, "How do girls benefit from a single-sex education?" A kindergarten teacher once told us about a parent who asked her, "Why do you teach reading *that* way?" The question sounded critical and would have been received more positively had the parent said, "Could you describe how you teach reading?" Another parent who was on a tour of the nursery school once asked, in front of the entire group, "So tell us the real truth. What's not so great about this school?" This parent was trying to be humorous but came across as confrontational.

Practical Wisdom for Parents

Here are some good ideas to bear in mind:

- Be on time for your appointment. Call ahead if you must cancel.

- Dress appropriately—business clothes are fine.

- Turn off your cell phone, beeper, pager, BlackBerry.

- Listen and look interested. Smile.

- Present your child in an honest, loving, and accurate way without bragging.

- Have both parents attend if applicable. If both parents attend, both parents should speak during the interview.

- Don't ask for special treatment or expect the school to reschedule your visit three times.

- If you have to call to cancel an appointment, don't be rude to the person answering the phone.

- Don't use first names unless the admissions director makes it clear that this is okay.

- Don't dominate or interrupt the tour guide or admissions officer with your questions.

- Don't look at your watch during the interview.

- Don't argue or strongly disagree with your partner.

- If you're asked about what your child likes to do, don't furnish a list of accomplishments or extracurricular activities. "Being read to" is a more appropriate answer.

- Don't criticize your child's current school or the school you're visiting.

- Don't name-drop. Don't assume the people you know or what you do impacts on the admissions process.

- Don't intimate that you will be very generous to the school. Never offer money during the admissions process.

- Don't ask where graduates of this kindergarten have attended college.

It's never a good idea to walk into the interview with a notepad as if you're writing an article, but it is a good idea to jot down your thoughts and impressions shortly after your visit. Some schools appreciate a short, specific thank-you note after a parent interview, but this isn't usually expected. If you do write, make sure you spell the interviewer's and the school's name correctly.

• Child "Interviews" •

Most schools will want to meet your child as part of the admissions process. This can be an intimidating prospect for any parent. The idea that after one brief meeting, your four- or five-year-old will be "evaluated" can seem unfair, if not downright unreasonable. Try not to feel as if your child and your parenting skills are being judged. This is not an "interview" in the adult sense of the word. A more accurate description is "a visit where your child is being observed at play and assessed for specific skills." It's a chance for the school to meet your child and begin to ascertain whether she'll thrive in their environment.

It can be easier if you know what to expect. Children are usually invited to visit a school as part of a small group. The visit lasts approximately forty-five minutes with teachers and possibly administrators in attendance. Some schools see children one-on-one. In almost every case, children will be expected to separate from parents. Most teachers and administrators are adept at putting children at ease, and many children we know actually enjoy their school visits.

Most visits are scheduled during the fall of the year prior to actual entry. It's important not to tell your child about her school visits too far ahead of time. Most children can be told the day before or even the morning of the visit. You can tell your child that she'll be visiting a school that she may attend when she's older. You can say that some of her classmates will also be visiting schools and that it's fun to see what other schools are like and what toys and games there are in their classrooms. You *must* reassure your child that although these visits are happening now, kindergarten won't be starting for a very, very long time. After all, your child only just started her pre-K year and is happily getting used to her new teacher and classmates. Young children live in the moment. We often hear children who have been on school visits telling their teachers that they're going to kindergarten tomorrow. Remind your child that she'll be in her current class for a whole year and that this means after the fall, the winter, the spring, *and* the summer.

Before you visit a prospective school, call ahead and inquire about the procedure for visits. Then, you can prepare your child specifically for what will happen, so she'll be more comfortable. Parents have told us that when they give children simple information—for example, that the school will give them a name tag—it's reassuring when this actually happens. You can tell your child that the grown-ups may ask her name or extend a hand for a handshake. Be positive and relaxed when you talk to your child about visiting. Let your child know that you expect her to cooperate and do what the grown-ups at the school ask her to do.

When visiting schools, your child should not be dressed as if she's going to a party. Comfortable, clean, and neat clothing is more appropriate. If your daughter is wearing a bracelet or fancy headband, she may become preoccupied with her accessories instead of the tasks presented to her. If your son has never worn loafers or a blazer, this is not the time to have him wear them for the first time.

Schools may schedule interviews in the middle of the morning or later in the afternoon. To allow for a calm morning with fewer transitions, it's best to keep your child at home if she has a midmorning interview and bring her to her current school afterward. One year, a child at the nursery school had to leave in the middle of a game on the playground to go to a school visit. He was streaked with dirt and took one look at his mother and bellowed, "I am not going to that school!" Most children don't like to leave when they're already engrossed in their day. If your child's visit is in the afternoon, it's helpful to arrange to pick her up a little early so that she can have a snack and quiet time before the visit. This allows time for washing the child's face and hands and changing her clothes, if necessary.

The most difficult part of the visit for many children is the moment of separation. Your child will have to separate from you in an unfamiliar place with an unfamiliar adult. She may worry that she won't know where to find you when the visit is over. Tell her beforehand where you'll be and what to expect so that she'll feel more comfortable. "When we go to visit the Hill School, we'll be meeting a nice teacher named Ms. Smith, who'll take the children to a classroom where you'll be doing some of the fun activities like you do in school. When it's time to come back, Ms. Smith will bring you to me and then we can go to your school/out for lunch/home." There's no need for both parents to accompany a child on a visit unless the parent interview or tour is scheduled on the same day. If it's the case that your child separates more easily from one parent than the other, you may decide that only one of you should attend.

Even with preparation, your child may not want to go with the teacher, especially if it's her first school visit or, conversely, if it's the sixth school she has visited in the past month. Remember that teachers will be experienced at encouraging children to feel comfortable and to participate. Even so, sometimes a small reward is a necessary incentive. "Small" is the operative word. If you bribe your child with a toy, she'll surely share this information with the admissions director. She may also sense how important the visit is to you and decide to exercise her power over the situation or become overly anxious. An ice-cream cone or an extra bedtime story are more appropriate rewards.

If your child is sick, you'll have to reschedule. A sick child will not be at her best and will likely infect everyone else in the room. Other than for reasons of illness, it's best not to reschedule a visit as it may be inconvenient for the school.

Whether children are seen in a group or individually, most schools have activities that they'll expect children to participate in. Typically, these include:

- Working on puzzles.
- Copying shapes.
- Drawing a picture of a person.
- Writing their names.
- Telling the teacher their birthdays and addresses.
- Listening to a story.
- Chatting with the teacher.
- Playing with other children.
- Working with manipulatives (blocks, Legos, pattern blocks).
- Having a snack.

All schools use these observations differently depending on the type of school and the expectations of that school. Some of the things that schools are interested in learning about your child are:

- Personality and temperament.
- Confidence and adaptability.
- Cooperative attitude.
- Social skills.
- Cognitive ability.
- Expressive and receptive language skills. (See chapter 5 for descriptions of these terms.)
- Small motor ability/writing or drawing skills.
- Independence and motivation.
- Focus and attention span.
- Maturity and readiness.

• Testing •

Many schools rely on some kind of standardized testing in order to learn something about a child's development and how she compares to her peers. Schools may use IQ tests such as the Wechsler Preschool and Primary Scale of Intelligence (WPPSI) or the Stanford-Binet. Others may use readiness tests such as the Gesell or the Otis-Lennon. IQ tests are administered individually to a child by psychologists, and readiness tests are given by trained professionals. Most tests take no more than an hour. It's important for a tester to know if your child is bilingual as this can affect how the test is evaluated.

These tests allow educators to learn something about a child's attitude toward learning, her ability to listen, focus attention, stay with tasks, and apply effort, perseverance, planning, and reasoning. Tests can measure a child's ability to comply with simple instructions; they can assess her self-confidence, as well as her language and visual motor skills. While testing can offer a degree of reliable information about a child's current skills and abilities, it should never be used as a long-term predictor of educational success. We know some parents who believe that if their four-year-old doesn't test well, this means he's never going to make it to Harvard. This is simply not the case. Many children whose test results are not outstanding go on to become excellent students. After all, this is only the very beginning of an educational journey that can last for the next twenty years and beyond.

It's good to keep in mind that test results are only used to supplement other information about a child. Schools are looking to create a complete picture in order to determine whether a child will be a good fit for their school. Testing alone could never reveal everything about a child as a learner or convey all her talents and creative abilities. The school will also be looking at reports from your child's current teacher and school director, as well as her interview and the information you have given. If your child receives glowing reports from her current school and does well in the interview, but wavers when she's tested, it's unlikely that the test will be weighed as heavily. Instead, the school will try to figure out the nature of the inconsistency. Was the child ill on the day she took the test? Was she coached? Was the tester unable to establish rapport with the child? Was the child afraid to make a mistake? Schools will look at the test as a part of the whole picture.

No early childhood educator will ever recommend that you have your child coached to prepare for testing. When children have been groomed for a test, the tester will know immediately. "I've played these games with Ms. Mandel" is an instant giveaway. Overpreparing your child actually invalidates the results of the test and hurts her chances for admission. You will have already given your child the best preparation for the test by sending her to a quality early childhood program and by being an active and involved parent.

What you *can* do to prepare your child:

- Read and talk to your child.

- Make sure your child gets adequate sleep.

- Encourage your child to be interested in the world.

- Involve your child in your everyday life.

- Answer questions.

- Help with problem solving.

- Expect your child to complete a task.

- Provide materials to help promote learning (puzzles, blocks, games, memory and matching games, and so on).

- Have expectations and set limits.

- Build confidence by allowing your child to do things for herself and to deal with frustration.

- Don't drill your child on skills.

- Don't talk to other parents about your child's test scores.

- Don't assume your child's test score is the definition of your child or her abilities.

Although it seems like a lot to expect such a young child to make multiple school visits, in our experience, children usually cooperate and handle the situation well. You can help your child to feel comfortable by appearing relaxed and confident about her ability to do this.

• Decisions •

Once all applications have been submitted and the interviews have taken place, the school's admissions committee will begin considering each applicant and family. Most committees are made up of admissions officers and school and division heads who use the information gathered from interviews, tests, school reports, and other observations to make their decisions. The idea of being judged by a committee made up of virtual strangers can make almost all parents feel uncomfortable. Remember that this isn't only about your child. The committee is going to make decisions based on many factors, some of which have absolutely nothing to do with your family. The school will be considering all kinds of criteria, including the need to create balanced classes that reflect their philosophy. They will want to balance the numbers of sibling and new applicants, girls and boys, and financial aid applicants, as well as making sure that classes are ethnically, religiously, racially, and geographically diverse.

After you've completed the application process, you can always write a letter to a school to explain that you're especially interested in sending your child there. It's not advisable to send this kind of letter to multiple schools. Another good piece of advice: Make sure you send the right response to the right school. We know of a number of parents who have written to their "first-choice" school and inadvertently sent it in the wrong envelope to another school.

After the committee makes its decisions sometime in early to late spring, schools will send out letters indicating an acceptance, a regret (a nice way of saying no), or a wait list. If your child is put on a wait list it can mean one of two things: First, your child was a highly qualified candidate but spaces were limited and your child will be among the first to be considered if a space opens up; alternatively, it may mean that your child was acceptable but may not be seriously considered if a space opens up. Contact the school admissions office to let them know that you're interested in remaining on a wait list. At this point, the school can let you know if the list is expected to move and whether you should you remain active on the wait list. They may discourage you if it doesn't look like there will be an opening. If you know someone well who is actively involved at the school, it won't hurt to ask your friend to call on your behalf.

When you receive notifications of acceptance or rejection, it's essential to stay open-minded and be flexible. There's no doubt that making decisions about the next step in your child's education can be stressful. The process often seems overwhelming, not least because the outcome isn't always within your control. If your child is offered a place at more than one school, remember that this is a personal decision and is yours alone to make. Often, advice from friends and family will probably only confuse you. If you ask your five-year-old child which school she would like to attend, her response will probably be motivated by the fact that she had a nice snack or happened to see a friend in the hallway. During this decision-making period, some schools will allow parents to revisit. This can be useful, especially if you are still undecided. If you're not interested in a school, you should call and decline its offer. You should only do this if your child has a definite place at another school.

It's important to keep in mind that there are no perfect schools. You may like some aspects of every school you visit and may find that there are aspects of every school that you don't particularly like. The best school isn't necessarily the school with the best reputation. Instead, you need to figure out which school seems most appropriate for the present needs of your child and your family. Don't forget that even if a school seems ideal, your child's needs may change (as can a school, staff, and program), and later you may need to reevaluate. We advise parents to stay focused on the next few years and not to make decisions based on what you think your child will require at age eleven or fifteen.

If your child isn't offered a place at the school that you'd set your heart on, you may need to take a step back and reassess your own expectations. You may have always imagined that your child would attend a small single-sex school where the children wear uniforms. Now you may have to adjust to the idea of a larger coed campus school. There is never only one "right" school for your child. Most children are extremely adaptable and will thrive in different school environments. Many parents we know who have been disappointed because their child wasn't accepted into their first-choice school call us in the fall to tell us how happy their child is at the new school and how much they like it there.

The investment of time and thought that you've put into this process can often distract you from what's truly important. Always keep in mind that it is you, your support, your values, and your appreciation of your child that have the greatest influence on her success in *any* school.

Getting Ready to Move On

• When to Tell Your Child About Her New School •

Once you know which school your child is going to attend, it's time to put the decision-making period behind you and focus on the present. If you tell your five-year-old now that she's going to kindergarten next September, her limited awareness of time may lead her to believe that she's going there next week. One mother we know rushed out to buy the new school's backpack after she received the acceptance in March. When she told her child, Grace, the news and gave her the new backpack, her daughter immediately went to her room and buried the backpack in the bottom of her closet. Grace took out her 92nd Street Y backpack, adamantly put it on, and proclaimed, "This is my backpack!"

In our spring meetings, we always remind parents that it will be months until the new school year begins and that letting your child know too soon can be confusing and upsetting for her. Children understand time sequentially and may need to focus on what's coming next. Your child will have a vacation and attend summer camp well before school begins. It's best to wait to talk about the new school toward the end of the summer, unless your child is asking specific questions.

• When Preschool Ends •

• Children's feelings

Children will anticipate the ending of school long before their teachers begin to discuss it with them. Each child may react differently. Some will be sad, some worried, others happy or perhaps oblivious. Toward the end of the pre-K year, we also tend to see a wide range of regressive behavior from children, such as crying, clinging, testing limits, and being more physical. At times, it can feel as if the children have already outgrown the classroom.

Sometimes children are anxious because they've heard negative information about "the big school" from their older siblings. Melissa loved coming to school from day one, but as her time at the nursery school drew to a close, she began crying at the end of each day. When we asked her mother what might be troubling her, it turned out that Joseph, Melissa's big brother, had told her that when she left the nursery school the big school was going to be *really* hard and she would *never* have any fun again. The mother reassured Melissa, explaining that her new school would be different, but she would still have time for friends and fun. The tears soon abated.

Your child's teacher will be sensitive to your child's fears and will build closure gradually to help prepare her for the ending of school. Teachers will inform the children when it's their last music class or library time. They'll discuss all the fun things the class did and learned throughout the year. Teachers may make a yearbook for the children, or help the children make collages from photos taken throughout their school year. Some classes make a list of things that the children who will attend next year should know about their classroom.

Often children can be nostalgic about this transition. At the beginning of each pre-K year, one teacher at the nursery school told her class on their eighth day of school that she wanted them to remember that day. She told them that she didn't know them very well yet, and they didn't know each other very well yet. But before long, they would know all about each other and would be best of friends. During the last week of school, Peter, a child in her class, raised his hand and said, "Remember when you told us in the beginning of the year to remember the eighth day? Now I wish we could go back to the eighth day again."

• Parents' and teachers' feelings

As school winds down, it's not just the children who are filled with mixed emotions but parents and teachers as well. Teachers often experience a sense of pride and sadness. They've invested so much energy and care in each child and in the whole class. While they feel gratified by the children's growth and accomplishments, the prospect of letting the class go can be hard.

For parents in particular, the ending of school is bittersweet. It means saying good-bye to a comfortable community that has fostered friendships with other parents and trust in a first school experience. As preschool draws to a close, it signifies the end of this phase of early childhood. Parents often feel nostalgia for the preschool years before school's even over. Your two-and-a-half-year-old who cried at the classroom door on the first day of school is now a five-year-old who dresses himself at dawn, excited to get to school. Your quiet, shy three-year-old, who wouldn't raise her hand in the group, is now a confident five-year-old who can stand up and lead her class in song. Looking back, you'll be able to see how far your child has come and how ready she is for kindergarten. A child in a pre-K class at the nursery school once said it most poignantly. The children had been growing butterflies from larva, and the teachers had taken the class outside to release them in the playground. The child said, "We're just like the butterflies. When we came here we were little, then we got bigger, and now it's time for us to go."

• Before Kindergarten Begins •

Even with all this careful preparation, parents often tell us that their children wake up the morning after school is over and ask, "Why aren't we going to school today?"

As a parent, you'll be tempted to prepare your child for the new school the minute she's finished her pre-K year. However, it's generally best to wait until a couple of weeks before kindergarten begins before talking about this with her. Some parents find it helpful to take a walk or drive by the new school. If the school sends you a class list, you can ask your child if she'd like a playdate with one of her new classmates so that she'll know a familiar face. (For some children, this is helpful, but for others, the prospect of playing with someone they don't know can cause unnecessary discomfort. You know your child best and whether she would benefit from this kind of playdate or not.) It can also help to familiarize your child with her teacher's name.

Children like to know that they'll still be able to see their friends from the previous school. You can remind your child that she can have playdates with her new friends and her old friends. She can talk on the telephone to her old friends, or you can help her write to them or send them an e-mail. One of the classes at the nursery school makes a telephone and address book each year. Parents tell us that their phones ring off the hook with long messages left on answering machines after school ends. Many children remain friends with their classmates for years after preschool.

• When Kindergarten Begins •

Once children have begun their new school year, parents need to know that it can take time to adjust and that every day will not be great. If you ask your child, "Did you have a wonderful day today." or "Do you love your new school?" you're setting up unrealistic expectations and inviting your child to give a negative response. It's much better to ask a more specific question: "Tell me something that you did at school today." "Who did you sit next to at snack?" "What did you have for lunch?" "Which story did your teacher read today?"

During the first few weeks of school, it's a good idea to limit after-school activities since your child will be tired at the end of the day. She'll need time to make new friends and see old friends. Most of all, she needs time with you.

You may find she regresses during this period, and you may see behaviors that you haven't seen in some time, such as whining, clinging, bed-wetting, or sleep disruptions. However, if you maintain consistency, set age-appropriate expectations, and reassure your child, before long she'll adjust and be back to her usual self.

After many years of responding to concerned phone calls from families whose children had just started kindergarten, we decided to invite parents back to school for an "Adjustment to Kindergarten" meeting. We held the meetings in early November, and parents remarked that if we'd scheduled them any sooner, they would have reported that their children weren't adjusting well. Now that six to eight weeks of school had passed, this was no longer true.

While the meetings were helpful for parents, we also learned a great deal about what this new experience meant for families. Many of the things that came up were consistent no matter where the children attended school. Parents reported that their children were tired, overstimulated, and having difficulty sleeping. One child said, "I can't turn my brain off." Another child said he was building a time machine to take him back to the nursery school. Although many parents and children were requesting playdates, some children were too tired to extend their day. Some parents suggested a half-hour "ice cream date" after school; others scheduled playdates on weekends when the children weren't as depleted. Others declined altogether and said that they would postpone making playdates until January, when they had a better idea of who their child wanted to play with. This was certainly helpful to the hesitant child who said, "It's hard for me to know what to talk to them about."

• Important Things to Know About Going to Kindergarten •

Teachers in a class at the nursery school once asked the children at the end of the school year what they thought were important things to know about going to kindergarten. Below are their replies. You may want to pass them on to your child. They constitute some of the best advice on preparing for kindergarten that we've ever heard.

"Raise your hand."
"Share."
"Listen to your teachers."

"When you don't get what you want, don't get upset."

"If you want to be friends with someone you never met before, say, 'Hi, my name is . . .' "

"You have to be nice."

"Smile."

"You can figure out how to work together when something is wrong."

"If someone is playing by themselves and is sad, say, 'I'll play with you.' "

"If you are feeling sad about saying good-bye, put a picture of the person that dropped you off in your brain."

"When it's time for your grown-up to leave, don't cry, because after they leave you're going to have a great time."

"If your mom is sad, tell her to put a picture of you in her brain. Tell her to do something with her friends."

Part Two

HOME

Chapter Seven

DAY-TO-DAY FAMILY LIFE

As important as school is to young children, the center of a child's life is his home and family. No matter where your child attends school, he's only with his teachers and classmates for three to six hours a day. The majority of his time is spent at home, and the influence of his family will be the single most important factor in his life. We tell parents that it's what you do on a day-to-day basis that provides the foundation children need to feel confident, successful, and eager to learn. It's the little things that count—sitting down to eat breakfast with your child in the morning, the loving hug before he leaves for school, the way you always read stories together before bedtime. You are your child's greatest influence and wherever he finds himself in the world, he carries you with him.

This isn't to say that day-to-day life with young children is always easy. As you will have already discovered, being the parent of a preschooler presents unique challenges. During the preschool years, children are changing and growing at an extremely rapid pace, and parents often find themselves running to keep up. Your child's probably testing limits on every level. He's asserting himself, wanting to establish his independence. He's finding out that language is powerful and that he can use words to test you. He has his own ideas and wants to do things his own way. Transitions become problematic at this age: When you ask your three-year-old to stop playing with his toys so you can help him get dressed, his defiance can be surprisingly forceful. It's inevitable that tears are going to be shed and tantrums thrown. At times, you may feel as if you're sharing your home with a mini-teenager.

Parents often tell us that they feel as if they've lived through a whole day just getting children dressed, fed, and out of the house in the morning—and that's before they've stepped into the office or returned home from dropping their children off at school. It's very easy for us to empathize. When we first met, we were working mothers who were trying to balance the considerable demands of family, home, and the responsibilities of our jobs. As we became friends, we found out that we were coming up against similar difficulties. We often felt exhausted simply by the prospect of the day ahead. At the same time, we were learning the importance of daily routines in family life, discovering that when we set regular bedtimes and mealtimes, things went more smoothly and there were fewer struggles. We were convinced of the wisdom of setting clear expectations for our children. We wanted them to say please and thank you and to know that whining would never get them what they wanted.

The more we talked, the more we found out how similar our backgrounds had been and how much this experience had influenced us as parents. We'd both grown up in fairly traditional homes where family life was stable and predictable from week to week. Our parents' expectations of us were clear and rules were consistent. Ellen fondly remembers the family meals that took place each evening, where no one ate until everyone sat down at the table. Her mother made a particular dinner each night of the week: Thursday was always fish night and roast chicken was on Friday. The house was immaculate; everything had its place, and it was expected that you cleaned up after yourself. Growing up, Ellen and her brother, Steven, knew that their parents were a united front—Mom and Dad worked together as a team, and you didn't question their authority. At the same time, family life was relaxed and enjoyable. There was a lot of laughter. Ellen's home wasn't a rigid place. Within its underlying structure, there was liveliness and a sense of fun to day-to-day family life.

Nancy's home was just as orderly, even though her mother had three energetic children to contend with. Nancy's younger brother, Barry, was particularly active and rambunctious—wherever he went, his toys and his mess followed him. In her mother's spotless home, this presented some challenges. But what might have become a chaotic situation simply didn't. All the children knew that cleaning up after yourself was the rule and they followed it. There was an order and a routine to everything you did. Each evening, the siblings were expected either to set the table or clear the table, and there was no discussion about whose turn it was or whether you felt like doing it. Whatever your mother and father said, you just did. When you sat down to eat, everyone said please and thank you, and you were expected to finish the food on your plate. When Nancy thinks back to those daily family meals, however, what she remembers most was the laughter. The dinner table was a noisy place where you had to fight to get a word in edgewise, but where you had a great time.

When it came time for us to raise our own children, it was only natural for us to be influenced by the way our parents had done things. Unlike our mothers, however, we were working outside the home as well. Both of our husbands worked long hours and weren't always available to help during the week. What we discovered was that structuring the day—as our parents had done—was essential to managing family life as working mothers and helped us to avoid feeling overwhelmed. Of course, we adapted things to meet the needs of our more modern lifestyles. We had less time than our mothers and more things to do. We learned to take shortcuts—having pizza and salad delivered when we didn't have time to go to the supermarket. Sometimes the floor wasn't exactly spotless and the laundry piled up, but we looked the other way because it was more important to spend that extra hour with the children. We may not have always made the meal from scratch, but we still made sure we sat down and ate as a family whenever we could and that our children developed a healthy attitude toward food and eating together. We wanted our children to be able to rely on their days to be as consistent as possible. Even if Mommy wasn't always home when they returned from school, they knew that the babysitter picked them up and that we'd be home in time for dinner.

Over the years, we've learned that there are enormous benefits to having day-to-day structure and routine in the lives of young children. We've seen that children who come from homes where there's a good sense of organization tend to do very well in school. When a child's family life is fairly predictable, when he sits down to eat with his family and has learned to ask politely for what he wants, he'll have a greater degree of comfort in the classroom. He enjoys the routines of the day, he knows how to talk to the other children at snack time, and he quickly learns to raise his hand before asking the teacher a question. In general, he's more likely to adapt well to new situations. He has a sense of confidence in himself and his place in the world. However, when bedtime varies from night to night, when there's no expectation to sit at the table for meals, and when parents regularly give in to whining, children tend to be very unsure of themselves in the structured environment of the classroom.

Routines, family mealtimes, respectful manners. You might wonder if such a traditional style of parenting has a place in the modern family, with its hectic schedules, busy parents, and equally busy children. But in fact, by organizing your family's day-to-day life in this way, you're helping to make life with young children much *less* hectic and stressful. When everyone in the family knows what's expected of them, it's much easier to get through the day with a degree of calm. When parents set clear guidelines for children and follow through on them, then children feel happier and more secure because they know exactly what's required of them. Conflicts, difficult transitions, oppositional behavior—all of these common problems could be alleviated with a little more structure. It may take time to establish clear guidelines for your family. It won't happen overnight. But with repetition and an established daily pattern, you'll help to ease the way for your child. And it'll make your life easier too.

Routines

Children are creatures of habit and benefit greatly from knowing what comes next. When nap time always follows lunchtime, and story time always comes after bath time and before bedtime, a child has a feeling of security that is essential to his sense of well-being. Some parents worry that they will be inhibiting their children if they "impose" a routine on them. This is simply not the case. From years of observing children, we have seen how much children like and *need* to anticipate what comes next in their day. In the classroom, each day follows an almost identical pattern, and within a few weeks, the children have learned it by heart. When we do need to change the structure of the day, which happens only occasionally, the children are always the first to protest. They're much happier when the day goes according to plan.

Routines help to decrease the need for arguing and nagging about things that need to be done on a daily basis. Instead of launching into a long explanation about why your child needs to get dressed, you can simply establish the routine of getting dressed after breakfast. Yet there is not one "right" day-to-day routine that fits all families. If you or your partner work outside the home and want a parent to be present to bathe your child and put him to bed, you may decide that bedtime is at 8 p.m. Another family may want to make bedtime at 7 p.m. and spend time with the children in the morning instead. The most important thing is that you establish a routine that works for your family and that you stick to it. If bedtime is at 7 p.m. one evening and 8 p.m. the next, you're much more likely to get into battles with a child who has figured out that bedtime is a movable feast. Consistency is key.

Here are some things to keep in mind when establishing routines:

- Parents ask us all the time: How long should it take to establish a routine? At what point should I give up if the routine isn't working? While it may take as long as a couple of weeks, it will definitely take longer than two or three days. If you give up because you feel a routine isn't working, you're probably not giving it enough time to be effective. Children learn from repetition, and you can't expect them to change immediately. With time, however, they will adapt.

- Some parents genuinely struggle with organizing a day around a routine. At school, we have the schedule pinned to the wall. Families have told us it helps them enormously when they do the same. When everything is written down in black and white, everyone can stay on the same page. Whether it's a mother, father, caregiver, or grandparent coming into the house to take care of the children, everyone can easily see how the day is organized. Children benefit from having this reminder as well. You can use drawings or photos of your child taking a bath, brushing his teeth, and putting on pajamas so that he can use these images to anticipate what comes next. Attach Velcro to the back of the pictures if you need to add or change something.

- Once you've established a structure to the day, you may need to adapt it to your family's changing needs. Ellen thought she had a good routine with Alice, but then Charles came along. The children were five years apart, and suddenly Ellen had the challenge of getting Alice ready for school while looking after an infant. She thought she could manage caring for Charles *and* getting Alice ready in the morning, but she was trying to do everything and feeling frustrated in the process. Together with her husband, Barry, she came up with a routine that worked better for everyone: Barry gave Alice breakfast and took her to school while Ellen dealt with Charles and waited for the caregiver before leaving for work. Barry usually worked late at night, so Alice and her dad benefited greatly from having this time together. And it left Ellen feeling much less frustrated.

- Often, as a parent, you tend to do what's easiest; then before you know it, this becomes the routine, even if it isn't working. When Nancy's children were preschoolers, she would get Michael dressed first while Alissa was watching TV. After a while, Nancy realized she was having more and more trouble getting Alissa out of the house in the morning. When it came time to get dressed, Alissa would start to whine and wouldn't want to turn off her program. Eventually, Nancy said to her, "The TV is broken; now let's get dressed." From that day on, the TV stayed off in the mornings, and it was much easier to get both children ready for school. Nancy had gotten into a routine that didn't work—otherwise known as a bad habit—and needed to change it.

• While it's important to establish daily routines for your family, it's equally important that you don't become a complete slave to your own regimen. We knew one mother who ran her home like the U.S. Marines. Her child would become incensed if we had to change the order of the school day for any reason. His teachers knew that if it rained and the children had to stay inside instead of playing outdoors at the allotted time, he would burst into tears. Routines are important, but if they're too rigid, your child won't learn to be flexible and to go with the flow when needed. Of course you can alter your routine, as long the structure is still in place. If it's your child's birthday, or his grandparents are visiting from out of town, then of course he can stay up later. When your child has discovered a new game that involves making shampoo hats in the bathtub, it's okay if bath time goes a little later that night. A routine should never become so entrenched that you forget to enjoy your time with your child.

Transition Times: Mornings and Evenings

During transition times—in the morning when everyone is leaving the house and in the evening toward bedtime—there's a lot going on and many families struggle to get through these moments. Young children have great difficulties with transition times. After all, it's adults who initiate transitions. Most children would be perfectly happy playing with their toys for hours without interruption. Children find it hard to jump from one thing to another without a warning and some extra time to adjust. When you establish a clear pattern to transitions, you can actually avoid meltdowns and defiance. It's helpful to leave enough time for transitions to take place—most young children resist being rushed, and you'll find that things go more smoothly when there's enough time to do everything at a child's pace.

• Mornings •

At school, we can always spot the family who has had a rough morning. The parent looks as if he or she has been through a war. The child is irritable and spinning out of control. This sets the tone for the rest of the day—a child who has a rough morning is much more likely to be unsettled in the classroom. If you can establish a regular routine in the morning, you'll discover that your child is more likely to have a smooth transition to the beginning of the school day and to enjoy his time in the classroom.

Morning routines for children involve getting dressed, washed, and fed. You need to determine how and when these things get done. Be practical about how much you can reasonably expect of your child and yourself. By simplifying the morning routine as much as possible, you can help decrease stress. It can help to lay out clothes, prepare backpacks, and organize bag lunches the night before so you have less to do in the morning. This will allow you to focus on gradually getting your child dressed, washed, and fed, rather than rushing him out the door.

Here are some other rules of thumb for making morning transitions easier:

- Assign tasks. During the mornings when there's so much going on, it can be extremely helpful to decide which parent or a caregiver will take care of which task. When one parent feeds the baby while the other dresses the older child, the older child knows what to expect, and the parents don't need to negotiate who's going to do what.

- Give your child either/or choices for breakfast and clothing options. When you ask a child, "What do you want for breakfast?" it's inevitable that he'll feel overwhelmed by too many choices. It's better to say, "Would you like cereal or toast?" Otherwise you'll only prolong the decision-making process. The same goes for clothing. By saying, "Would you like to wear your red shirt or blue shirt?" you're involving your child in making a choice without wasting a half hour dissuading him from wearing his Spiderman costume.

- Keep the TV turned off. Families often tell us how much easier they find the mornings when the TV is off. This gives everyone the opportunity to communicate without distraction. It also makes it much easier to leave the house without getting into arguments about "wanting to finish watching this one program."

- Eat breakfast together. Make sure one parent is sitting down with your child to eat breakfast. When you sit with your child and the TV is off, you can focus on him and his needs for that day.

- Pick your battles. You may want your child to put on his own socks in the morning, but if it's becoming frustrating and difficult, and you're feeling rushed, this might not be the best time to insist on independence.

- Say a good good-bye. Whether you're leaving to go to work or your child is leaving to go to school, you can remind him that you'll see him at dinner, or you'll call when he gets home, or you'll pick him up at school. This will ease the separation and help him understand when he'll see you next.

- Establish a clear schedule for drop-off and pickup at school. Children need to know what's happening on any given day. If the person who takes your child to school varies, you need to set up a routine for how this gets done. Then, if your child is whining and saying, "Mommy, I want you to take me!" you can say: "Mondays the babysitter takes you, and tomorrow I take you."

- Let your child know what's happening after school. Children are comforted by knowing the after-school routine. In the morning, you can tell your child, "You have a playdate," or "I'll be picking up and we'll have lunch together," or "Daddy's going to take you to gym class."

• Evenings •

Evening routines involve eating dinner, bathing the children, and putting them to bed. This is often a problematic time for families since everyone is tired and depleted at the end of the day.

Here are some good rules of thumb to help evening routines progress more smoothly:

- Give yourself time to adjust. Parents who work outside the home often tell us how difficult it can be to go from the environment of the office to a home where a young child is waiting. What typically happens is that the moment a parent walks through the door, the child starts whining and making demands. He misses you and needs you, and you haven't been there. Meanwhile, you're feeling guilty and don't want to start the evening with a conflict. You may need a few minutes to collect yourself before you enter the house at the end of the day. If you're feeling stressed from work, it can help to sit in the car with your eyes closed listening to a song or to take a walk around the block before going in.

- Develop a reunion ritual. If you're making contact with your child after many hours of being apart, it can help enormously to have some kind of special greeting to show your child how happy you are to see him. Your child is looking for your time and attention. Instead of saying, "Why is there such a big mess on the floor?" you can have a hug and some quiet time for talking instead. You can ask your child to clean up the mess later. This is the time for a reunion, not an argument. If you walk in the house and the phone is ringing, your coat is still on, and your child is trying to get your attention, you have to make some choices. First of all, take off your coat. Let the machine answer the phone. Greet your child with a hug and stay at his eye level for a few minutes. Reading e-mail and listening to your messages can wait. You and your child need to be together in this moment so that you can reconnect. You can talk to your child about your day and ask him about his. The most important thing is to spend a little uninterrupted time with him when you first get home. When you do this, the chances are he'll be much less likely to demand your attention when you have to return a phone call later in the evening.

- Allow your child to participate in the preparation of meals. You can involve your child in getting dinner ready or setting the table so that you have the opportunity to be together and share the responsibility. He can tear the lettuce for the salad, add the ingredients as you are preparing, or wash the vegetables.

- Sit with your child as he eats. Even if you can't do this as a family, or you're waiting to eat later, it's still important to sit down with your child. This is a time for learning manners and having conversations.

- Begin the bedtime ritual at least an hour before bedtime. As the evening progresses, you need to slow the pace and quiet things down as you transition toward bedtime. Every family needs to develop rituals that are consistent from day to day and allow children to gradually ready themselves for sleep. You need to take charge of these routines and be clear about what everyone will do each night. Keep things calm. We often hear mothers complain about fathers who walk in the door at bedtime and roughhouse with the children: Jumping on the bed and playing horsey does not contribute to a smooth transition to bedtime. Instead, this transition period can include taking a bath, brushing teeth, reading stories, talking and cuddling, or listening to quiet music. If you come home late from work and feel the need to spend time with your child but have to keep him up past bedtime to do this, it's even more important to maintain a calm and relaxed atmosphere. If your child is tired, you might decide to spend special time together in the morning instead.

- Keep the TV turned off. It's never a good idea to watch television before bed—even the mildest shows are stimulating for a young child. One mother with a child at the nursery school was concerned that he was waking up every night crying hysterically. It was difficult to calm him down enough to get him back to sleep. When we asked her if there was anything new or different in his day, she mentioned that he was asking for his *Dumbo* video on a daily basis and that he usually watched it after he finished dinner and before bed. We suggested that she stop showing it to him. Within a day or two, the night terrors stopped.

- Take turns bathing your children and putting them to bed if you can. During bath time, children feel relaxed and soothed and often open up and talk more easily about their day. It's nice for the whole family if parents can alternate the bath and bedtime ritual so that each parent gets the opportunity to bond during this time. When we think back to our time with our own young children, we can still remember exactly how it felt to wrap a child up in a towel after a bath, the softness and the closeness, the fresh smell of clean skin, and how delicious it was to dry them off, then to put them in their pajamas. We wouldn't have missed this part of our family's daily ritual for the world.

- If you have more than one child, figure out a routine that allows you to divide your attention. It can be hard to read a bedtime story to your older child while your two-year-old is whining for your attention. Try staggering bedtimes, even if it's only by fifteen minutes. Your older child can play quietly in his room while you put the younger one to bed. You can tell the older child, "You can stay up later because you're older," and meanwhile the younger one is getting more sleep.

Bedtime and Sleep Issues

For families with young children, bedtime is often the most challenging part of the day. Everyone—parents included—is tired and arguments can often ensue. At our parent meetings, this is one of the topics that comes up regularly and causes the most frustration. We've listened to hundreds of parents as they tried to figure out strategies to help their children go to sleep and stay in bed. It's clear to us that there's no one method that works for all families, but parents who have the greatest success are those who establish consistent bedtime routines, stay with those routines until they are well established, and whose children know what's expected of them.

No parent needs to be reminded of the benefits of a good night's sleep for young children. A tired child won't be able to cope the next day and will easily become irritable and upset. We've seen how much this can affect children at school. When a child lacks sleep, he'll find it much more difficult to concentrate and to retain information. This was the case with Julie, a four-year-old in one of the nursery school's classrooms. The teacher noticed that Julie was having problems remembering the names of the letters of the alphabet. Some days she could remember them and other days she couldn't. The inconsistency was puzzling to the teacher, who spoke to Julie's parents about it. The teacher discovered that Julie's bedtimes were very irregular and her parents often had to wake her in the mornings so that she wouldn't be late for school. The teacher realized that when Julie was tired, she struggled with her letters, and on the days when she was well rested, she could easily name them. When Julie started going to bed at the same time each evening and got enough sleep, her ability to retain information became consistent.

If you have to wake your child up in the morning, it may mean he's not getting enough sleep. You should think about whether his bedtime needs to be earlier. Parents have told us that when they put children to bed earlier, this often avoids the overtired stage and their children sleep longer and better. Children at this age need ten to twelve hours of sleep nightly. Typical bedtime for three- to five-year-olds is between 7 and 8 p.m. When you have to wake a child up in the morning, he won't be well rested and may become irritable and tired, especially toward the end of the day. Also, you may end up rushing the morning in a way that doesn't get the day started on the right foot.

Practical Wisdom for Parents

At around three years old, children are going through a period of transition where they're starting to give up their daytime naps. If your child is older than three and a half, is still napping during the day, and is taking longer and longer to settle down at bedtime, you should start shortening his nap times so he'll be tired in the evening and can get to sleep more easily. By setting a regular bedtime and bedtime ritual for your child, you're helping to ensure he falls asleep without struggles.

Other tried and tested ways to help settle your child to sleep:

- Reading one or two stories in bed before sleeping is a calm and relaxing ritual that children have enjoyed for generations. Children feel comforted by hearing the same stories over and over again, and your child may want you to read *Goodnight Moon* as part of his bedtime ritual for years to come. One parent we know added to this experience by putting photos in a book of her child getting ready for bed—taking a bath, putting on pajamas, brushing teeth, reading a story, and then sleeping. Another mother we know told stories about when she was a little girl and the things that happened to her: Sometimes the little girl was naughty and sometimes the stories had a purpose to illustrate something that had happened that day.

  When reading or telling stories to your child at bedtime, however, it's important that you set a time limit or stipulate the number of books and stick to this. When you tell your child beforehand to choose which books he would like to read, this gives him some control. But when you allow him to ask for more and more stories, this will only prolong the process of getting him to sleep. Two stories are generally enough. When he asks for one more, you can always say, "Let's put that one aside and we can read it tomorrow night."

- Some children like listening to music or hearing you sing to them at bedtime. By playing or singing the same tune nightly, you're creating a good sleep association for your child. If you are going to play recorded music, however, make sure the volume is turned down low and that it's soothing. One mother we know would sing about her child's day: "Jamie got up in the morning and went to school, played with his friends, had spaghetti for dinner, took a bath and brushed his teeth, got into bed and said goodnight to his room and his toys."

- Many children need a special object like a favorite stuffed animal or blanket to help them to sleep. Nancy's daughter, Alissa, liked to cuddle

Nancy's pillow—she said she liked it because it smelled like Mommy. Other children may prefer not to have the distraction of objects. A parent we know actually asked her daughter what she thought would help her fall asleep. Her daughter said, "I think I have too many stuffed animals on my bed. I think I'll put some on the floor." Magically, it worked.

• When None of These Work •

No matter how hard you try, some children will resist going to sleep and will claim they're not tired even when you know they're exhausted. Many children use bedtime negotiations as a way of asserting control over you and their world. This is one of the greatest challenges that parents of young children face. It may be that your child resists going to sleep because it means separating from you. He might be struggling with nighttime fears or have difficulty learning to soothe himself. Sometimes, it'll be that he's overstimulated—although he looks and feels wide awake, he desperately needs to sleep.

Many parents have talked to us about the frustration and exhaustion they feel at a long, drawn-out process of bedtime. If your child is refusing point-blank to go to sleep, it can be very hard for a parent to handle, especially if you're also feeling tired. You'll need to remain as calm and firm as possible. Bedtime is bedtime, period. Don't engage your child in negotiation as this will only stimulate him further. Stick with your plan and be consistent.

Some parents lie down next to a child to help settle him. At first, this seems like the easiest way to get him to finally close his eyes and fall asleep. By lying next to him, he feels that you are near and finds it much easier to relax. You may find that you enjoy this time to cuddle, especially if you've been separated from him during the day. But what can happen is that over a period of time, a five-minute snuggle can turn into a struggle where your child won't let you leave. Be aware of habits that keep children from learning to soothe themselves at bedtime. There's nothing wrong with lying down next to your child, but if this turns into an extended period of time and you're frustrated and missing out on time for yourself or to be with your partner, you'll need to adjust your nighttime routines. Many exhausted parents end up falling fast asleep alongside their children. Ellen remembers looking into Charles's room only to find Charles wide awake and her husband, Barry, fast asleep next to him.

If your child is accustomed to having you lie next to him before bedtime, he's probably going to cry when you try to change this habit. Many parents are uncomfortable with leaving a child to cry himself to sleep. If this is the case, over a period of days, gradually shorten the time you're lying down with your child. You can put your hand on your child initially so that he still feels you're near. You can move to the side of the bed, and from the side of the bed to the chair.

One parent gave us the following piece of advice that we have passed on to many other families: Try telling your child that he doesn't need to fall asleep right away but he has to stay in bed. The pressure to fall asleep can often keep a child awake, so tell him, "You can cuddle with your animals, rest, or snuggle, but you have to stay in bed." Parents have informed us that when they say, "I'll come back to the bedroom to check on you in a few minutes," the child is often asleep when they go back to check. You may want to leave on a night-light or some soothing music. One parent told us that she leaves a flashlight and two books on the bed. You can also record yourself reading your child's favorite story and put that on before leaving.

Most importantly, remember that over time it is possible to adjust your child's sleeping habits. With patience, persistence, and consistency, you'll be able to establish good bedtime rituals and routines, and your child will begin to find going to sleep—and staying asleep—much easier.

• Night Fears •

Another problem we regularly hear about from families is the issue of night fears. Children have many fears and their imaginations are very active, particularly at bedtime. Sometimes fears will increase as children are going through periods of growth or change. A move, a new caregiver, a new sibling, or a new school can disrupt your child, causing him to have nightmares that wake him up during the night. These dreams and anxieties are very real to him, and you need to listen and reassure him that you'll keep him safe. You can say, "Tell me about the dream; it will get it out of your head and make it go away." Don't deny the existence of monsters; it won't work. Be prepared to check the closet and under the bed for monsters and look like you mean it. Try devising an imaginary "monster catcher" or "monster repellent" to help soothe your child. If he's afraid of the dark you may need to put a night-light or dimmer switch in your child's bedroom, or leave the door ajar.

You can also read stories about night fears to your child. Mercer Mayer's book *There's a Nightmare in My Closet* is a favorite with young children. It deals with a little boy's nighttime fears by allowing him to take charge of the monster. First, the little boy tries to frighten the monster, but then the monster gets frightened, so the boy invites him to bed with him. Books like this one can be very soothing for young children.

• Staying in Bed •

Many children will awaken during the night and want to get into their parents' bed, especially during the period when they're transitioning from a crib to a bed. (Most children are in a bed by age three.) This can be a very difficult habit to break. Most parents find that if they walk their child back to bed and don't talk or give him any attention while they do so, he'll stop this habit after a short time. If your child insists on getting into bed with you, you can always try placing a blanket on the floor and letting him sleep there for a while so that he can gradually adjust to going back to his room. When a child learns to sleep in his own bed and his attempts are praised or rewarded with a sticker, he feels a sense of accomplishment. This is one way that children begin to feel confident about themselves and their growing independence. One family found that singing a special song to their son in the morning after he stayed in his own bed the whole night helped give him the incentive to remain under the covers. The most important thing is to stick with your plan and not to give in to your child in the moment because this is easier for you.

• Early Mornings •

Many children will wake up very early in the morning, sometimes because their rooms are too bright. You can try putting black-out shades in the bedroom so that your child doesn't wake up as soon as the sun rises. If your child has gotten into the habit of rising very early, you can tell him to play quietly in his room. One family put a Post-it saying "7:00 a.m." near the digital clock so the child would know not to go into his parents' bedroom until that time. Bear in mind that if you get into the habit of giving your child breakfast very early in the morning, he may develop the expectation that he should eat at that time every day. Even if your child wakes at 5 a.m., breakfast doesn't need to be until 7 a.m.

Mealtimes

We've learned from our parent meetings that many families do not sit down for a regular mealtime together. In many families, dinner is squeezed in between other activities, the television is turned on during the meal, parents come home from work too late to eat with their children, or children are allowed to snack in different areas of the house. We've even heard about parents who feed their children dinner in the back of the car on the way home from after-school classes. It's true that family life is busy and that often it's not possible to cook a full meal or to have every member of the family present. Even so, you shouldn't underestimate the importance of structured mealtimes.

When talking about this subject with parents, we always cite a survey that aimed to find out what all National Merit Scholars had in common. The results of the survey showed that, without exception, all of these outstanding students came from families who ate together three or more nights a week. Other studies have shown that children from families who eat together are less likely to be susceptible to drug abuse, eating disorders, depression, and teen pregnancies. It's clear that a family meal isn't only about eating. By giving your family this time together around the dinner table, you're sending a powerful message to your child about belonging and identifying as a member of a family unit. When a child feels connected to a family in this way, he's much more likely to take on its values. During family meals, children learn how to interact in a social setting, they learn to share and to cooperate, and they find their place in the family dynamic. They absorb table manners by watching you and modeling appropriate demeanor. They begin to have an appreciation for the art of conversation. They learn to enjoy food and the social interactions that take place at mealtimes.

Even if your family is unable to gather for a meal every night for practical reasons, children should always be sitting at a table with an adult while eating (as opposed to sitting and eating while you do something else or wandering around the house with food). The television should be turned off. When you sit with your child, you're showing him that you value this time together. You can talk about your day, and have him talk about his. You can teach him beginning table manners and encourage his self-help skills—by the age of three, your child is ready to use a fork and spoon on his own. Most young children are unable to sit for more than fifteen to twenty minutes at a time, but when you sit down at the table with your child, he's more likely to stay in his seat for a little longer. If you're talking on the phone or glancing across at the TV while eating, your child will doubtless lose his focus also. A booster seat can also help. As your child becomes better able to sit still, you can gradually lengthen his time at the dinner table.

If your weeknights are busy, it's still important that you find time to gather around the dinner table for a meal with the whole family at least once a week (or more if you can). Although family dinners during the week can be difficult to arrange, Saturday or Sunday brunch or a Sunday dinner may be more manageable. It's pleasurable to make your own family traditions surrounding this meal. Lay a special tablecloth or place a vase of flowers on the table. Assign age-appropriate tasks for each family member such as setting the table or helping prepare part of the meal. When you sit down to eat, have everyone take turns sharing the best and worst stories of the week. If you don't have time to prepare food, you can eat out at a favorite restaurant, spending time together without the distraction of preparing and cleaning up afterward. By creating rituals such as these, you're making memories that your child will treasure as he grows.

During special mealtimes, it's important not to bring up other conflicts—the dinner table is not the place to discipline your child about another issue unrelated to dinner or for one child to tell on another child. On the other hand, don't become overly idealistic—if you expect every family meal to be a "happy meal," you'll be disappointed. A dinner table is a place for fun, but it can also be the setting for conflicts and fights as each member of the family jostles for position within the group dynamic. You can help to manage this by making sure everyone has a chance to speak and that each family member is listened to respectfully. One mother tells us that she gives her children "talking time" by either starting from the youngest to the oldest or the other way around.

• What's on Your Child's Plate •

All parents want their children to be healthy. Even so, providing nutritious meals for your young child is challenging. Young children are often picky eaters. They want control over what they will and won't eat, and they have limited patience for sitting in one place. Many parents feel pressured about what and how much their children eat. You may find yourself spending family mealtimes estimating the nutritional value of your child's food consumption rather than actually talking to him. If you are too focused on quality and quantity, you may undermine the potential pleasure of mealtimes. It's very easy to turn your dinner table into a battlefield.

The first thing you need to do is create a relaxed atmosphere around food. You'll be setting yourself up for daily conflict if you're worried about your child finishing everything on his plate. If you complain in front of your child that he never eats enough or if you withhold foods out of a concern that he'll get fat, then you're ensuring that your child senses that food is a powerful issue. It's possible that he'll begin to use this knowledge to gain control over you and the situation.

Here are some good rules of thumb for helping your child develop healthy attitudes about food:

- Think about the whole week rather than the individual meal. Although nutrition is important, it's better not to fixate on the nutritional value of a single meal. When Ellen's two children were small, they were both very picky eaters. She was concerned about how much they were eating and what kinds of foods they consumed, so she asked her pediatrician for advice. He told her, "Don't focus on individual meals—think about what they are eating over the course of a week." This reassured Ellen and mealtimes became less tense. As her children matured, they became healthy eaters who enjoyed a variety of foods. Your pediatrician will be able to tell you if your child is healthy and growing.

- Understand that children eat less than adults. In fact, most preschool-age children don't eat three full meals a day. A child may eat very little on one day and much more the next. He may eat a good breakfast but very little at lunch and dinner. Children are overwhelmed when you put large amounts of food on their plate. It's better to offer small portions and have them ask for more rather than forcing them to finish. If your child has only taken a small nibble of food, you can always entice him to eat "three more bites" or "just half" so that he doesn't feel under too much pressure to finish everything. Some children are grazers and prefer small minimeals frequently throughout the day. If your child is eating in this way, you need to offer healthy choices like cut-up apples, cheese, and carrots, or yogurt.

- Avoid giving your child too many food choices. Many parents turn into short-order cooks in the attempt to please their children and get them to eat. While the "parent-as-chef" is well meaning, a variety of choices can be overwhelming for a small child. At school, we've seen children bring lunches with five different kinds of food. They stare at their lunch, not knowing where to begin, rarely eating more than half a sandwich and a few bites of fruit or cheese. Parents need to take charge of what a child eats. If you've given your child a choice of pasta or chicken for dinner, and he asks for something else, you can say, "I can make that for you tomorrow." Don't fall into the trap of appeasing your child's whims. When a child always determines what he eats, it's rarely about the food and more about asserting himself.

- Don't become overly anxious when your child wants to eat only one thing. Children often want to eat the same foods over and over. As long as the preferred food is healthy, you can relax. Most children will eventually move on to something else. Rather than turn this into a big issue, you can try making light of the situation. Suggest to your child that you have an "upside-down day." Put on his pajamas and let him eat breakfast for dinner; call it "Brinner." Last night's pizza can be breakfast. Sometimes it works if you give a child his favorite food while introducing a small portion of a new food on the side. Even the most determined parent, however, may find that their child holds his ground. When Nancy's son, Michael, was young, he went through a phase of eating only cinnamon toast. He wanted cinnamon toast three times a day. Nancy wanted to find some way of getting him to eat other things. She told him, "I have a great idea. How about we have scrambled eggs with cinnamon toast!" Michael replied, "That's a great idea, Mom. But let's forget about the eggs." Nancy had to have faith that Michael would mature and develop new tastes, and eventually he did.

- Don't deprive your children of sweets and junk food altogether. Most parents worry about children eating too many sweets or junk food, and of course you should have healthy snack choices in your home. Cereal, dried fruit, juice pops, or pretzels are excellent alternatives to cookies and ice cream. However, when children are denied candy or cookies, they often crave these forbidden treats, developing an unhealthy interest in them. When these children go on playdates to friends' houses, they may gorge on the things that they're not allowed to have at home. We'll never forget the time we found a four-year-old who was never allowed sweets sneaking a cookie from the garbage. It's fine to allow your children treats occasionally.

Practical Wisdom for Parents

- Present food in a fun or different way. If your child's a picky eater, it can be very difficult to persuade him to try something he's not familiar with. Children will be more likely to eat a new food if you prepare it imaginatively. Struggles with food are a common theme at our parent meetings, and these are some suggestions that have worked for the parents of picky eaters: sandwiches cut with cookie cutters into shapes, raw vegetables with a dip or on toothpicks or wooden skewers to make kabobs, turkey and cheese rolled up and closed with a toothpick. Nancy's children loved to help make "fruit faces" out of all kinds of fruit (or vegetables) cut in fun shapes.

- Avoid talking about dieting in front of your child. When you talk about your own weight in relation to the way you look and feel about yourself, you're sending a powerful message. We've heard four-year-olds say, "I can't eat the bagel; it will make me fat." In a society that values thinness and where dieting is common among adults, it's very important for parents to talk about food and food choices as they relate to *health* and *growth*. What constitutes a healthy diet for an adult is not a healthy diet for a child—children need balanced meals that include some fats and carbohydrates. As a parent, you need to help your child understand that food is the fuel that makes him grow. You can talk about how milk, cheese, and broccoli help make his bones strong. Carrots help keep eyes healthy, and meat and chicken strengthen muscles. One four-year-old we know was eating lunch at school and reported proudly to his teacher that he had a protein and a complex carbohydrate in his lunch. His parents had taught him an important lesson and some fun words to show off at school.

- Be aware of your child's weight without turning it into an issue. If your child seems to be over- or underweight, you should ask your pediatrician if his weight is typical for his age. Review healthy food options with your doctor and assess if your child is getting enough physical activity and nutritional content from week to week. Don't discuss these matters in front of your child, or he may become anxious or develop an unhealthy attitude toward food.

- Allow your child to help you in the kitchen. You may find that your picky eater will try new foods if he's involved in making them. Children love to cook and to be in the kitchen with you. When children cook, they learn to measure, they pour, they stir, they cut, and then they can eat. By cooking foods, children also learn about different cultures, family history, and nutrition and health. There are many wonderful cookbooks that are geared to children's tastes and interests, and some of these are listed at the end of this chapter.

Manners

As parents and as educators, we've always believed that manners are much more than a matter of simple convention. Manners are an important way of teaching children to be respectful and to show consideration of others. At school, the children learn to be polite as part of the everyday classroom experience. When the teacher greets a child with, "Good morning, Olivia," Olivia is learning to make eye contact with her teacher and to respond, "Good morning, Ms. Claire." At snack time, the children thank the child who brought the snack and are expected to say please and thank you when they ask for more. They learn to raise a hand before speaking and not to interrupt when someone else is speaking. Teachers model polite behavior so that the children can learn by example. Teachers will also make a point of noticing and commenting when children are polite, kind, or helpful toward each other.

Of course, children whose parents have begun to teach them good manners at home have a head start when it comes to integrating into the world of the classroom. When a child learns to ask nicely, he's much more likely to be listened to and to be helped by others. When you give your child a good grounding in basic manners, you're helping to ease his way, not just in the classroom, but in the wider world, when he visits his friends or relatives.

Often parents assume that it's okay to wait until a child is older to begin to teach basic manners or that this is something that children will naturally acquire over time. Although it's important to model polite behavior for your child so that he can learn by example, it's equally important to actively teach manners as well. There's no time like the present. As soon as your child learns to say, "I want," you should remind him to ask, "Please may I have?" and to say, "Thank you."

• Basic Table Manners •

By age three, children should be eating with a spoon and fork and not with fingers. Once your child is able to eat independently, you can start to teach basic table manners. Children learn by example and will imitate the behaviors they see. When you sit down for dinner with your children and model appropriate table etiquette, they'll pick it up by watching you, as well as listening to your instructions. Here are some expectations you can begin to have for your child at this age:

- Have your child put his napkin in his lap and show him how to use it.

- Encourage him to sit in his seat with his feet under the table and not up on the chair.

- Have him sit for fifteen to twenty minutes without getting up.

- Have him wait for everyone to be seated before beginning to eat.

- Remind him to chew and swallow before speaking.

- Encourage your child to close his mouth when chewing.

- Remind him that food should stay on his plate.

- Instead of reaching and grabbing for something, he should say, "Please pass . . ."

- If your child doesn't like what's on his plate and says, "That's disgusting!" you should tell him he doesn't need to comment on it, but can put it to the side of his plate.

- Have him ask to be excused before leaving the table.

- Have him help clear plates and cups after eating.

• Coughing, Runny Noses, Nose Picking, and Burping •

It's inevitable that young children will cough or sneeze without covering their mouths, that they'll pick their noses in public, and that they'll burp without saying excuse me. When you see your child do any of these things, it's a good idea to teach him to do otherwise. You're actually showing him how to be considerate of others.

- Coughing and sneezing. At school, children are taught to cough into the crook of their elbow so that germs don't spread to their classmates. This is better than covering mouths with hands, which spreads germs. If your child's cold is at the infectious stage, of course you should keep him at home.

- Runny noses and nose picking. We've all seen the child who stands helplessly while mucus drips from his nose and down his face. In the classrooms, tissue boxes are easily accessible to children, and they're taught to wipe their nose, throw the tissue in the garbage, and wash their hands. When children pick their noses (which they will), we offer them a tissue. After all, no one wants to hold hands with the child who just picked his nose.

- Burping. Children think burping is funny. You need to teach your child to say, "Excuse me," following a burp. If the burping is repeated and purposeful, don't let your child think this is amusing or you'll have a perpetual burper in your home.

• Interrupting •

Young children like to say what's on their minds, and they need to say it right away. It can be very hard for a young child to wait to speak. Even so, you need to teach your child that it's polite and considerate not to interrupt. You can say calmly, "Hold the thought in your mind, and I will listen to you when I've finished speaking." Most children don't understand the meaning of the phrase, "Excuse me." Instead of waiting until you've finished talking, they'll say, "Excuse me, excuse me, excuse me," until they get your attention. If you want them to learn to wait, you have to tell them that you'll listen to them when you're finished. If you break down after the eighth "excuse me" and respond to the request, you're sending the message that it's okay to interrupt.

• Whining •

The tone of voice your child uses—especially when asking for things—is very important. Children whine and often use a nasty tone when making demands. There is probably nothing more grating to a parent than a whining child, and it follows that many parents will give in to the demand just to put a stop to the whining. However, if you do relent when this tone is used, you'll only encourage your child to use the tone again. When your child whines in the classroom or at another child's house, it's going to be much more difficult for him to get along with other children and adults. By requiring your child to talk in a polite voice, you're teaching him a much more effective way of communicating.

Some children may not understand exactly what you mean when you tell them not to whine. One parent we know explained to her child that "whining means talking and crying at the same time." This helped him to understand what she meant. You can also say, "I can't understand you when you whine. Please talk to me in your big boy voice." Another way to send the message that this is wrong is to ignore the whining. Remember that when you start to whine back at your child, you're just raising the ante. Nagging your child about this is actually the adult equivalent of his whining.

• Responding When Spoken To •

Some children are uncomfortable making eye contact and will be reluctant to speak to people they're unfamiliar with or haven't seen for some time. If this is the case with your child, it can help to explain it to him in this way: "When you look at someone, that person will know you're listening, and if you don't answer, the other person's feelings may be hurt." When you excuse your child by telling people that he's shy, you're labeling him in a negative way rather than building his confidence and encouraging him. You can start by asking him to make eye contact with and respond to family members and teachers so that he can gain comfort, then build it up gradually from there.

• Hitting and Name-Calling •

It's not unusual for children to get angry or frustrated with their parents or caregivers and to hit them or call them names. Children will do this. But when you allow your child to hit you or call you names without correcting him, you're sending the message that you approve of this behavior. When a child calls Daddy "stupid," and Daddy ignores the behavior, the child may think it's fine to use this language with others. It's very important that you let your child know in a firm, definitive voice that this is unacceptable behavior: "Name-calling is not allowed." Once we observed a three-year-old in one of our classes hitting his mother in the hallway at school because she'd left his special toy at home that day. His mother didn't address his hitting and even apologized for "forgetting." We weren't surprised when the teachers reported to us that this child was hitting his classmates when he didn't get what he wanted.

• Rude Remarks •

Children are observant and usually say whatever they're thinking. When your child says in a loud voice, "Mom, that lady is fat!" he's not intentionally being hurtful or rude. But he does need to be taught that when he's speaking about how a person looks, he should tell you in a very quiet voice or wait until the person leaves. You can teach him that it's okay to think things but not to say something out loud if he thinks it might hurt someone's feelings.

Children's natural curiosity will often cause them to comment on differences, including skin color. While it can be mortifying to hear a child make a comment about this, in fact, this is a good opportunity to teach your child that all people are different. By handling your child's remarks in a matter of fact manner, you are sending a message that differences exist without making a judgment. It's helpful to read your child books that show diverse people and cultures. When you point out the many ways people are different and yet alike, children gain a greater understanding of the world around them.

• Saying Thank You •

When you teach your child to say thank you, you're teaching him to appreciate the effort and caring of someone else on his behalf. Whether it's saying thank you for a playdate at a friend's house, for a gift or a meal, or to a waiter in a restaurant, your child benefits in so many ways when he uses these words. By saying thank you, he gets something back and feels good about himself because others will acknowledge his appreciation and consideration. When your child says thank you without prompting, remember to compliment him in order to encourage this good behavior. Your acknowledgment and expectation encourage him even further.

• Being a Good Role Model •

Young children are like sponges and naturally absorb all that they see around them. When you're on the bus and give your seat to an elderly

Practical Wisdom for Parents

woman or smile and say thank you to the checkout person at the supermarket, your child is watching and learning. If good manners are part of your family life and you expect your child to be polite and understand polite behavior, he'll logically pick up good habits. It's immensely gratifying when your four-year-old reaches to shake someone's hand because he's seen you do this, or puts his napkin on his lap at a relative's house without prompting. When you see this, you know you have been a good role model.

Recommended Books for Parents About Family Life

Raising Resilient Children	Robert Brooks
Siblings Without Rivalry	Adele Faber and Elaine Mazlish
The Childhood Roots of Adult Happiness	Edward M. Hallowell
Raising Good Children	Thomas Lickona
The Blessing of a Skinned Knee	Wendy Mogel
Nurturing Good Children Now	Ron Taffel
Parenting by Heart	Ron Taffel
Healthy Sleep Habits, Happy Child	Marc Weissbluth

Recommended Books for Children

BED AND BEDTIME

Musical Beds	Mara Bergman
My Big Boy Bed	Eve Bunting
I Am Not Sleepy and I Will Not Go to Bed	Lauren Child
Time for Bed	Mem Fox
My Own Big Bed	Anne Grossnickle Hines
Bedtime for Frances	Russell Hoban
Just Go to Bed	Mercer Mayer
What a Bad Dream	Mercer Mayer
Otto Goes to Bed	Todd Parr
10 Minutes till Bedtime	Peggy Rathmann
What's Under My Bed?	James Stevenson
Billy's Big-Boy Bed	Phyllis Limbacher Tildes
Can't You Sleep, Little Bear?	Martin Waddell
The Napping House	Audrey Wood
How Do Dinosaurs Say Goodnight?	Jane Yolen
Mommy, I Want to Sleep in Your Bed!	Harriet Ziefert

Day-to-Day Family Life

Chapter Eight

THE PEOPLE IN YOUR CHILD'S LIFE

Over the past twenty-five years, we've watched the concept of family change significantly. The majority of families are no longer made up of a mother who stays home and a father who goes out to work. In many families, both parents work outside the home, or the father may stay home while the mother goes out to work. There are single-parent families and families where parents are sharing custody after a divorce. Same-sex parents are common, as are blended families in which the parents have remarried and are bringing up their children together. In some families, grandparents or aunts and uncles may be involved in raising a child, but often relatives live far from one another, and parents rely on friends and caregivers for support and a sense of belonging.

Although we raised our own families in New York City, we both grew up in small towns, with mothers who stayed home and fathers who went out to work. Coincidentally, we both had an aunt, uncle, and cousins living just across the street. There was always an extra pair of hands to help with child-care, shopping, and the daily routines and chores of family life. When we were growing up, there was no such thing as a playdate. We didn't need them. We had our siblings and our cousins across the street to keep us busy. When we became parents ourselves, however, life was very different. We didn't have our extended families so close by. Ours was an urban lifestyle, living in a big apartment building with few neighbors who had young children. It could have been an isolating experience. We were lucky. After we met and became friends, we managed to effectively replicate the communities of our childhood. We watched each other's children, we'd check to see if the other needed milk or bread when we went shopping, and we used the elevator as the conduit for a cup of sugar or an egg when we ran out. As busy, working mothers, we depended on each other, our husbands, as well as our care-givers, to help with the children and the demands of everyday life.

In the time since we were bringing up our own children, the pace of family life has increased enormously, with parents often working long hours and with less time to devote to family and home. Over the past twenty-five years, divorce is quite common, and families in general have become more fractured, with relatives often living in different states or overseas. We regularly hear parents saying that they wish they had more help, more time, and less stress. When we listen a little longer, however, we're struck by the familiarity of their concerns. Parents tell us about sibling battles and about the complications and conflicts with their partners about raising children. They tell us that they're irritated when grandparents give unwanted advice and feel frustrated by not being able to "do it all." We empathize. After all, siblings have always fought. Partners have always argued. Grandparents have always wanted to interfere. And parents have always felt overwhelmed at times. What we have begun to realize is that although the structure and pace of family life has changed a great deal, many of the difficulties that parents face on a day-to-day basis have remained the same across generations.

Whatever your family's structure, you may imagine that there was a more perfect time when life was simpler and less stressful. Modern families are busy, and the demands on parents seem to increase daily. But no matter who's in your family or how much time you have for your child, there's no such thing as the ideal, perfect family. All families experience disagreements, stress, disappointment, and bumps along the way, and they always have. It's how you handle these challenges as they come along—and they will—that determines the quality of your family's life. In our parent groups, we always stress the importance of giving up the idea of perfection. When you're no longer imagining the "perfect" parent or family, you can put your energy into being a good enough parent for your family.

Setting Priorities in Family Life

One of the greatest challenges parents of young children face is how to set priorities. How do you divide yourself between your children, your home, your work, your partner, your other family members, and yourself? Maintaining balance is a constant struggle. If you always put your work before your children, of course your family's life is going to suffer. If you always put your children before your work, and if you fail to prioritize your health and your other relationships, then everyone suffers. We've seen many families that have become excessively child centered, where the children call the shots, dictating every aspect of family life. When this happens, parents inevitably become overtaxed and may neglect their health, well-being, and other important relationships.

It can be very hard to balance the demands of home, work, and family. Many parents feel guilty about time spent away from the children and want to compensate for this when they're at home. While it will always be difficult to juggle priorities, it's very important not to let guilt get in the way of being an effective authority figure for your child. Your feelings of guilt may cause you to give in to your child's demands even when those demands are unreasonable. You might hang up on an important call in order to instantly gratify your child's wish to watch one more DVD. You might immediately succumb when a child says, "I only want Mommy to dress me!" even though you need to get ready for work. You might forgo dinner with your partner because your child cries when she's left with the babysitter. When this happens, your child is getting the message that she's the most important member of the family. If family life always revolves around its youngest members, children aren't given the chance to learn that they're part of a unit and that there will be times when they need to acquiesce to the group's needs. By teaching your child that she's a member of a team, rather than the star of the show, you're setting up a much more realistic expectation for her as she begins to find her way in the outside world, where people may not always be able to gratify her every whim.

As a parent, you need to help your child understand that each member of the family is important. You can do this by setting clear limits, explaining to her that you need to finish the phone call before you can help her, that you aren't the only person who can do things for her. It's important for grown-ups to have time together alone. If you're in a relationship, a regular date night can be a great way of keeping your connection and the channels of communication open with your partner. A dinner out, a walk in the park, or a movie can give you a much needed break and the chance to enjoy being together. Although it can be hard to do, you should also consciously carve out time for yourself, even if it's only for half an hour a week. Go for a child-free coffee with a friend, a quick workout, or a walk alone. Offer to look after the children so your partner can do the same. When both adults in a family take time to care for their relationship, health, and sense of well-being, it follows that stress levels decrease and the ability to cope increases, which means everyone benefits. And it'll make your child feel good when she sees that you're more relaxed and that her parents can take pleasure in each other's company.

When you're home with the children, remember that family time doesn't have to mean the whole family is together. It can be healthy to spend time with your children individually. If there are two adults and two children in your home, one parent can have a special lunch with one child and the other child can stay home with the other parent. When you take this time to bond with your child one on one, you get to know each other as individuals and can forge a deeper relationship.

You can't do everything, however, so when balancing priorities, you need to pace yourself and set reasonable goals. Think about your week and what will work best for each member of the family. Sometimes this will mean compromising with your partner or doing less than you originally intended. If the bed gets made after the children go to school, or your trip to the dry cleaner has to wait a day because your child desperately needs a nap after school—give yourself permission to change your plan and don't criticize your partner if he or she occasionally does the same. Sometimes staying home and playing quietly with your child instead of rushing to make a dance class on time is the better choice.

Part of your job as a parent is to create a sense of family where each member is valued and respected and has a responsibility to the family as a whole. We've seen that when family members try to treat each other with respect and caring, and when parents create an atmosphere of support and understanding, family life becomes more pleasurable. When compromise and discussion are part of your lives together—and when you attempt to resolve disagreements constructively—your child is learning lessons that she can carry with her through life. A child who grows up in an environment like this has wonderful models for how to interact and get along with others.

You and Your Partner

Parents frequently talk to us about the difficulty of sharing the responsibilities of raising their children. Whenever there are two parents involved in bringing up a child, you can guarantee that there will be two perspectives regarding just about everything. One parent may have high standards for appropriate clothing, while the other may be happy to let a child go out with his jacket on inside out. One parent may be lax about rules on sweets or watching TV, while the other sets the rules and keeps them. One parent may always want to have the children be busy and physical, while the other may appreciate that the children are sometimes tired and need to be home to rest. Bringing up your children together is bound to present challenges. After all, you and your partner come from different homes with different parents and values. You have different personalities and temperaments. You may have different religious or cultural backgrounds. And if you are a man and a woman, you'll certainly have different perspectives on things.

When you first moved in together, you had to learn how to compromise, how to tolerate each other's day-to-day habits, how to blend work schedules, and how to juggle competing family commitments. After your child was born, you had to learn to adjust and compromise all over again. Children come into your lives and take over. In these early years, the demands on you and your partner are intense, both physically and emotionally. You may be less resilient because you're tired and stressed. You're more likely to feel vulnerable and snap at the slightest provocation from your (equally exhausted) partner. It's inevitable that you and your partner will disagree about how to raise your children at times, and when you find yourself in the midst of a conflict, it can be hard to keep perspective. It can help to remember that you are both in the same boat, even if you have different opinions sometimes. And maintaining a sense of humor about the struggles of family life helped enormously.

Some other good things to keep in mind when sharing the responsibilities of child rearing with your partner:

- If you and your partner have different approaches to child-rearing duties, this isn't necessarily a bad thing. Children learn so much from each parent and benefit from being exposed to different parenting styles. If one parent becomes the "expert," however, and insists on everything being done his or her way, the other parent is likely to feel criticized and may become less involved. What often happens is that the parent who's taking on the majority of the parenting becomes resentful, even if the burden is self-imposed. Periodically, you should assess the division of labor. If you find yourself doing morning, evening, and weekend duties because you like to do things your way and don't trust your partner to handle these things, it's time to take another look at the situation. There's no need to compete for the "best parent" award. In fact, when this happens, your child actually loses out because she needs to see both of you as effective and loving parents. In a good parenting partnership, parents complement one another and understand that they can bring different qualities and skills to the mix.

Often the parent who spends the most time with the child will naturally take on the role of expert. It can be good for everyone when the other parent takes over. Nancy's husband, Richard, once took the children to Washington, D.C., during Michael and Alissa's school vacation. Nancy couldn't go with them since she had to be at work. Everyone in the family was a little nervous about this extended period of time together without Mom. In the end, it was a good experience for everyone to know that Daddy could manage the children's day-to-day needs. Michael, Alissa, and Nancy almost never bring up the fact that Richard left all of Alissa's pants in the hotel after they went on to Williamsburg.

- While your child needs to see both of you as individuals, at the same time, you need to make sure that your child understands that you and your partner are on the same team when it comes to issues of discipline, health, and safety. If a child doesn't get her way with one parent, you can bet she'll try the other parent. If Daddy says no to the fourth cookie and Mommy automatically says yes, without finding out how many cookies had been agreed upon, both parents lose out because you've undermined your authority. Such mixed messages are very confusing to children, who thrive on consistency. In order to be effective, you'll often need to present a united front. The things that you need to agree about include health and safety issues, bedtime, food choices, TV watching, and how you will celebrate holidays. If you and your partner can anticipate and discuss these issues in advance, it can help to avoid conflicts when they arise.

- Other things will come up in the moment, and you may not know how you feel about them until that point. If you do feel upset or conflicted about how your partner has handled a situation, you need to decide how important it is to address it with him or her. Pick your issues—you don't need to turn every grievance into a cause for conflict. If Daddy is fine with mismatched clothes or stays in the park for an extra half hour, this may not be the place for the two of you to take issue. Remember that it's how you deal with conflict that counts. The manner in which you and your partner cooperate and compromise is just as important as the decision you come to as a result. If you find yourselves having disagreements in front of your child but you can resolve your issues without anger or criticizing each other, your child will have positive role models for dealing with conflict.

- However, there may be times when you become angry at one another and lose control while your child is watching. Remember that this is very frightening to young children and causes them untold worry and anxiety. Children will report to teachers, "My daddy yelled at my mommy and it scared me." It's best if disagreements about emotionally charged issues take place in private and out of earshot of your child. As a side benefit, when you wait to discuss your problems until your child has gone to bed, this gives both of you time to cool off and think about matters. Something that was important in the heat of the moment might seem less critical an hour later when you're more likely to listen to each other's point of view and come to an understanding or solution.

- Of course, that's the ideal. Sometimes you can't avoid arguing in front of your child. If this happens, you need to reassure her that grown-ups can argue but still love each other. You can support this claim by giving your partner a hug or a kiss. This is a case of actions speaking louder than words.

Grandparents

When you think back to your own childhood, you may find that some of your strongest memories are connected to the visits you made to your grand-parents. Often, it's a grandparent's home that provides the center for family gatherings and traditions. Nancy remembers how her grandmother would always fry a pan of onions or bake her special cookies before the grandchildren arrived so that her house smelled good for their visit. For Nancy, just the smell of those familiar foods cooking still stirs memories and creates feelings of connection.

When the child-grandparent relationship works, it can be an enormous boon for the whole family, and that includes you. After all, your child's grandparents are some of the few people who share your unconditional love and interest in your child. You may find that your own appreciation of your child is enhanced when you see the happiness she brings your parents. Ellen remembers that when her parents came to visit, they would walk right in without saying hello to her—they were so eager to hug their grandchildren. Ellen didn't feel hurt. She loved watching the joy in her parents' and children's faces as they greeted each other. For your mother and father, becoming a grandparent can be a much-anticipated milestone in their lives, bringing with it a newfound source of pleasure and pride.

If you're fortunate to have parents who live nearby—and with whom you get along—they can be a vital source of support, helping you with child care and stepping in when you need an afternoon to yourself. While some grandparents may play a large role in a child's life (and some may even be custodial), there are others who only see the children once or twice a year. When grandparents offer to spend time alone with the children—whether it's on a regular basis or intermittently—this often works best when they look after one child at a time. One grandmother told us that she wanted to take her eldest grandchild to the theater, but her daughter insisted that the other grandchild, who was much younger, attend as well. During the play, the younger child got frightened and insisted on leaving, which ruined the day for everyone. It would have worked better if the grandmother had been allowed to see the children individually on separate days.

Sometimes the grandparents resent being asked to look after their grandchildren because they feel they've already finished with child rearing. This can be distressing for you, but it's important to overlook your own sense of hurt and still find ways for your child and her grandparents to build a relationship. You can suggest a family meal together at your home or at a restaurant. Regular phone calls or bringing your child for short visits are good opportunities to create closeness. It's often the case that grandparents who are initially uncomfortable around young children adjust to their role over time. When your child is older, her grandparents may become more involved when they can share interests, such as going to the theater, museums, or ball games.

Some other good things to keep in mind when dealing with grandparents:

- If you feel at all upset by the way your parents interact with your children, remember that your reaction may be complicated by your memories of how you were raised. If you see your mother being very indulgent with your child, you may feel unsettled and even jealous when you remember how strict and withholding she was with you. If you see your father criticizing your child, you may find this triggers strong associations of paternal disapproval from your own childhood. It can help if you try to see your child's relationship with your parents as separate from your own. In a way, it makes sense that your parents' relationship with your child would be different from the relationship they had with you. A grandparent is no longer responsible for the day-to-day pressures of child rearing and can simply enjoy time spent with the children. It's not unusual for people who were very strict parents to become putty in the hands of their grandchildren.

• Your relationship with your partner's parents is also going to change as your child grows. You may find you have to adjust your expectations of your in-laws in their role as grandparents. Don't expect them to be the same as your own parents. If you end up comparing your in-laws to your own parents or holding them up to your ideal of a grandparent, you may be disappointed. Every grandparent in the family is likely to have a completely different style. If you can find ways to treat your in-laws respectfully and include them whenever possible, you may discover they have many things to offer your child, and you'll be better able to foster her relationship with them.

• Sometimes you may get unsolicited advice on parenting from your child's grandparents. This may feel like criticism, and it's only natural to feel upset and vulnerable. As a parent, you're going to feel strongly and have your own ideas about how to raise your children. Your own parents and your partner's parents may have very different ideas about these things. When the advice is given infrequently, and you don't think it's helpful, it's best to politely ignore it and carry on doing things as you think best. If the advice giving persists and continues to make you feel uncomfortable, you can say to the grandparent in question: "I know that this is important to you, but we have talked about it and this is how we feel." If it's an issue to do with health, discipline, or education, you can always blame the higher power: "This is how the pediatrician/teacher advised us." Remember, it's okay to agree to disagree. Your parents made their own mistakes raising you, and you'll surely make your own mistakes along the way—it's just part of being a parent. At the same time, you may want to consider if there's any validity in a suggestion that you initially rejected. It might be the manner in which the information was imparted that created difficulties for you, rather than the information itself.

- When it comes to family rules and discipline, grandparents should know what you expect of your children when they're in your home. If you don't allow TV or a treat between meals, you should explain your rules in advance of a visit to your home so that grandparents can comply. On the other hand, when your child is visiting her grandparents, you need to support their rules and be a little flexible. Don't worry too much about consistency in this instance—your child will understand that the rules at home and the rules at Grandma's house are different. If Grandma allows food in the living room or gives a cookie before dinner, this won't harm your child. In fact, children delight in the special indulgences of their grandparents. Parents often worry that their children will be "spoiled" by grandparents. Unless grandparents are your child's full-time caregivers, this simply won't happen.

- If your child is spending a lot of time with her grandparents or if they're her principal caregivers, you'll need to give them the authority to discipline her. You can say, "When Grandma's here, she's in charge and she knows the rules and you need to listen to her."

- Whenever possible, encourage your child's grandparents to share family traditions, stories, memories, and recipes with you and your child. These are the ties that bind families and provide continuity. Your child will love to look at photographs of you when you were a child and photographs of grandparents when they were younger. When grandparents tell stories about what life was like in the past, your child learns to find her place within a larger continuum. Even if one or more of your child's grandparents passed away before she was born, it's still important to talk about these people. When you keep a grandparent's memory alive, your child will have a sense of who that person was and will maintain a connection to an older generation and another time in her family's history.

Caregivers

From discussions at our parent group meetings, we realized that we were missing a piece of the puzzle: We weren't directly communicating with caregivers—the people who have a most important role in the lives of many families. To address this, we started having a yearly meeting with caregivers to discuss the children's development so that caregivers would have a better idea of what went on at school and what they could do to support growth and learning. We were moved and amazed by their reactions. Caregivers felt included, respected, and valued. When communication between caregivers and the school improved, the children benefited greatly. Caregivers and parents also became more consistent in their expectations for the children, which helped everyone. In your own family, the more specific and open you can be with your child's caregiver, the easier this relationship will be for you and your child.

A caregiver can be a nanny, babysitter, housekeeper, or au pair. Whether she lives with you or not, whether she works for you every day or only occasionally, your relationship with this employee who comes into your home to look after your children is more complex than you first might assume.

You need to share information about your child and your expectations with the caregiver as often as possible. Issues related to your child's behavior or feedback from school about her growth and development should also be discussed. When you set aside time to talk with a caregiver, you'll both have an opportunity to bring up problems that arise and make plans for a consistent approach.

It's important to think of yourself as an employer and to treat your child's caregiver professionally and with respect. Caring for children is a very demanding job, and it's vital that you build in realistic expectations. An exhausted caregiver who has too much housework won't be able to care for your child in the way that you'd like. In addition, when you're respectful of the caregiver, you're teaching your child an important lesson about relationships and helping to ensure that your child will be respectful as well.

Here are some other good rules of thumb for working with your child's caregiver:

- When hiring a caregiver, trust your instincts about whether you feel comfortable with this person. You must check references—and know who those references came from. On the other hand, even the caregiver with the most impeccable references may not have the personality that feels right for you or your child. Does the caregiver smile and exude warmth? Is her appearance clean and neat? Can she communicate in a clear and intelligent manner? Does she establish an easy rapport with your child? Does she feel like the kind of person who will be a good fit for your family? Are you comfortable with her as a role model for your child?

- Make certain the caregiver you choose has good skills in the language of your family. Some parents will hire a caregiver who speaks another language so that their child will become familiar with a second language. This can be problematic if the caregiver spends many hours a day with your child. In some cases, a child's language development can be inhibited if a caregiver is unable to sufficiently communicate with her. If a potential caregiver doesn't have the facility with language to handle an emergency situation, you should not hire that person.

- Establish a professional relationship with this person from the start. Discuss the exact job description in advance: salary, vacations, benefits, sick days, overtime, and how you would like your family's privacy handled. In order for a caregiver to do the job effectively, you must be very clear about what the job entails. You need to define the hours, the number of children, and the basic duties (which might include doing some housework, cooking for the children, driving or transporting children to playdates, or going on appointments). You'll need to discuss how you expect to handle money for daily expenses. You'll also want to make clear your expectations about making personal telephone calls, watching TV, entertaining friends, and going shopping or to someone else's house while with your child.

- Remember that you'll have to be available to orient a new caregiver in the first week or so. Caregivers need to know the details of your child's schedule—what time is lunch, nap time, bath, and so on. We're always surprised when a new caregiver arrives at school to pick up a child and has to ask the whereabouts of the classroom.

- Have a clear plan, discussed and written, for emergency situations. All emergency and contact telephone numbers should be posted near the telephone. Some parents enroll caregivers in CPR and first aid classes. Some communities offer caregiver courses, and you may decide to sign up a new caregiver for one of these.

- Assess the role of the caregiver as your child grows. Now that your child is a preschooler, you may still have the same caregiver that you had when she was an infant and toddler. Remember that preschoolers are much more mobile; they need more intellectual stimulation; they require new forms of discipline; and they need encouragement in learning self-help and language skills. This sets up a whole range of challenges for a caregiver. You may discover that the babysitter who was great with your newborn is less competent when it comes to caring for your three-year-old. While you can't expect her to immediately adapt, if, over time, this caregiver is unable to adjust to these new demands, you may want to consider a change.

- Work with the caregiver to maintain an approach that's consistent with your own. If you're feeding your two-year-old with a spoon but the caregiver's letting her eat with her fingers, your child is receiving mixed messages. A parent who's uncomfortable with disciplining a child may hire a caregiver who's a strict disciplinarian, and this can also be very confusing for children. If you feel strongly about a method of discipline, watching TV, food, or other aspects of child care, these feelings need to be spelled out clearly and agreed upon with the caregiver. Sometimes children will ask questions about sensitive topics such as sex, death, or religion—you need to let the caregiver know how you want these handled.

- Help the caregiver to establish her authority. If you hear your child saying to her caregiver, "You're not my mommy; I don't need to listen to you!" you must intervene and support the caregiver in order to reinforce her authority. If you disagree with her about how a situation has been handled, it's important that you wait until your child is out of the room to talk about this. When you're alone with the caregiver, you can explain why this issue is important to you and what you expect from her. If you get into a disagreement in front of your child, you're only confusing your child and lessening the caregiver's effectiveness. You don't have to agree on everything, but it's very important to empower a caregiver to carry out your expectations in your absence.

- Be aware that the transition times in the mornings and evenings are difficult for families. In the mornings, remember to make a point of warmly greeting the caregiver and having your child do the same. This sets the tone for everyone's day. If you're arriving home at the end of the day, remember you don't always have a context for what's taken place while you've been away. Be careful that you don't undermine the caregiver's authority by jumping to conclusions. If you come home to find your child in her room having a time-out, it's inevitable that she'll tell you, "Nora [the caregiver] was being mean to me!" If you then say, "It's okay; you can watch TV now," without checking to see what happened to cause the time-out, you're sending a very confusing message to your child. Instead, you can say, "Why do you think Nora gave you a time-out?" Then you can check with Nora to see what happened. When you know the facts, you can say to your child, "Nora gave you a time-out because you hit your brother. You know hitting is not allowed. You need to go back to your room until I come in."

- Don't be afraid to end the relationship with a caregiver if necessary. Most parents would rather avoid changing caregivers, especially when the child feels a strong attachment. We've seen parents extend a problematic situation rather than ending it because they feel dependent on the existing relationship and are worried their child would become upset if that person left. Maybe you no longer need child care when your child starts attending school for a full day, or the caregiver who was great with your toddler can no longer cope with your four-year-old. Perhaps the caregiver doesn't listen to you or refuses to work with you in the best interests of your child. If your relationship with a caregiver isn't working out for whatever reason, a change can be a positive thing for your family. Remember that you are the most important person in your child's life and, when the situation is handled sensitively, your child will adapt.

- Pay attention if someone informs you of something he or she has observed of your child's caregiver. Sometimes parents get upset or defensive if friends, family, or teachers report negative things about a caregiver. Find out more about the situation; then you can respond by clarifying your expectations to the caregiver, if needed. If you aren't comfortable with an explanation or if it happens again, you should consider ending the relationship.

- Give your child a chance to say good-bye when a caregiver leaves. Whether leaving is your decision or the caregiver's, children need to have closure. It's helpful to tell your child what's going to happen a few days before the caregiver leaves. Your child can make a card or buy a small gift to say good-bye. She may want to have a photograph of herself with the caregiver. If you are parting on good terms, it's nice to have your child and the caregiver write or call each other periodically.

- Help your child gain closure when her caregiver leaves suddenly. Sometimes a caregiver may leave and you'll have no warning and won't be able to prepare your child. A parent at the nursery school had this problem when her long-term caregiver left suddenly. When this happened, the mother was also pregnant and the child was adjusting to a new year at school. As a result, Rachel, aged three, was having separation difficulties. She cried when leaving the house to go to school and clung to her mother and cried when it was time to say good-bye at the classroom door. We suggested that mother and daughter write a letter to the caregiver so that Rachel could express her feelings and experience some closure. This is what Rachel dictated to her mother:

> Dear Sophie,
> I miss you. I love you up to the moon and back. Please come back. I for-give you. I love you. I miss you.
> Rachel

Afterward, a weight was lifted. Although the mother didn't have an address so that she could mail the letter, the act of writing it helped Rachel. The child's anxiety dissipated and she became more comfortable separating from her mother and more like herself again.

New Babies

If you're expecting another child, you'll probably discover that this stirs up feelings of conflict for you. You may wonder if you're doing something that will upset your first child. You may be concerned that you couldn't possibly love the next one as much as you do your first. You may be worried about your time and whether you'll be able to give each child adequate attention. Will you have to rearrange your home, your work schedule, and time with your partner?

All these concerns are natural. Almost every parent we've ever met has worried about these things when expecting a second baby. It's true that having another child will create many fresh challenges. On the other hand, there are so many benefits for your family:

- If you have siblings yourself, and you get along with them, you know that the bond between you is unique. Only you and your siblings share your upbringing and your parents. When you have a sibling, you have someone with whom you can share memories or family issues. Now that you're expecting a second baby, you can look forward to watching your children grow up together so that they can develop this special bond.

- There are also practical advantages. A sibling means that your child has a playmate who's always accessible. You may find in many ways that it's less time-consuming to have a second child when your older child is there to entertain the younger one.

- One of the true joys of having a second child is the realization that you can love another child just as much as your first.

Although there's bound to be a period of transition as your older child becomes used to sharing your attention with a baby, this isn't to say that your older child can't adjust quickly. In the classroom, we've seen every kind of reaction to new siblings. Some children are excited and proud and want to show photos to the teacher and class. Other children will respond to the teacher's question, "Did something special happen in your family yesterday?" by saying, "Yes, I got a new doll." There are children who are naturally maternal and want to help out with the baby. Others have no interest whatsoever. Some children will have a reaction to the pregnancy and will be fine once the baby is born, and others are oblivious to the pregnancy and have a reaction when the baby arrives.

There are many things you can do to help ease your child's adjustment:

- Wait to tell your child that you're pregnant. Although it's natural to be excited and to want to share the good news with your older child or children, it's usually best to hold off. A three-year-old is unable to understand the concept of nine months and will think that the baby is arriving tomorrow at the latest. Since she's unable to comprehend the time frame, she'll be asking you every day, "Is the baby coming today?" It's better to wait for as long as possible, preferably until around the time you really begin to show, before telling your child. (Be aware, however, that she may sense something's up long before she's told. It's possible that she'll overhear a telephone conversation or a remark between adults. When parents tell us that they're having another baby but their child doesn't know, we'll often hear that child telling another child, "My mommy's having a baby.")

- When you do tell your child, be honest with her about what's happening. Children will often ask for a baby brother or a little sister. If your child makes you promise to give her a baby brother, you need to explain that nature will decide and not you. She may also ask questions about where the baby is growing and how it got there. If these issues come up, it can be tempting to make up a story so that you won't have to deal with talking about the difficult topic of sex. In fact, it's important to be honest with your child or she may become confused in the long run. You don't have to say very much. Answer the question being asked and wait for further questions. Your child will only ask as much as she wants to know or is able to understand. This is also a good opportunity to introduce appropriate language for body parts. If you say you have a baby in your "tummy," your child may want to know why you've eaten her new brother or sister. Instead, you can tell her that a mommy has a special place in her body called a "uterus," where the baby grows.

- Avoid any other changes around the time of your due date for the sake of your older child. If you're planning to move, toilet train, or change a caregiver, it's better to do this earlier in your pregnancy or wait for a while after your new baby is born. If your children are close in age, you may be planning to transfer your older child out of her crib in time for the new baby's arrival. We recommend that you buy a new crib for the baby if at all possible. Although it seems expensive and impractical to have two cribs, when you move your older child out of her familiar crib at this time, you may be creating unnecessary problems for yourself. Your older child is already going through the enormous adjustment of having a new sibling, and a change of bed at this time can cause sleep disturbances.

- Make sure your child has realistic expectations about the new baby. Some children think that the new brother or sister will come home from the hospital and play ball with them. Your child needs to know that babies are "boring," that they only sleep, cry, and eat and can't do anything for themselves. There are many wonderful children's books about babies that you can read to your child to help her get used to the idea. Some of our favorites include *McDuff and the Baby* by Rosemary Wells and *Julius, the Baby of the World* by Kevin Henkes. On the other hand, if your child isn't interested in talking about her new sibling's arrival, it's okay to drop the subject. Follow your child's lead as to how much she wants to talk about this.

- Prepare your child for your hospital stay. A few days before your due date, you can let your child know that you'll be away for a short time in the hospital. Tell her that you'll be able to talk on the phone or have a visit if it's permissible. Some hospitals have a predelivery visit for siblings, and you may decide to take your child to one of these.

- Make sure to maintain established family routines and expectations. When your older child is adjusting to a new sibling, it would be unfair to let her stay up later or give into her demand to eat cookies before bedtime if you don't usually allow her to do this. Although you may feel badly that you're no longer devoting all your attention to your older child, in fact, she needs as much calm and consistency as possible during this transition period.

- Include your older child in caring for her new baby brother or sister. You can ask her to bring you a fresh diaper or to help with a bottle. This will make her feel included and that she has a responsibility as the "big sister" in the family. Don't assume it's okay to leave your older child with the baby alone, however. Your older child may feel excited but conflicted. She may "hug" a bit too hard or try to pick up the baby in an effort to be helpful. When your child goes to touch the baby, instead of saying no, you can talk to her about "gentle" hugs and touches.

- Set aside time to be with your older child one on one. Even though you're busy with the new baby, remember that your older child will need your undivided attention during this transition period as much as you can spare it. You'll be able to do this more easily if you can designate a specific time each day, and your child can look forward to your time together. If your older child is becoming angry or jealous of your attention to the baby, you should understand that this is natural and that you don't need to feel guilty. You can help your older child by giving her the words to express her feelings: "I know you're upset when I need to feed the baby, but I'll play with you as soon as I finish." You can reassure her by saying that mommies and daddies can love two children just like she loves both mommy and daddy. You can also remind her that as the "big girl" in the family, she has special privileges like going to a movie or out to lunch, which babies can't do. When visitors come to see the new baby, encourage them to be sensitive and give some special time or a gift to your older child as well.

- Expect that your older child will regress to baby behaviors after the new baby arrives. These may include using baby talk, wanting a bottle, and having toilet accidents and sleep difficulties. It's best not to punish regressive behavior during this transition. Instead, you can praise your child when she demonstrates independence and grown-up behavior. Even though she's taking a few steps backward, it's important that you continue to support her growth. If your child's been toilet trained or hasn't been using a bottle for some time, don't be tempted to give in to diapers when she wets herself or to relent when she whines for a bottle.

Siblings

If there are two or more children in a family, you can guarantee that sibling issues are going to arise. One Thanksgiving, Alice's class was asked to draw a picture of some things they were thankful for. Alice was five years old and Charles was still a baby at the time. Alice chose to draw a picture of herself with her mother and father. Ellen asked Alice why she hadn't included her baby brother. Alice replied, "Hmmm, I like Charles. But I'm not thankful for him."

Like Alice, your child may not always be thankful for her baby brother or sister. Around the time your younger child becomes more mobile and starts to intrude on your older child's life, it's inevitable that problems will occur. At some point, the baby's going to snatch your older child's toy, or the two children are going to want to watch different DVDs, or your older child is going to exclude the younger one from her play. The good news is that sibling relationships serve as models for other relationships in life and help children learn to deal with conflicts. When she has a little brother or sister your child will quickly learn to share, compromise, express feelings, take responsibility for others, handle frustration, and problem solve. Even though all siblings fight, you can bet that they still bond together to form a united front on occasion, at least when it comes to opposing their parents.

If you expect peace and harmony between siblings, you're setting yourself up for frustration and disappointment. Siblings have always fought and always will. Fighting doesn't mean your children don't love each other. Often, children will fight because they're bored or simply because they enjoy it. Many children fight to get their parents' attention. Fighting is usually intolerable for parents, and your instinct is going to be to intervene in order to solve the problem. Here's your dilemma: You want to break up the fight, but by doing so, you're giving your children the reaction that they were looking for in the first place. Try not to rush in too soon to fix the problem. Sometimes the most effective way of ending a fight is to ignore it or to stand back and see if your children can resolve things on their own.

Of course, when the fighting becomes physical and someone might get hurt, you must intervene. You can always send the children off to separate rooms or tell them they're not allowed to play together for a specified amount of time. This will give them time to cool off. Left to their own devices, however, children will often find their own way of working through sibling difficulties. When Nancy's children were young, Alissa went through a period of being physically aggressive with her older brother. Nancy told Michael that he should never let Alissa push him and that he could tell her in a firm voice that he didn't like it. This was hard for Michael, as he was a gentle-natured child. One day Nancy came home and Alissa greeted her at the door saying proudly, "Mommy, I'm a moron!" Nancy asked, "Who told you that?" She replied, "Michael did." Nancy asked, "What did he say it meant?" Alissa answered, "It means I'm good at sports!" Clearly, Michael had figured out an amusing way to get back at his little sister.

To follow are some good rules of thumb for dealing with sibling conflicts:

- If you do have to break up a fight, try not to play judge and jury. Unless you've witnessed the entire exchange, it's going to be impossible to know exactly what happened to cause the dispute. Each child will want to tell her side of the story and will want you to agree with her point of view. Your children will have engaged you, but there's unlikely to be any resolution that satisfies either child. Although you should listen to what your children are trying to tell you, it usually doesn't help to play referee. Instead, try to concentrate on the solution, not the problem: "If you both want to watch different TV shows, how about we watch a DVD that you both want to see instead?" As much as possible, involve children in finding solutions to their conflicts: "You both want to watch different TV shows. How do you think we can solve the problem?" When you do this, you're teaching your children to problem solve and settle conflicts on their own. These are the tools they'll need to negotiate social relationships outside the home when you're not there.

- Don't reward tattling. When one child tells on another child, you may feel that you have received valuable information about a situation and even thank her for bringing this to your attention. If you do this, however, it will encourage your children to tell on each other rather than resolving conflict for themselves.

Practical Wisdom for Parents

- Give children incentives or consequences when they're playing together to help avoid conflict: "If you can take turns with the truck, I won't need to take it away." Often it helps to use a timer for taking turns: "Your sister can play with the truck for five minutes, and then you can play with the truck for five minutes."

- Principles of sharing and respect need to be underlined regularly. The word "fair" can be a complicated concept for young children, and you'll need to explain to them exactly what it means. You can say, "We can watch your TV show today and your brother's tomorrow. That's fair." "Fair means no name-calling or hitting." "You can say that you're angry or upset, but you should never hit or call names. That's not fair." Fair doesn't always mean each child is treated exactly the same at all times. Fairness may be determined by the situation or age of the children: "Your sister can play with the toy because she asked nicely for it instead of grabbing." "Your sister can stay up another half hour because she's older than you are."

- If you notice your children sharing or playing nicely with each other, you should compliment them on it. When you praise cooperation as it occurs, children learn that it feels good to compromise and share.

- Maintain clearly established rules. If an older child is taking advantage of a younger one or a younger child is ruining something that the older one has been working on for days, make sure everyone knows the rules: "The rule is that you don't tease your little brother when he can't run as fast as you." "The rule is that you don't knock down the Lego tower your big brother is building." Let your children know that physical and emotional hurting will not be tolerated. Have family meetings to discuss problems and review rules. If necessary, write down the rules.

- Don't insist that siblings always play together. Each child needs time to play alone. Even if siblings share a room, you can give them spaces that are their own and agree that certain prized possessions aren't for sharing. This is a very effective way of avoiding conflicts before they begin.

- When your children fight, try to stay calm. Don't raise your voice. If you become upset and get involved in the argument, the fight will only escalate. Instead, keep your voice level, and guide your children away from the area where the conflict is taking place. Go into another room if necessary, and have the children sit down before you speak to them clearly and calmly about the issue. If you take your children's attention away from the problem, everyone is better able to move on.

- When children fight, both parents need to present a united front. If one parent is trying to problem solve while the other one is trying to find out what "really happened," then children are going to become confused and the conflict will be prolonged.

- When children are fighting, you can always try to distract them with another activity or by telling a story or by being silly. You can say, "It looks like you need to take a break from this game. Let's have a snack." Children have short attention spans. When you engage your children by telling them a story about when you were a child and what would happen to you when you fought, they may quickly forget what they were fighting about.

- If all else fails, seek advice. If your family life is suffering because of sibling conflict or it seems as if a child's self-esteem is being harmed, it's helpful to consult your pediatrician, teacher, or school director. It may be that you need to get additional assistance from a mental health professional who can help you come up with strategies to deal with this situation.

• Treating Siblings as Individuals •

As your younger child grows, you may discover that she has a very different temperament from your older child. You might assume that you should treat both children equally. In fact, your children are individuals and you'll need to tailor your parenting to suit their individual needs. This means you'll have to treat them differently at different times. Ellen's eldest, Alice, was an exceptionally self-regulating child who didn't need many rules and reminders. Her younger brother, Charles, however, tested limits and needed much more guidance from his parents. Nancy's eldest, Michael, would tell her if he'd watched too much TV and would turn it off himself or actually say, "I've watched too much TV this week. I won't watch next week." Alissa, meanwhile, had to have constant monitoring of her TV time or she would never turn it off. It's fine to have different approaches and standards for each of your children. In fact, it may be essential.

Some other good ideas to keep in mind:

Practical Wisdom for Parents

- Parents often forget that children of different ages need to be encouraged in different ways. It can be hard to keep track of the actual developmental level of each child. You may forget to raise the bar for your younger child because you think of her as the baby of the family. On the other hand, you may expect too much of her too soon because you're always comparing her to her older sister. You may expect your older child to have too much responsibility for her sibling or to accommodate the younger child's demands. If you're unsure whether you're responding to your children in ways appropriate to their developmental levels, you can seek advice from your child's teacher or pediatrician.

- As a parent, it's your job to foster your children's relationships with one another and to encourage their cooperation. If your naturally shy child feels that you always compliment her big sister's confidence, then you may be helping to create resentment between the siblings. Each child in your family needs to be respected and loved for who she is as an individual. If you observe each child and encourage each one to develop their innate abilities, your children will feel less competitive and that you value them as individuals. Your children are going to have different strengths and interests; it's how you value those interests that will help in building a strong sense of self and reduce feelings of competition between siblings. If one child is musical and another child loves sports, then both interests need to be respected equally. For example, it may be the case that in your home the arts are deemed more valuable than physical activities, so the child who is good at sports may feel her talent isn't as important as the child who is good at music.

- Although it's important that you identify each child's interests and tendencies, it's equally important to avoid labeling your children at such an early stage in their lives. When you identify your children as "the shy one," "the athletic one," or "the funny one," you're comparing your children and setting up expectations that can be hard for them to live up to. Your children may resist developing other aspects of their personalities or other interests as a result.

- However hard you try to treat each child fairly, there will always be times when one of your children turns to you and says, "It's not fair" or accuses you of favoring one child over another. All you can do is to make sure you accept and respect each child as an individual and that each child feels that she has an important place in your family. Even though sibling relationships are frequently wrought with competition and arguments, in our experience, the benefits far outweigh the difficulties. Although our children experienced sibling issues when they were younger, we're happy to report that, as adults, they've remained good friends, communicate often, and enjoy spending time in one another's company.

Recommended Books for Children

FAMILIES

I Loved You Before You Were Born	Anne Bowen
My Dad	Anthony Browne
My Family Is Forever	Nancy Carlson
So Much	Trish Cooke
I Already Know I Love You	Billy Crystal
Now One Foot, Now the Other	Tomi dePaola
Wilfrid Gordon McDonald Partridge	Mem Fox
I Love You Like Crazy Cakes	Rose Lewis
The Family Book	Todd Parr
Let's Talk about It: Adoption	Fred Rogers
All Families Are Special	Norma Simon
Who's in a Family	Robert Skutch
Our Granny	Margaret Wild

SIBLINGS AND NEW BABIES

The Pain and the Great One	Judy Blume
I'm a Big Brother	Joanna Cole
I'm a Big Sister	Joanna Cole
The New Baby at Your House	Joanna Cole
Will There Be a Lap for Me?	Dorothy Corey
Before You Were Born	Jennifer Davis
The Baby Sister	Tomi dePaola
Julius, the Baby of the World	Kevin Henkes
Hi New Baby	Robie H. Harris
A Baby Sister for Frances	Russell Hoban
Titch	Pat Hutchins
I Love You the Purplest	Barbara M. Joosse
Over the Moon	Karen Katz
Peter's Chair	Ezra Jack Keats

Practical Wisdom for Parents

Chapter Nine

DISCIPLINE:

Setting Limits, Saying No, and Accepting No

It's a fact. Young children will whine, cry, have tantrums, bite, scream, use bathroom talk, pretend they can't hear you, interrupt you, ignore you, fight with their siblings, refuse to stay in bed, and say no when you ask them to finish their dinner. Don't worry. It's not that you have a problem child; it's just that you have a child. At times, your preschool child is going to behave in ways that seem specifically designed to try your patience and test your resolve. At this age, your child wants and needs to assert himself as an individual. He's discovering the power of his ideas, words, and desires. When things don't go his way, he'll protest, cry, and even throw a tantrum. Parents often tell us that the "terrible twos" aren't as terrible as the all powerful three- or four-year-old who wants to rule the world.

This brings us to the difficult issue of discipline. We've never met a parent who didn't struggle with this problematic aspect of parenting. On the one hand, you're dealing with a child who wants to assert himself, whether it's at the dinner table, at bedtime, or in the cereal aisle at the supermarket. No parent wants a child who whines or bites or has tantrums. On the other hand, we've seen many mothers and fathers who falter when it comes to handling these behaviors. Even the most successful adult who commands enormous respect in the workplace can waiver when faced with a three-year-old who wants a lollipop on the way to school. If you are struggling with setting limits for your child, it's only natural to feel unsure. It can take time to find your voice as a parental authority, and you'll probably make mistakes along the way as you discover what works for you and your family. We tell parents that they don't need to be perfect. Children are resilient and will survive your mistakes if you do two things—love your children unconditionally *and* set limits for them.

When we talk about discipline, we remind parents about the root of the word. Somewhere along the way, the word "discipline" acquired a negative connotation and got confused with the word "punishment." In fact, "discipline" actually means "to teach" (it has the same root as the word "disciple"). You wouldn't feel uncertain about teaching your child the alphabet or how to count to ten. Yet many parents feel ambivalent about teaching a child appropriate behavior. We've seen children who know every fact about dinosaurs or how to tell a Pablo Picasso from a Jackson Pollock, but they haven't learned that it's wrong to interrupt, use disrespectful language, write on the wall, or hit the babysitter. If a child hasn't been taught how to behave, this can actually hamper his growth in all areas, as he's not going to be appreciated by his teachers or accepted by his peers.

Children aren't born knowing what's acceptable and safe. They don't know how to control themselves. As your child grows and begins to interact with the world in a more independent way, it's up to you to teach him how to control his impulses. All children will misbehave and test limits. It's their job. It's your job to provide the boundaries so that your child can grow up feeling secure, both physically and emotionally. The world is a large and often frightening place for young children. Without clear boundaries, they can feel out of control and unsafe.

It's not just children who suffer but parents too when the youngest member of the family is allowed too much control. If your child is ruling your home and all the adults in his life are afraid to confront him for fear of a tantrum or tears, it's time to take charge. You can feel confident that your child will benefit when you are firm with him. As educators, we've seen that children whose parents set limits for them are much more likely to enjoy school and do well there. These children have been given a chance to develop a sense of right and wrong; they're more respectful of others, they can manage and understand their feelings, and they're able to cooperate and become responsible members of a classroom. What we've seen is that children who lack discipline at home tend to struggle in the classroom. They can feel anxious and confused at the expectations of their teachers and have trouble making friends. Over a short period of time, the same children who struggled at the beginning of the school year quickly gain confidence and blossom when their teachers set clear expectations for them. When their parents follow suit and have consistent expectations at home, these children continue to grow and their good behavior persists.

As parents, we were lucky to have "easy" first children. Alice and Michael were both fairly self-regulating. They didn't need us to constantly make rules for them, and they rarely tested limits. This left us unprepared when our second children, Charles and Alissa, came along and needed us to continually give them rules and to always remind them who was in charge. At first, we often gave in to our more assertive younger children, hoping that this phase would pass. Over time, we realized that Charles and Alissa actually needed us to take charge. One day, four-year-old Alissa decided to put her foot on the table while the family was out having pizza. Nancy promptly said, "Please take your foot off the table." Alissa responded by saying, "It's my foot and I can put it wherever I want." Nancy said, "I have something funny to tell you. Your foot belongs to me and goes where I say for the next fourteen years." In that moment, Nancy realized she had found her voice as an authority with Alissa. Ellen also took a while to find a discipline style for her youngest child, whom the family used to jokingly call, "Charles in charge." What Ellen recognized was that if she allowed her son to continue to rule the house, life at home would become progressively more miserable, and eventually Charles would have a difficult time at school. In the long run, it paid off. When Charles was a teenager and his parents said no to an unsupervised spring break trip, although he wasn't happy, he accepted their decision since this wasn't the first time he'd been disappointed in this way. If Ellen and her husband hadn't established their authority when Charles was a developing child, they wouldn't have been able to say no when they were confronted with a much bigger issue down the road.

It's up to every parent to find his or her own discipline style with each individual child. You'll need to know your child's personality and your own instincts as a parent. You'll need to figure out what's important for you as a family. You'll need to act as a role model, teaching your child good behavior and self-control by example. You'll need to have patience and know that you can't change a pattern overnight. It's true that discipline takes hard work and consistency over days and years, but it's also true that it's worth it. Although it's never enjoyable to say no to your child, what you'll find is that life at home becomes much more pleasurable as a result. Your child will love you more for your strength and your consistency. And you will like your child more.

Why Is It So Hard?

If the benefits of discipline are so essential for children, why are parents so hesitant and unsure of themselves in this respect? Many parents are uncomfortable about taking on the role of authority. Meanwhile, children are very

Practical Wisdom for Parents

savvy and will quickly figure out when you really mean something. If you're feeling ambivalent, your child will sense this and quickly learn that he can control the outcome. When you recognize the roots of your ambivalence, you can address this and become more confident in your role as the authority in your home. Some of these root causes can include:

- ### Fear of emulating your parents

  Parents often worry that if they are "too strict" with their children they'll be emulating their own parents. If your parents were strict disciplinarians, you may be determined to be a different kind of mother or father. You may want to be more nurturing, more understanding, more respectful. But the danger of this reaction is that you may also become overly permissive and passive. If the youngest members of the family are dominating your household and you have to plead for good behavior rather than expecting it, then it may be time to reassess the limits you're setting for your children.

  Some parents are more inclined to take charge. Perhaps you had few rules growing up and wished that your parents had been clearer and firmer. As a result, you may impose too many rules on your child or say no arbitrarily. These parents may rely on punishment as opposed to positive reinforcement. What we have seen is that children of overly punitive parents often become anxious and unsettled as they try to please their parents.

  Somewhere between the two extremes is a balanced parent who is clear, firm, consistent, and kind. Although it's not always easy to strike this balance, being a parent will require you to find your own voice, regardless of your own parents and their parenting style.

- ### Wanting your child to be happy

  As a parent, of course you want your child to be happy. It's only natural to try to protect children from any unhappiness or distress. But you also need to be aware of the role that frustration and disappointment play in every child's healthy development. If your child never experiences what it feels like when things don't go his way, he won't ever learn to cope with life's challenges. We tell parents that a child's most problematic day at school may be the day when he learns the most valuable lessons.

  It's unrealistic to think children need to be happy all of the time. When you always give in to your child's demands, you may feel that you're making him happy, but you may actually be making him less resilient. You're depriving him of the opportunity to feel the disappointment and frustration that comes from accepting limits. When you say no to your child, it's unlikely that he'll be pleased. On the other hand, if you don't set limits for him, you may actually be negatively influencing his ability to feel happy in the long term. Life is fraught with small and large problems. The more a person is able to cope with these challenges, the more content he's going to be with life.

• Fear of inhibiting your child

Some parents fear that if they set limits for their children, they'll hamper a child's creativity, that by disciplining him, they'll cause him to become inhibited and unable to express himself fully. It doesn't always follow that a child who's allowed to make his own decisions is the child who's the most creative. In fact, children who are given too many choices can easily become overwhelmed and unable to make decisions for themselves. They may feel burdened when they are always given the responsibility of having to make a choice.

We tell parents that when children don't have limits, their creativity can actually be stifled. Alex's parents used to ask him what he wanted to wear in the mornings before coming to the nursery school. His answer was usually, "My astronaut costume." His parents didn't want to inhibit him by saying no. However, when Alex wore the costume to school, it was hard for him to participate with his friends since he only wanted to play astronaut and avoided joining in other kinds of imaginative play. During music and story time, he was distracted by the silver cuffs Velcroed to the sleeve and was unable to undress himself when he needed to go to the bathroom. Instead of enhancing his creativity, his parents had ensured that he was unable to fully participate and explore other creative experiences. Your child can't always know what's best for him. He needs you to take on the role of the adult and to make decisions in his best interests.

• Fear of not being liked

It's only natural to want your child to be able to come to you and talk about problems and to see you as a friend. But the fear of not being liked often prevents parents from establishing their authority. Without authority, you become incapable of setting limits. Children need their parents to be parents, not best friends. You can have a loving, close relationship with your child without having to give up your role as a parent. It's true that your child won't thank you for being firm or saying no, but he may give you a hug or kiss when you least expect it because he feels safe and loved due to your strength.

- **Wanting to take the path of least resistance**
  Children have immeasurable energy and tenacity to challenge you and test your patience. When you've had a tough day and you've asked your child to put his toys away for the fourth time, it's going to seem easier to do it yourself. But if you don't address these patterns as they arise, you're actually sending the message that it's okay to act this way. Although it may seem easier in the short term to put away the toys, you're only setting yourself up for more problems in the long term when the behavior has a chance to become entrenched and then takes longer to undo.

- **Lack of confidence**
  Some people genuinely lack confidence and have trouble asserting themselves. If you're soft-spoken and nonassertive, it can be hard to be definitive with your child. When you recognize how much your child needs you to be self-assured and firm, however, it can bring those qualities out in you. As you gain confidence and strength in this role, both you and your child will benefit.

The Basics: What Parents Can Do to Set Good Limits for Children

Once you understand the wisdom of setting limits and are confident in your ability to assume authority for the sake of your child, you've already gone a long way toward effective discipline. Here are some basic guidelines that will help you at every level:

- **Find a balanced discipline style that works for you and your family.**
  When parents discover a discipline style that works for their family, the benefits are immeasurable. Kate was a four-year-old who struggled through her day at the nursery school. She had difficulty sharing the markers at the drawing table, complained about her seat at meeting time, refused to put her coat on to go outdoors, and was unable to compromise in play with the other children. The reasons for Kate's difficulties became clear when we watched how her parents dealt with

her demands before and after school. Anytime Kate wanted something, she would whine, cry, and eventually throw a tantrum until she got her way. Her parents would plead and beg her to stop; this was rarely effective. Not only was Kate unhappy at school, her parents were upset and frustrated. We suggested that the parents seek counseling, as they were evidently very uncomfortable about establishing their authority. Once Kate's parents were able to be clearer about their expectations and consistent in their responses to her behavior, their daughter became more able to accept adult authority and more flexible in her relations with her classmates. Kate quickly became happier at school, and the family's home life improved.

At the other end of the scale, we've seen parents who are overly strict and whose children become anxious as a result. One day at the nursery school, three-year-old Jenny was crying hysterically at dismissal. When we questioned her, we learned that she couldn't find her hat and was fearful of her mother's reaction. When we spoke with her mother, it turned out that the week before, Jenny had lost her mittens, and the mother had become furious and canceled her playdate. The mother also told Jenny that the next time she lost something, she would take away her favorite doll. Although this mother was trying to set limits for her child, Jenny wasn't able to focus on keeping track of her possessions as she was too concerned with the threat of punishment. We suggested that the mother give her child reasons for looking after her possessions and offered suggestions on how to do it: "Jenny, you need to keep track of your mittens. If you don't have mittens, your hands will get cold. If you put them in your pockets as soon as you take them off, you'll always know where they are. Do you have any other ideas?" We noticed that in the future, Jenny no longer became upset when she did something that she feared would earn her mother's disapproval.

• Be consistent and persistent.

One of the most important things you can do for your child is to be consistent and persistent. If you say one thing one day and another the next, your child won't learn what you expect of him. If you give in too easily, your child may fall into patterns that are difficult to undo.

Your child will benefit from firm repetition over time. When Alissa was three, she began asking Nancy for ice cream for breakfast. The first morning the answer was no. The second, third, and fourth mornings, it was still no. By the fifth morning, Nancy thought, "Why not? It won't kill her to have ice cream one time. It has milk in it. . . ." Although

Nancy was on the verge of giving in, she quickly came to her senses. It wasn't about the ice cream. It was a test. Would Nancy say no and stick to it? Once Alissa understood that "no" meant "no," she stopped asking for ice cream.

Many parents tell us that they've tried to change a behavior but that "it didn't work." When we ask them how long they tried, they'll say, "a day or two," and we know that this was why they didn't see results. It can take time to change patterns, especially when your child has been used to doing something. There are no shortcuts here. You'll simply have to stick with your plan until your child gets the message. This can be exhausting, frustrating, and annoying for you, but when your child finally understands that you mean business, you'll be amazed by the change that takes place.

- **Set rules.**

You can't set limits unless you have clear and specific rules for children. Without rules, children won't be able to learn to regulate themselves and control their impulses. It often surprises parents when we tell them how much children at the nursery school enjoy the classroom rules. They love to repeat them back to teachers and often become indignant at any infractions. Children are very concrete and respond well when the adults in their lives are unequivocal. Rules help children to feel secure, and that the world is within the control of the adults around them.

Rules should be appropriate to your child's age, they should be understood by your child, and they should be consistent and reinforced by all the adults in your home. If you let your child walk around the house with juice one day and the next day tell him he can only drink in the kitchen, you're sending conflicting messages and setting yourself up for problems down the line. You should try not to make rules in your home that you, your spouse, and the other adults caring for your child cannot agree on. Children will easily be able to sense who is the wimp in the family and go to the person who gives in easily to demands. This certainly undermines the parent or caregiver who's working hard to establish clear expectations and consequences.

You don't need many rules, but rules that involve children's health and safety should be absolutely nonnegotiable. You wouldn't let your child cross the street alone, eat only unhealthy foods, play with sharp objects, turn on the stove, or put something in an electrical outlet. These are obvious dangers to your child. Less dramatic issues of health and safety are just as important. Some of the other areas where you'll need to establish clear rules include bedtimes, bathing, brushing teeth, doctor visits, school, food choices, appropriate clothing for the weather, putting toys away, and sitting at the table while eating. The rule of "no hurting" needs to be the law in every home.

In all other respects, it's up to every family to set their own priorities about what rules are necessary for a happy home. You might let your child have a cookie once a week; another family might allow one cookie a day. You may decide on no TV; another family may allow one TV program a day and DVDs on the weekends. Pick the things that really matter to you and stick with them—you don't want to make an issue over everything. You can determine what's most important to you but relent on the things that matter least to you. While brushing teeth should be nonnegotiable, it's okay to let your child go to school wearing mismatched plaids and stripes if that's what he chooses. If everything's a battle, you and your child will become frustrated and you won't enjoy your time together.

It can be very helpful to involve your child in making the rules for the family. When parents and children work together to come up with the rules and when they write them down, the child feels involved and is more likely to remember and understand what's required of him. Once you've established the rules for your family, then you can simply refer to The Rules, letting them become the "higher authority." If you are someone who's uncomfortable with authority, this helps shift the emphasis away from you and onto The Rules. Referring to The Rules is less confrontational and more impersonal, and it helps avoid power struggles with your child, as children respond well to the idea of an indisputable higher power. When your child doesn't want to brush his teeth, you can say, "The rule is teeth are brushed before a story." When your child says, "I want another DVD," your response is, "Our house rule is one DVD a day." We often tell parents to use school as the authority as well. When you tell your child that you know he puts the toys away or hangs up his own coat at school, this will help you to reinforce a rule and send a coherent message.

Many parents find it works well to post The Rules in a prominent place in the home. One family we know has their rules in number order posted on the refrigerator, and when an infraction occurs, the other children simply say, "Sebastian didn't do number three." Even though these children didn't know how to read yet, they had learned The Rules and knew their order. Children like to know that The Rules are for everyone, as this establishes fairness.

At other times, your child won't like it when you enforce or remind him about The Rules. He may show his extreme displeasure by crying or yelling. Don't give in—your child will feel safe and loved when you are calm and consistent and when he senses that you are strong and sure of yourself. If you waiver and seem uncertain, he'll challenge you and feel out of control.

The Rules can extend to other people's children when they are in your home or in your care. One parent told us about the time she was asked to drive another child home from day camp. When the child got into the car, he refused to wear his seat belt. He said that his mother didn't make him wear one. This mother simply said, "In my car, we wear seat belts. That's the rule." The child then buckled his seat belt.

- **Don't negotiate.**
  When you say "no" to your child and you really mean it, it's still the case he'll want to negotiate with you. This is what children do. But if you're engaging in constant back and forth discussion with your child, he won't know where you draw the line. One family we know told us that they had gotten into a pattern of always negotiating with their daughter, Kara. It had reached a point where Kara had become very good at this, and arguments about day-to-day things would go on and on. One day, Kara's father had had enough. He turned to his daughter and simply said: "We don't negotiate with terrorists." Once the parents became clear with Kara, the lengthy negotiations subsided.

- **Adjust your expectations for different children in your family.**
  All children are different and will react differently to your style of discipline. Some children will respond to a raised eyebrow or a stern tone of voice; others may need a consequence or a time-out to reinforce appropriate behavior. Often one child in the family will respond very differently than another, and you'll have to adjust to meet his individual needs.

How to Help Prevent Confrontations and Conflicts Before They Occur

There are numerous things you can do to prevent confrontations and conflicts before they happen, thereby making your life easier. These include:

• Establishing Routines •

Young children need routines. At this age, they rely on consistency to help them manage their world. Routines are comforting, letting children know that there's a plan. If your child can anticipate what comes next, he's more likely to cooperate with you, transitioning well into the next activity. When routines aren't clearly defined, children won't be able to handle the practical aspects of everyday life easily, and you'll find yourself spending a great deal of time arguing and negotiating about when and how things get done. See chapter 7 for tips on how to establish routines.

• Anticipating and Preempting Problem Behavior •

Why do young children cry, whine, have tantrums, protest, get frustrated, and melt down? They may be tired, hungry, overstimulated, frustrated, looking for attention, coming down with an illness, or unable to express their feelings. Maybe you've just had a new baby, moved into a new house, changed caregivers, returned from a trip, or had an illness or death in your family. If you think about the possible causes of these behaviors, you may be able to anticipate and eliminate some of them.

Things that trigger oppositional behavior include bedtime, clothing choices, food choices, going to the toilet, cleaning up, shopping, talking on the telephone, turning off the TV, and transitions in general. You won't always be able to avoid some of the situations that cause challenging behavior, but there are things you can do to preempt conflicts and outbursts. If you're prepared, you'll be better able to deal with your child's reaction.

> **situation:** You're going to the supermarket and it's close to lunchtime. Your child will inevitably whine as you approach the cereal aisle because he's beginning to be hungry.
> **anticipation:** You could plan your outing for after lunch, or you could bring a small baggie of your child's favorite cereal to have as a snack.

> **situation:** You plan to go to the shoe store after school, but when you arrive, your child is tired and cranky.
> **anticipation:** You can avoid a meltdown in the shoe store by having a

quiet rest at home first or stopping at the library to read a story beforehand. Once your child rests and regroups, your trip to the shoe store will surely be a happier experience.

---

situation: You have a physically active child who can be aggressive when overstimulated. You pick him up at a birthday party to find that the children are running around throwing jellybeans at each other. Now he wants to go to his friend's house for a playdate.
anticipation: You firmly and calmly say, "We're going home now, but I'll call Paul's mother later to plan a playdate."

---

situation: Your newborn baby needs to be fed, and your jealous three-year-old wants you to read him a story as you get ready to feed the baby.
anticipation: You can set up a book with an audiotape and have him snuggle next to you on the couch while you feed the baby. Once the baby is fed, you can ask him to pick out a book for you to read.

---

situation: You're talking on the telephone, and your child keeps interrupting you. He can't wait because he feels that he won't remember what he was going to say if he doesn't say it that moment.
anticipation: You can tell him that he isn't allowed to interrupt you. Tell him he can hold his thought in his brain and you'll listen to him when you hang up. When you hang up, make sure you give your child your full attention.

---

situation: Your child wants to wear his shorts to school, even though it's the middle of winter.
anticipation: You can remove his summer clothing from the drawer and place the items in a box on a high shelf.

• Breaking It Down •

You'll need to be very specific when telling your child what to do if you want to avoid a confrontation. It's important to be aware that young children don't respond well to vagueness and generalizations. It can help to break down your expectations into smaller tasks. Instead of saying, "We're leaving the house. You need to get ready to go now," you can say, "Put the Lego in the Lego box and come put your coat on." At the same time, young children have difficulties processing too many directions at once. If you tell your child four directions in one go, he'll only focus on the first or last one he heard.

• Working Alongside Your Child •

Most children will be more responsive if you work alongside them to help things along. A child who is reluctant to clean up can be encouraged when you turn the task into a game or a challenge: "You pick up the blue blocks, and I'll pick up the red ones." "Let's see if we can clean up everything on the floor before the timer goes off." "I bet you can put all the little cars in the box before I count to ten." Four- and five-year-olds are competitive and love a challenge, and you can capitalize on this by using games as an incentive. Three-year-olds are more likely to respond to a song or a timer. Teachers in the nursery school use a sand timer in the three-year-old classrooms so that the children can actually see how much time they have left.

• Giving a Warning •

Many children are reluctant to shift gears without some kind of preparation. When you give your child a warning before changing activities, you allow him to make the transition less abruptly. You can say, "You can finish the puzzle you're working on, and then we'll have a bath." This allows your child to anticipate what you need him to do and gives him a chance to comply. It's sometimes helpful to ask your child to repeat what you've just told him so you can be sure he's understood you.

• Giving Either/Or Choices •

Remember that too many choices can be overwhelming for a young child and give him too much control. Either/or choices let your child make decisions while allowing you to control the outcome. Sometimes there should be no choices. The teachers at the nursery school often tell the children, "You get what you get and you don't get upset." Children love this rhyme and quickly accept this simple and clear message. We often hear them repeating it to themselves and to each other.

• Using Distraction or Humor •

Another good tactic is to use distraction or humor to prevent a confrontation or a meltdown. You can change the subject, walk into another room, or come up with a new plan: "I have a great idea! Let's see what secret game is hidden in your room!" Be dramatic. Children have short memories and will soon forget the thing that was bothering them a minute ago. Humor is an equally effective strategy. Be a little silly. When your child demands ice cream for breakfast, tell her, "Yes! Let's have ice cream, and then meatballs and spaghetti, and then let's put birthday cakes on our heads!" It's possible to be playful in this way without being sarcastic and without imitating or mocking your child.

• Getting Your Child on Your Side •

Let your child know that you're on his team. Instead of saying, "I want you to go to bed," try saying, "If we go to bed now, we can have an extra story." Instead of getting into a power struggle, you've hopefully managed to get your child on your side.

• Reinforcing Good Behavior •

While it's necessary to respond to negative behavior, it's equally important to recognize and reinforce your child's good behavior. Children feel proud and encouraged when the adults in their lives notice when they're doing the right thing. When you see your child cleaning up his toys without any prompting, you should "catch" him in the moment and reinforce his good actions: "I see you put your toys away. Your room looks very clean." This isn't praise exactly; it's letting your child know that you appreciate that he did it, which reinforces the good behavior. Another "catching" strategy is to remark on a certain behavior to your partner or friend while your child is within earshot. If you're on the telephone, you can say, "Ethan helped me feed the baby today and put his jacket on all by himself!" You can bet your child will glow with pride at your words.

• Avoiding Overpraise •

It's very easy to fall into the habit of complimenting a child on small things that should simply be expected of him. Many well-meaning parents are concerned that if they don't constantly praise their child, they will lower his self-esteem. But when you consistently applaud your child for things that aren't actual achievements, you're actually lessening the positive effect of praise. Over time, the message of praise—"You did something good," or "You need to do that in the future"—loses its validity. Your child will begin to look for external approval every time he puts on his coat or brushes his teeth. In the classroom, we see children who are overpraised at home asking teachers or other children, "Is this okay? Do you like my picture?" rather than relying on intrinsic feelings of self-worth.

Most young children like to please the adults in their lives and respond well to specific praise. When praising, it's essential that you compliment your child for real accomplishments. Your child will know if the praise is undeserved and feel uncomfortable if he senses that what you're telling him isn't true. It can be confusing for a child when he hears praise that isn't genuine or is overly exaggerated. If you're in the playground and you hear yourself saying, "Good job going down that slide!" you know that you've gone too far. Gravity, not your child, is doing the work.

It's a good idea to state the behavior you're acknowledging, commenting on your child's actions, not her general conduct. Instead of saying, "You're a good boy," you can say, "It was nice that you shared your cookie with your friend." Tell your child how you feel about his good actions: "I appreciated that you came to the dinner table the first time I asked you." Encourage a sense of pride in his own accomplishments: "You must be so proud that you put your shoes on all by yourself." Another way to show your approval is by a warm smile or a gesture. At school, we've observed how effective this kind of approbation is when used in a classroom. The teacher calls the children to the rug for a morning meeting. The children form a circle independently. The teacher waits, slowly looks around the circle, smiles broadly, nods her head in approval, and comments, "Look what a wonderful circle you made!" The children smile proudly, sit up straight, and feel pleased with themselves.

Child-Tested Discipline Tactics

Even if you have established routines, made rules, set clear limits, and tried to avoid conflicts, the reality is that your child will still misbehave. When he does, the way you respond to him reinforces your expectations for appropriate behavior and guides him toward more acceptable conduct. You should try to stay calm and firm.

When you need to tell your child no or to correct a behavior, here are some simple tactics you can use to make sure your message is effective:

Practical Wisdom for Parents

• Come Down to Your Child's Level •

When telling your child no or asking him to do something, you need to make sure you're being heard. If you really want your child to listen, you must get on his level, make eye contact, and use his name. If you're calling from the next room, it's very easy for your child to ignore your request. Sometimes it's not that your child is deliberately ignoring you, it's just that he's so absorbed in what he's doing that he can't hear you. Pick an optimal moment to state your expectation, when you have his full attention.

• Find the Right Words •

Young children respond best when the language you use is simple, clear, and concise. The words you choose are critical in getting your child to listen and respond to you. By choosing words carefully, you're setting a good example for your child.

You need to be aware that what you say can be damaging to your child's self-esteem, however. Words are very powerful and can be hurtful. When you blame or shame your child into doing what you want, he'll respond out of fear and stop internalizing what you're trying to teach him. That doesn't mean you shouldn't be firm or have consequences for misbehavior. It means you have to be thoughtful. You need to state your expectation and how you want him to change without blaming or shaming him.

If your child draws on the wall with markers, for example, your temptation may be to shout at him and simply take the markers away. When you do this, however, your child isn't learning about appropriate behavior or how to take responsibility for what he's done. You need to firmly tell him that markers are for drawing on paper and that you're upset that he messed up the wall. Then you can tell him that he needs to help you clean the wall and that if he does this again, you'll take the markers away for one week. In this way, you're teaching your child that what he did was wrong, you're holding him responsible for repairing the "misdeed," and you're also giving him a warning and clear consequence if he does it again.

When you tell your child what he *can* do instead of what he *shouldn't* do, it's usually more constructive and effective. When you state your expectations clearly and describe the behavior in question, you send the message that it's not the child you disapprove of, but his actions. This way you can set the limit and teach what you expect without having to always say no. In general, words like "always" and "never" should be avoided.

blame response: "You're impossible. You always lose your hat."
alternative: "I'm upset that you lost your hat again. When you take your hat off, it needs to be put inside your coat sleeve. Let me show you how."

---

blame response: "You're a bad girl. You ruined my work by scattering my papers on the floor. Why did you do that?"
alternative: "You need to play with your own paper. Come and help me to gather up my papers and put them back in order. Then we can find you your own special paper to play with."

---

blame response: "Never squeeze your baby brother like that!"
alternative: "Babies don't like squeezing; you can gently touch him this way."

---

blame response: "That's terrible that you hit your brother. Don't ever do that again."
alternative: "You know that we don't allow hitting in this house. Use your words, not your hands."

• Use the Right Tone of Voice •

Be very aware of your tone of voice. If you say softly in a singsong questioning manner for the fifth time, "Sweetie, please clean up your toys?" your child is going to think that this is a request, not an expectation. When you state clearly and firmly what you want your child to do, he'll be much more likely to comply.

For generations, children have always responded to: "By the time I count to five, you need to . . ." This works, not because there's any magic in the numbers, but because adults sound as if they mean business when they say this. It's certain you'll get your child's attention if you use his name. Parents tell us that if you really want a child to know you mean business, you should use his middle and last name too. Your child will sense if you are uncertain. Even if you are wavering on the inside, you need to give your instruction or reprimand with outward conviction if you want your child to respond.

Yelling, on the other hand, is usually ineffective. When you raise your voice, it probably means you've lost your patience and are feeling out of control. If you asked once in a gentle manner and were ignored and your next response is to become frustrated and yell at your child, you've missed the middle ground of being firm and strong. If you use your businesslike voice from the first request, you're more likely to have an impact. If you think about a scale of one to ten, you can modulate your level of intensity to around a five.

• "Blah, blah, blah": When Your Child Tunes You Out •

Too much talking or explaining isn't always helpful to a young child. Children need adults to be clear and concise. If you're giving your child a long-winded explanation about why he needs to wear his raincoat, you're giving him too much information. Instead of a long statement, "If you go out in the rain, you're going to get wet, and then I'll have to bring you home and change your clothes," what he really needs to know is that he must wear a raincoat when it rains. "It's raining. Put your raincoat on" is enough information. In the same way, it's much more effective to tell your child, "No grabbing!" than it is to tell him, "It isn't nice to take a toy away from another child." Sometimes a single word, "Shoes!" gets your point across more effectively than, "You need to put your shoes on so we can leave the house in time for school."

Often the best language is no language. There will be times when it's better to pick up your child and sit him on the chair rather than discussing why he needs to sit at the table to eat a snack. A parent once told us about the time she asked her son three times to turn off the water after he'd finished washing his hands. When he refused to respond, she walked over and turned off the water. She was surprised by how easy it was and how unnecessary it was to have asked him three times.

Sometimes the most effective solution is to ignore the behavior, rather than calling attention to it. If your child is doing something harmless although annoying, you may find it loses its appeal if you ignore it. Often, if a child has been told not to do something, he'll do it deliberately in order to get your attention. We've all seen children sticking out their tongues, blowing bubbles in milk, or jumping on the bed even though they know it's forbidden. Your response needs to be appropriate to the action. If something is simply annoying, don't overreact; it's not worth going into battle over. You can leave the room or refocus your attention on your child only when he stops. If ignoring doesn't work, try distraction or redirecting your child. You can give him permission to do it two more times and then, "That's it!"

Of course, some behavior can't be ignored. When your child is doing something harmful or destructive such as hitting another child or throwing objects, of course you'll have to intervene.

• The "Look" •

Every parent needs to develop a stern expression that sends a silent but powerful message. Your "look" can speak louder than your words. By raising your eyebrows and looking powerfully and directly at your child, you can effectively send the message that you disapprove. Children are very sensitive to facial expressions and can "read" them even before they have language. By showing disapproval or anger through your look, you instantly tell your child what you mean.

• Time-outs •

Time-outs can be a very effective tool for helping children understand that a particular behavior is unacceptable. A time-out removes your child from the situation, stops the behavior, and helps both of you regain self-control. Time-outs should not be overused or used when a child does something accidentally (such as spilling juice or wetting his pants).

Children need a calm, firm warning in advance of this punishment: "If you do that again, you will need to have a time-out." Then, if the behavior continues, you should:

- Explain simply that he must have a time-out because he didn't stop when you told him to.

- Move him to a quiet place with no toys or distractions.

- Have him sit no longer than one minute for each year of his age (three minutes seems like forever to a three-year-old).

- Refuse to engage in conversation with your child or respond to crying or whining during the time-out.

- Hold him firmly if he seems to be out of control.

- If he refuses to stay in the time-out, be firm and start it again from the beginning.

• Give Consequences and Follow Through •

When you are dealing with young children, it's necessary to give them consequences for negative behavior so that they can predict what will happen if they break a rule or misbehave. Consequences need to be logical, brief, and immediate. Young children live in the moment. If your child grabs a toy away from another child in the sandbox, and you punish him by eliminating his bedtime story five hours later, this won't make any sense to him. Removing him from the sandbox will. Make sure you follow through. If you say you're going to remove him from the sandbox and then you leave him there for another ten minutes, you're sending him the message that he can ignore you.

Sometimes it works to let your child continue with his actions and learn from the consequences of what he's done, rather than trying to stop him. For example:

- You've planned an outing to the park but your child refuses to put on his coat. You wait a short time, then tell him that you can't take him outside without his coat. If he still won't comply, you simply stay home. The next time you plan to go to the park and the coat issue comes up, you can remind him about the last time and that he didn't get to go.

- Your child goes to a friend's house for a playdate. He only wants to play firefighter and his friend wants to play another game. They agree to play firefighter first and then the other game. But when it's time to change activities, your child refuses and cries. You try to coax him to accommodate the other child but he won't. You can tell him you have to end the playdate early since he didn't cooperate, and you can tell the other child, "I'm sorry Tom didn't play your game; maybe next time he will." When your child wants to play with this child again, you can remind him what happened the last time.

• Use Incentives Judiciously •

There are times when offering a small incentive for a task well done or a change of behavior can be useful as a motivator. The promise of a few more minutes of extra playtime or one more story can inspire your child to do something to which he's resistant and this can reinforce positive behaviors. Make sure the incentive is small and appropriate, however. You don't need to promise your child a trip to Disney World—a sticker or extra time with a parent is enough.

Incentives can be in the form of a reward or the promise of a reward. Both rewards and promises can motivate behavior, but be careful that you don't fall into a habit of overusing them. If your child starts asking for a reward for routine things such as putting on his shoes before leaving the house or brushing his teeth in the morning, it's gone too far.

Some behaviors will take a long time to change, especially if your child's bad habit has been around for some time. Sticker charts are an effective tool for tracking your child's progress over a week or so. It's helpful to involve him in the process of making the chart, writing the expectation at the top and choosing the stickers. This technique often has dramatic and positive results. Andy, a four-year-old in one of the nursery school's classrooms, would often hit the other children when he was frustrated or didn't get his own way. Together with his mother, Andy's teacher developed a positive reinforcement plan to encourage a change in his behavior. His teacher would give him a sticker at the end of each day if he did not hurt his classmates. When he had five stickers in a row, his mother would take him to the library where he could borrow one or two books as a reward for good behavior at school. Andy's mother knew he loved books and this would be a great incentive. In a short period of time, we were amazed at the change in his conduct.

Another reward system that can work, but which takes longer to achieve, is the "marble jar." This helps encourage a change in behavior while teaching your child about the pleasures of postponed gratification. For instance, if you're struggling every day to get out of the house on time for school, tell your child that for each morning he's ready at the specified time, he's allowed to put a marble in the jar. When the jar is full, he'll receive a reward you've previously agreed on (an extra DVD, a special toy, baking a cake with you). This allows your child to fail on one day but get back on track and accomplish the goal the next.

One parent we know puts pieces of paper in a box with special rewards written on them, such as "a trip to the park," "inviting a friend for dinner," or "baking cookies." When the child accomplishes a goal, he gets to pick a paper and have the surprise special reward.

Children love stickers or small toys as rewards, but don't forget that your hugs and approval are what they value most.

• Avoid Empty Threats •

When disciplining your child, you should avoid using threats that you can never follow through on. When you say, "If you don't stay in your seat, we are never going to a restaurant again!" or "I won't take you to Florida on vacation if you don't clean up your room!" your child will quickly learn to ignore your threats. Children are clever—they can easily understand which threats are real and which are empty. If your child senses that consequences won't happen immediately, you're not going to help change the behavior. It's more realistic if you follow through on your threat and if it has a direct correlation to his behavior: "If you can't remain at the table in the restaurant, we'll need to go home." "If you don't clean up your room, you can't have an extra story at bedtime."

Other Typical Problems and What to Do About Them

• "I hate you, stupid-head!" •

Somewhere between the ages of three and five, you're very likely to hear your sweet, adoring child say, "I hate you, stupid-head!" or words to that effect. What this usually means is: "I don't like what you just told me to do. I'm feeling angry and testing the power of words. I'm looking for your reaction." Children don't enjoy having limits imposed on them, and you shouldn't expect them to respond happily when you discipline them. Although it's normal for a young child to say, "I hate you, stupid-head," he needs to know it's unacceptable to talk to people in this way. If you allow your child to speak to you or his caregiver disrespectfully, you send him the message that you approve of this behavior.

It can be helpful to give your child alternative and acceptable words to express his feelings. Children enjoy language, they love experimenting with interesting words, and they're often capable of learning alternative ways to describe how they feel. When you rephrase the sentiment and show your child that there are many ways to express himself, you're helping him to put names to feelings. By explaining to him the meaning of words such as "angry," "upset," "frustrated," "disappointed," "embarrassed," "jealous," "lonely," and "worried," you're giving him the vocabulary he requires to gain emotional maturity.

• Bathroom Talk •

At this age, when children are experimenting with language, "bathroom talk" is exciting, inviting, and inevitable. When children use "bad language," they discover how powerful words can be and how useful they can be when they want to get your attention. It's very natural for children to do this, and it usually starts around age four. When your child tells you at the dinner table that you're a "poop-face," remain calm and don't overreact (or laugh). Instead, send him a clear message that these words are not appropriate. Say clearly and in a matter-of-fact tone, "Bathroom words belong in the bathroom and name-calling isn't allowed." Another approach is to let your child know that these words are unacceptable and, if he must use them, he should do so in private where no one else can hear. Giving him permission to use "bad" words under these conditions usually puts an end to the excitement of doing something that's forbidden.

When it comes to curse words, you are your child's best role model. If you don't want your child to use profanities in your home, at school, or at another child's home, be careful that you don't say these words in front of him. There's nothing more embarrassing than hearing your three-year-old repeating your favorite obscenity in the supermarket.

• Tantrums •

We've all witnessed it—a child wailing, screaming, waving limbs around, completely out of control. Although you were probably told that your two-year-old would outgrow his tantrums by age three, it's normal for some preschoolers to throw the occasional tantrum. At two, your child didn't have the language or self-control to handle his very powerful emotions and frustrations. Your preschooler, however, can use words to express himself, and by this age, you can expect him to have greater self-discipline. When children older than age three continue to have regular tantrums, it's usually because they've learned that this behavior has been effective with adults in the past.

When a tantrum happens, it's tempting to give your child attention or give in to his demands. This tells your child that he can manipulate you and that tantrums work. Instead, you should make sure he's physically safe—away from furniture or any other potentially hurtful objects. Sometimes you can hold him close to you while you allow him to get the tantrum out of his system. During a tantrum, it will be impossible to talk to him or reason with him—you'll just have to wait for it to run its course. When you set limits for your child, give clear instructions, and have consistent expectations, he'll be less likely to throw tantrums in the first place.

• When a Parent Loses Control •

Sometimes children can try the patience of even the most sanguine parents, and it's only natural to lose your cool from time to time. If you find that you're starting to lose control, you can give yourself an adult time-out and physically remove yourself from your child. This will take the attention away from the behavior and allow you to have a cooling-off period. By going into another room and closing the door, you're sending a very strong statement to your child that you don't approve of what he did. An adult time-out should never be used when a child might physically harm himself or others if left alone.

If you're at the end of your rope and your child continues to pester you, it's only natural to snap. When he keeps whining for you to put on his DVD while you're in the middle of a call—even though he knows he's not allowed to do this—it's very natural to slam the phone down and shout at your child. If you regret using particularly harsh language, simply apologize. You can say, "I'm sorry I lost my temper and yelled at you. I was upset with what you were doing." You shouldn't apologize for disciplining your child, however.

If your child puts himself in danger, you may find that you have a surprisingly powerful reaction. When Charles was three years old, he loved to ride his scooter as fast as he could down Seventy-ninth Street. Ellen would always run behind him cautioning him to stop at the curb, and Charles would always go as close to the edge as he could. One day, while Ellen was running behind him, he went off the sidewalk and into the traffic. Ellen panicked, lifted him off the scooter, and smacked his bottom. This wasn't a reaction that Ellen had considered, and she certainly didn't feel good about how she'd reacted in the heat of the moment. Although it made an impact on Charles, the smack didn't send him a good message about self-control. Later, when Ellen had calmed down, she apologized to Charles and explained that she'd reacted badly because she was so frightened that he was going to get hurt. While Ellen's reaction was perhaps understandable in this circumstance, spanking should not be used as a discipline tool. If at all possible, when you start to feel out of control and emotional, you should physically remove yourself from your child and take an adult time-out.

By disciplining your child, you're teaching him self-control, respect of others, and how to handle difficult situations in ways that involve words, not hitting. If you spank your child or use some other form of physical force, you're sending the opposite message. Research shows that spanking can actually increase your child's antisocial behavior as he may mimic your behavior and end up hitting others. Ultimately, you may be harming his self-esteem, and you certainly won't have shown him an appropriate way of handling anger and resolving conflicts.

• When to Seek Professional Help for Your Child •

All young children will misbehave and test limits. If your three-year-old screams because you won't give him a candy, he's simply exhibiting normal behavior for a child of his age, and the best thing you can do is to set clear limits for him and wait to see if he grows out of this behavior when he learns to express himself better. But if your four- or five-year-old is still regularly having passionate, lengthy tantrums, doesn't respond to consistent limits and consequences, and is regularly physically aggressive and destructive, it may be time to seek help. If your child's behavior is continually disrupting your family life and is interfering with his progress at school—and if he shows no signs of growing out of this—you may need some form of outside intervention.

The first thing you can do is to ask for advice from your child's teacher or some other adult whose opinion you value. You need to find out if this behavior is appropriate for his age and what you can do to change that behavior. But if the behavior persists and the strategies discussed with your child's teachers have little or no effect, it may be time to seek advice from a mental health professional. Your pediatrician or school director will be able to direct you to appropriate resources. If your child has physical symptoms that accompany behavior issues, you should definitely check with the pediatrician.

If you decide to seek professional help, it's important to keep your child's school informed since teachers may have useful information to share and can benefit from any strategies suggested by a therapist. We find that when the family and the school work on these issues together and communicate often, the child's behavior changes more rapidly. If you don't feel comfortable with the psychologist or other professional that you have seen, don't give up, but try to find someone who's more compatible with your child and family. For more information on this subject, you can refer to chapter 5 of this book, which describes children's development.

• Raising the Bar for You and Your Child •

As your child grows it's essential that you regularly reassess your expectations for him and that you raise the bar periodically. You'll be surprised at how capable he becomes when you expect more from him and how proud he'll feel when he accomplishes something new. In order to set reasonable expectations for your child's behavior, you need to understand what children are capable of at each stage of development. If you allow your four-year-old to behave in the same way as your two-year-old, you'll only be holding him back. Some of the ways you can learn about appropriate expectations include reading books about child development, talking to teachers, and observing your child's friends. You can also refer to chapter 5 in this book, "Understanding Your Child's Development."

When children know what's expected of them and how to behave, they feel safe, secure, and confident in themselves and the world around them. Children love and depend on the adults in their lives to provide them with boundaries and consistency. This is the time in a child's life when internalizing discipline takes hold, enabling him to meet the challenges and expectations he'll find as he ventures outside the home. It may seem hard at times and that you're making your child unhappy in the moment, but in the long term, what you're actually doing is giving him a gift. It takes time and patience to change habits and patterns of behavior, but stick with it—the rewards are immeasurable.

Recommended Books for Children About Good and Bad Behavior

Hands Are Not for Hitting	Martine Agassi
What Makes Me Happy?	Catherine and Laurence Anholt
When Sophie Gets Angry—Really, Really Angry . . .	Molly Bang
The Way I Feel	Janan Cain
How Are You Peeling? Foods with Moods	Saxton Freymann
I Was So Mad	Mercer Mayer
I'm Sorry	Sam McBratney
Where the Wild Things Are	Maurice Sendak
When I Feel Good about Myself	Cornelia Maude Spelman
When I Feel Angry	Cornelia Maude Spelman
When I Care about Others	Cornelia Maude Spelman
Words Are Not for Hurting	Elizabeth Verdick

Chapter Ten

DEVELOPING MORALS AND ETHICS IN CHILDREN

As parents, we want our children to be good. We want them to feel empathy and to treat others with fairness and respect. We want them to grow up understanding the difference between right and wrong. In other words, we want to raise moral and ethical human beings. If you ask most parents what they want for their children, however, they'll usually say, "I want them to be happy and I want them to succeed." Happiness and success are wonderful goals. But if you place these qualities above all others, you may forget to prioritize the essential value of being a good person. What we have seen is that many parents don't spend enough time asking the question, "How do I raise a good person?" "Good" in this context is very different from simply behaving well. Basic goodness for young children has to do with the concepts of kindness, decency, fairness, empathy, respect for others, and the difference between right and wrong—common values we can all share.

Parents of children this age are often so concerned with a child's intellectual and physical development, it's not surprising that they sometimes neglect to think about her moral education. They may assume that this is something that can wait until later or that it's the job of the school or religious institution. Many parents take it for granted that goodness is a natural instinct in children and therefore doesn't need to be taught. In fact, every child has within her the potential to do both good and bad. In the morning, your child may spontaneously give her friend a hug when that friend is crying. Later in the day, she may grab her brother's toy and make him cry. It's your job as a parent to show your child how to distinguish between these two actions: the good action of the morning and the bad action of the afternoon. You can't assume that she'll figure out the difference for herself. She needs adults to help her develop her judgment during this time when her desires are more powerful than her ability to control them. In other words, you can't just expect goodness from your child. You need to teach it, value it, model it, and reinforce it.

Children at this young age are very egocentric and don't naturally consider how their actions will affect anyone other than themselves. When our boys, Michael and Charles, were four years old, they were playing in Ellen's bedroom, jumping on her bed. Of course, we told them to stop. We reminded them that this was inconsiderate to Mrs. Herman, the sweet eighty-five-year-old lady who lived on the floor below. Boys being boys, they kept jumping. A little while later, the doorbell rang and it was Mrs. Herman asking politely if the banging could stop as she was feeling unwell. Both of us went into the bedroom and told the children to stop immediately and that Mrs. Herman had come all the way upstairs from her sickbed because the noise had disturbed her. We told Michael and Charles that they needed to apologize right away, so we sat them down and helped them to write a note to Mrs. Herman, which they then delivered themselves. We could see that the boys felt terrible about what they had done, but when Mrs. Herman told them the next day how touched she was by their note, they soon felt good about themselves. At this young age, Michael and Charles didn't have the experience to predict how their actions would affect others. When they were held accountable and shown a way to repair the damage, they learned that their actions had consequences. We're proud to say both our boys have grown up into men who are respectful of others.

Never underestimate your child's ability to be considerate. Children at this age are beginning to move from a completely self-centered view of the world to a more outwardly directed one. At school, your child is becoming part of a larger community and is learning to work in cooperation with others. Her teachers will consciously try to create classrooms that are caring communities, always complimenting the children when they do something kind. They'll often talk about who's absent from school and include that child's name in the morning song. They may encourage the children to make a phone call to a sick child or teacher or have the class create a get well card. The children are asked to thank the child who brings in a special snack, and when another classroom invites the class to visit, the teacher helps the children to send a thank-you note. Some classrooms will have a chart to record when a child is helpful to another child. Many classrooms recycle and talk about what they can do to protect and take care of their world. One class at the nursery school takes a "garbage walk" around the block looking for litter and graffiti. Parents have told us that their children have become much more aware and careful about putting garbage into trash cans as a result.

During these preschool years, you'll have many opportunities to offer your child similar guidance. As she makes this transition from toddler to child, it's up to you to continually reinforce realistic expectations for her so that she can grow into an understanding of what constitutes good behavior. If you offer your child direction and act as a role model right from the beginning, she can and will begin to learn. She may not always be able to act in accordance with principles of goodness, but she will begin to absorb them. You can't wait until she's five years old to start this. The groundwork needs to be in place long before then. When you do pay attention to this area of your child's development, you're doing something very important. You're aiding in the essential formation of her conscience and building a foundation for ethical behavior and respect for others that will last a lifetime.

What You Can Do to Guide Your Child Toward Ethical Behavior

Some children are ready for ethical guidance sooner than others, but a child will never be ready unless you help her. There are some simple steps you can take to begin guiding your child.

• Establish a Code of Ethics •

As a parent, it's up to you to establish your family's basic code of ethics. These can be as simple as: We don't hurt each other, we take care of each other, we treat one another with respect, we use kind words, we help others, and we're fair. Environmental values may also be important to your family: We recycle, we don't litter, and we try not to be wasteful. For younger children, you'll need to be the one to set the rules; by the age of four or five, your child is probably old enough to be involved in creating your family's essential moral guidelines. When you have a code that everyone in your family tries to abide by, you can refer to it as the higher authority: "That's Our Rule."

• Acknowledge Your Child's Kind Acts •

When your child spontaneously does the right thing, you need to acknowledge this good behavior. When her baby brother drops a toy and starts to cry and your older child picks it up and gives it to him, you should comment on her helpfulness. If your child asks to make a card for a sick grandparent, make sure to send it. When you notice and respond positively to kind or good actions, you actively reinforce these behaviors. Your child doesn't need a reward for her good acts. When she learns that it feels good to do something good, she takes the first step in her moral development.

• Hold Your Child Accountable •

By holding your child accountable when she does something wrong, you're helping to teach her the difference between right and wrong. If your child deliberately rips a page of a book, you need to make sure that she understands this is not the way to treat a book and that she's spoiling the book for others. Just as you should compliment a child for doing something good, your child needs to feel badly if she's done something wrong. In this way, she owns *all* of her behavior and learns to make the right choices in the future. We've heard parents say that they are concerned they'll damage a child's self-esteem if they're too "critical" of a child. But if you don't expect your child to have good behavior, it's likely she'll continue to be inconsiderate and won't be liked by the people around her. This will be very damaging to her sense of herself in the long term.

• Catch Your Child in the Moment •

When you see an opportunity to teach good behavior, you should "catch" your child in the moment. Don't wait until later. One day, Ellen was outdoors on the school playground when she saw Christina, a three-year-old, picking up a pink beaded bracelet from the ground. Ellen immediately went over and asked, "Is that your bracelet?" Christina replied, "No, but I can have it." Ellen explained that the bracelet belonged to someone else and asked Christina to come with her to see if anyone had lost it. "No," insisted Christina. "It doesn't belong to anyone out here." But Ellen was firm, saying, "Let's go and see." Together they went over to a group of girls and, sure enough, Katie's face lit up when she saw her bracelet. Christina's reward was Katie's beaming smile and thank you as she handed back the bracelet. Ellen used this moment as a teaching opportunity to show Christina that giving something back can feel good, even when you really want to hold on to it.

• Help Your Child to Repair the Hurt •

When your child makes a bad choice, she needs to have the opportunity to repair the hurt or wrongdoing. The child who tears the page from the book should be shown how to tape it back in. The child who pushes her little brother so that he bumps his knee can help bring him a cold pack and give him a hug. For a very young child, the words "I'm sorry" are not always meaningful. Acts of kindness such as giving a hug, making a drawing, or helping to rebuild the block structure that she knocked down can be much more meaningful.

• Motivate Through Love •

When a child behaves badly, your reaction needs to be calm and considered. The best way to motivate your child to be good is through love, not fear. For example: You notice that there's a small pile of soil where a plant used to be and when you ask your child what happened, she says she doesn't know. Later, you find the uprooted plant hidden in her closet. You have two options here. You could get angry because your child lied to you, but if you do this, you run the risk of making her fearful of displeasing you in the future and covering up her actions again. Or you can confront your child and ask her to help you replant the plant, thereby showing her how to repair the damage. You could explain to her that if she makes a mistake or has an accident in the future, she can always tell you what has happened. You need to disapprove of her behavior while still reassuring your child that you love her.

• Be a Good Role Model •

As much as what you say, your actions form the basis for your child's values. When your child sees you call a sick friend, take care of an aging parent, or offer help to someone in need, she'll learn from your example. On the other hand, if you don't always model moral behavior, or you send conflicting messages about moral issues, you may confuse or even upset your child. A parent with a child in one of the nursery school's five-year-old classrooms told the following story. One day, she and her son, Matt, were getting on a bus. The mother didn't have enough change for both of their fares. Up until then she'd been giving Matt the change to put in the fare box himself. This time she said, "Just walk on. It's okay." When they sat down, Matt got very upset and said to his mother, "I thought you said I have to pay now that I'm five. Isn't that bad that I didn't pay?" This parent quickly learned that how you act is just as important as what you say to your child.

• Teach Your Child the Value of Her Possessions •

We live in a materialistic society where there are many wonderful products designed specifically for young children. It can be tempting for parents and grandparents alike to shower children with new toys, clothing, and accoutrements. However, when you do this, you run the risk of bringing up a child who is overly materialistic or takes her material possessions for granted. We've all seen the child who has more toys than she knows what to do with. As a parent, there's much you can do to help your child appreciate what she does have—thereby helping her to enjoy and value her things more.

- **Keep fewer toys on the shelves.**
  In the classroom, we keep the numbers of things on the shelves to a minimum. We find that the children are much more productive and play for longer periods of time when they're not overwhelmed by too many choices. Your child is more likely to play creatively when she has a smaller number of toys to choose from. You can always put some toys away and rotate them regularly.

- **Don't immediately replace a toy when it breaks.**
  If something is so easily replaceable, you're denying your child the opportunity to learn about its value. It's okay for your child to experience a sense of loss. When you wait before buying the new toy, you help inspire her to take care of her belongings the next time.

- **If your child wants a new toy, tell her she can wait for a special occasion (a birthday or a holiday).** You can say to her that she can put the toy that she wants on her "wish list." This way you are delaying gratification, allowing her the pleasure of anticipating receiving the toy, and helping her to enjoy the toy more when it arrives.

- **Tell people that it's okay *not* to get your child a gift.**

  We know parents who decide they don't want to have gifts at their child's birthday party. Another idea is to ask friends and family members for a favorite book for your child, instead of an elaborate present. Many parents choose to put a few gifts away in order to save them for another time or to give to charity.

What Do Children Understand?

When you're guiding your child toward conscientious behavior, it can help to try to see the world from a child's point of view. When your child does something "wrong," she's often simply acting on impulse and without malice. When she sees a toy car that she wants, she takes it. When she sees a person in a wheelchair in the supermarket, she asks in a loud voice, "Why can't he walk?" When she knocks down another child's blocks, she doesn't understand why this would make him cry. In order to be judicious in your expectations and explanations, you need to know how much your child can understand.

Here are some good things to bear in mind:

• Preschool Children Think in Very Concrete Terms •

For a young child, right and wrong are black and white concepts. You're either a good guy or a bad guy. For example, when two children are playing in the playground and one child accidentally bumps into the other, the child who was bumped declares, "He pushed me!" It doesn't matter that the bumping was accidental. Your child perceives the action as deliberate, and she can't be convinced that bad things happen unintentionally. Even so, you can gently explain to her what took place: "James didn't see you. You were running and bumped into each other. It's no one's fault."

• Young Children Tend to Think that the Greater the Physical Damage to Something, the Greater the Infraction •

For example, breaking a china vase with a gigantic crash or causing a child to fall down and scrape her elbow seems much worse than being mean to someone. Children need to have it pointed out to them that words can hurt as much as a scraped elbow.

240

• Children This Age Are Able to Understand that Rules Shouldn't Be Broken •

Children love to win and will often change the rules of a game in order to avoid losing. You can remind your child: "We agreed when we played the game that these would be the rules." When you say this, you are teaching about fairness.

• A Child's Idea of What is Wrong is Directly Connected to Whether She Thinks She'll Be Held Accountable •

Young children will be good if you are consistent in your disapproval of their wrongdoings. When your child won't include another child in her play and you excuse the behavior by saying, "Oh, what's wrong? Are you having a bad day?" you're not teaching her to take responsibility for her actions. In the same way, if you reprimand your child for this action one day but fail to do so the next, you're sending a confusing message and letting your child know that it's okay to exclude others from the game.

• At This Egocentric Age, Children Are Often Unable to Immediately See Things from Another's Point of View •

A young child simply can't put himself in someone else's shoes. It's no use saying to a four-year-old: "How would you feel if Lara knocked your blocks down?" Instead, you need to draw attention to a recent occurrence and give her a concrete example: "Remember how you felt when Lara wouldn't let you play house yesterday?" In this way you are helping her internalize what it feels like to have your blocks knocked down, thereby guiding her toward empathy.

Lying, Stealing, and Cheating

When a young child lies, steals, or cheats, it doesn't mean she's morally corrupt. This is simply part of her normal development. At this age, it's inevitable that your child will tell you something that you know to be untrue. It's likely that she'll take something from her classroom that doesn't belong to her. When playing a game, she'll doubtless want to change the rules and play her own way. When you respond to these actions, you need to be aware that your child isn't deliberately doing something wrong. It's important not to be overly punitive. Instead, use this as an opportunity to gently teach.

• Lying •

Your child's ability to distinguish fantasy and reality is still quite blurred at this age. Young children are magical thinkers—their wishes are often expressed as reality. A child this age loves to exaggerate. She may say, "I'm stronger than my dad," or tell you that she has a big sister when she's the eldest in the family. If you reprimand your child for lying or you dismiss the fantasy, you're missing a valuable opportunity to remind her of what's real. You can say, "I bet you'll be as strong as Daddy one day," or "I know you wish you had a big sister." When you rephrase rather than accuse, you acknowledge her feelings and wishes without making her feel badly for having her fantasies. As she learns to distinguish what's real and what's not, this stage will pass.

• Stealing •

We're never surprised when parents report that they found Lego pieces from school in their four-year-old's backpack. When a young child takes something that doesn't belong to her, it's often her way of connecting to a place or person that she likes. Instead of punishing your child for stealing, you can gently remind her that the things she's taken belong to someone else. Next, you need to help her return the item without making her feel ashamed (a child who feels excessively embarrassed won't want to return a stolen possession in the future). This is a good time to explain the concept of borrowing. Finally, you can talk to her about the difference between "wanting something" and "taking it without asking." Don't use the word "stealing" in this context. Your child isn't thinking in these terms. Instead, you can help her to understand the concept of "something that belongs to you" and "something that doesn't."

• Cheating •

This is a concept that very young children are not developmentally capable of understanding. Before you can hold your child accountable for deliberately cheating, you need to be certain that she's mature enough to have internalized the whole concept of "rules in a game." Young children love to win. They'll invent rules as they go along for the express purpose of winning. We've heard children say to each other, "Do you want to play the regular way or the cheating way?" One parent we know told us about her youngest child, who always declared, "I won!" in a running race, even if he lost. This child wasn't cheating. He simply didn't understand what it meant to lose. You can help your child by pointing out that it's fair to play by the rules. You can also avoid this issue by choosing to play simple cooperative games where the goal is to finish and not to win or lose.

Developing Empathy

For years, child development experts thought that very young children did not have the capacity for empathy. However, recent research has shown otherwise. For our part, we've seen very young preschool children comforting a classmate or sharing their most precious toy with a special friend. We once heard a two-and-a-half-year-old in one of the nursery school's classrooms tell his friend, who was crying for a mother, "Don't worry. She'll be back after snack." Young children *are* capable of empathy, especially if they're guided toward it.

There are many things you can do to help your child to become a more empathic being:

• Foster Respect at Home •

When parents create an atmosphere of mutual respect at home, children learn how people can live and work together. By balancing adult needs with children's needs in your home, by creating small chores for children, and by praising kindness when it happens, you're helping to build an environment where everyone is respected.

• Call Attention to the Feelings of Others •

It's very important that you talk to your child about how her actions affect others. If your child throws sand in another child's face in the sandbox, explain to her how her action made the other child feel. "When you threw the sand, it hurt him and made him cry." If you yell at your child and say,

"What did you do?" you're not helping your child understand that her actions were the cause of the other child's distress. Instead, you can point out the other child's facial expression and talk about how he might be feeling. By the time your child is four years old, she should be able to take responsibility for causing another child to become upset. That connection has to be made before empathy can exist.

• Be a Good Role Model •

The most important influence on a young child's ability to develop empathy is the adults around her. When your child is surrounded by empathetic and understanding parents and teachers, she has daily opportunities to learn from acts of caring and talking about feelings. In time, she'll learn to better understand her own feelings and the feelings of others.

Empathetic parents and teachers:

- Give affection and show respect to children.

- Are helpful to others.

- Call attention to the feelings of others.

- Help a child to identify her feelings.

- Give reasons for rules that involve consideration of others.

- Explain to a child the implications of her behavior.

- Underline that kindness is important.

- Expect a child to be considerate of others.

- Point out examples of acts of kindness and empathy.

- Show approval when a child is being empathetic and disapproval when she's not.

Volunteering as a Family

When your family volunteers to help others, you're benefiting in many ways. Not only are you spending time together; you're also teaching your child about the value of community service. When your child is thanked for volunteering or sees that others are pleased by her actions, she's learning that it feels good to help others. If the volunteering involves contact with others who are less fortunate, she can gain an appreciation of her own privileges. Above all, when you volunteer with your child you are teaching consideration and compassion for others.

Some age-appropriate activities include:

- Helping clean up a local park or picking up trash.
- Planting in community gardens or playgrounds.
- Visiting the elderly.
- Making holiday cards for the homebound.
- Delivering meals to the sick.
- Donating toys or books to hospitals.
- Bringing food or clothing to a shelter.
- Participating in runs/walks for various causes.

Valuing Goodness

When you show your very young child how to care and how to respect others, and when you set limits and lead by example, often what you're doing is paving the way for her good behavior in the future. It can take hard work and years to build your family's values. The results won't always be immediate. Sometimes, however, the results *can* be more instant. We've seen that when a child's goodness is valued and nurtured at home and at school, amazing things can happen.

Recently, we received this letter from the parent of Ben, a four-year-old at the nursery school. Ben's teacher had been teaching the children about the Jewish New Year, a time when it's traditional to perform acts of kindness and good deeds (mitzvahs) so that the year can get off to the right start. Although the teacher had been teaching the children about goodness, this was something that the child's parents were reinforcing at home as well. The parent wrote:

On Friday Ben was so excited about the New Year. He talked a lot about all of the good stuff you can do at the beginning of the year. He spoke about being kind, and about mitzvahs. I thought this was very sweet and asked him where he learned so much about the New Year. He said, "At school." As the day progressed he stuck with the theme of helping and being kind and came up with an idea. He told me he would like to blow up red balloons, put them in a garbage bag, and give them out to people on Saturday morning. I asked him, "Why balloons?" and he said, "They make people happy and it's a nice thing to do for others." So on Saturday morning, Ben blew up the balloons and I tied them for him. After we had a full garbage bag of balloons, off we went.

As Ben walked down the street he would say to me, "Can I ask that person?" and I would say, "Of course." So from 76th Street to 79th and back we proceeded to do good for others. Ben reminded me that it's important not to just *think* about good things but to *do* good. As we passed the "Ready, Willing, and Able" men from the Doe Foundation, Ben said, "How about them, Mom? They pick up our garbage every day. I think they would like a balloon." Before I knew it, the men were smiling with red balloons in their hands. Ben also asked the fruit stand man if he would like a balloon as well.

When we were just about done, my child asked me to help him with something else. I said, "Sure, what can I do?" He said, "We need to make a chart. We need to chart how many balloons we gave out. We need to keep track of all of this because it's important that we do this again next year, and we need to know exactly how many balloons to blow up and how many people to make happy." It was very important to him that I help him put a chart together. He insisted on counting the people, balloons, and documenting it all in the chart.

I could have never dreamed of such a day. Ben's kindness was felt by many and the gesture was so kind. I admired his confidence to speak to others and express himself so well. All of which will be documented in a chart for next year. What can I say? The core of his being has been so nurtured and developed through his early education experience at school and at home. I only pray each day it continues to grow and flourish for all of my children.

Recommended Books for Children About Morals

The Boy Who Cried Wolf	Aesop
Clifford's Good Deeds	Norman Bridwell
Stone Soup	Marcia Brown

Developing Morals and Ethics in Children

The Great Kapok Tree	Lynne Cherry
The Empty Pot	Demi
The Little Red Hen	Paul Galdone
Giants Have Feelings, Too	Alvin Granowsky
Lilly's Purple Plastic Purse	Kevin Henkes
The Mountain That Loved a Bird	Alice McLerran
Yo! Yes?	Chris Raschka
Horton Hatches the Egg	Dr. Seuss
A Tree Is Nice	Janice May Urdy
A Chair for My Mother	Vera B. Williams

Chapter Eleven

SELF-HELP SKILLS AND INDEPENDENCE:
"I Want to Do It Myself!"

Now that your child is preschool age, he's going through many adjustments, and so are you. For the first few years of your child's life, it's been your job to take care of all his most basic needs: getting him dressed in the morning, feeding him, changing his diapers, and everything else that goes along with being the parent of an infant or toddler. As your child begins school, however, your role needs to adjust in order to allow him to become more independent. Most schools expect that by the time your child is three, he'll be well on the way to dressing himself, feeding himself, and transitioning from diapers to underwear. It's up to you to help your child take on these challenges so that he'll be able to handle school and feel confident and competent when he's not with you. This is a time to begin thinking about your child as moving away from toddlerhood and into early childhood—which also means weaning him from "baby things" such as bottles, pacifiers, cribs, and security blankets.

We tell parents that the months between two and a half and three years of age are an ideal time to begin to teach basic self-help and independence skills. You have a window of opportunity during these months when your child will be most receptive to your guidance. After age three, it generally becomes much more difficult to introduce these skills. Older children tend to be more self-assertive, and their habits have had time to become entrenched. Parents often ask us when exactly is the right time to begin teaching their child to dress and feed himself independently and to be toilet trained. This can vary from child to child. Look for signs of readiness. Many children will begin to tell you, "I want to do it myself!" and you can follow their lead. If your child tries to do something alone or asks to be shown, it's a good indication that he's ready. However, there are other children who prefer to hang back and don't show signs of readiness. These children may need adults to lead the way.

Often, it's not just children but their parents who need a little nudging. We've seen many well-meaning parents who hold off when it comes to teaching self-help skills. Many parents find themselves helping a child get dressed or feeding him his dinner even when the child's old enough to do these things for himself. After all, it's much more convenient to do something for your child rather than allowing him to do it himself. When you're rushing to leave the house, and your child's insisting on putting on his shoes and struggling to figure out which shoe belongs on which foot, of course your instinct is to do it for him. No parent enjoys watching a child struggle, and it's always going to be easier and faster to help. You may hope that the child will figure these things out in time, simply by emulating the adults around him. While it's true that your child learned to crawl and walk quite naturally, when it comes to dressing, feeding, and toileting, these skills must be taught, supported, and encouraged. In general, you're going to have to resist the temptation to jump in so that you give your child the opportunity to learn from his attempts.

It's very easy to get into the habit of doing things for your child. When you feed him from a spoon or help him put on his sweater, it can feel like you're doing your job as a parent. It's not that you're deliberately undermining your child's independence; it's just that you're both used to doing things this way. When Nancy's daughter, Alissa, was four years old, she was in the habit of calling out, "Mooooommmmy, come wiiiiipe me!" when she was on the toilet, and Nancy always did. One day, Ellen, who was Alissa's teacher at the nursery school, was visiting and heard the calls. "What are you doing?" Ellen asked Nancy. "She wipes herself at school." This was a case of Nancy forgetting to raise the bar of expectation. Mother and daughter had fallen into a habit even though Alissa no longer needed Nancy to help her in this way.

Other parents may resist teaching self-help skills because they have a degree of reluctance about letting go of the baby stage. At age three, Ellen's youngest, Charles, would still throw his arms up in the morning as if to say, "Dress me." Ellen found she kept dressing Charles even when he was old enough to do it for himself because Charles was her "baby." When Charles finally learned to dress himself, Ellen could see that she had been underestimating his capabilities. He enjoyed his newfound independence, and his confidence grew as a result. It's only natural to feel ambivalent about your child's increased independence. As your child grows, it can feel like he's going to need you less. You can't help your feelings, but even so, you need to keep in mind how much your child will benefit from your belief in his abilities.

When we speak about self-help with parents, we always remind them just how important these skills are for a child's sense of self-esteem. We've seen parents who place enormous importance on a child's extracurricular activities, yet forget to prioritize basic self-help skills. From our years of working in early childhood education, we have seen that children at this age gain much more from learning to feed or dress themselves than they ever could from playing a sport or learning a foreign language. Children feel such a sense of pride in their new ability to take care of themselves. When a child knows that he's able to put on his coat, eat his snack, and go to the bathroom without adult help, he has a feeling of confidence and competence that has a positive effect on every other aspect of his learning and growth.

What You Can Do to Support Your Child's Independence

• Maintain Consistent Expectations •

When teaching self-help skills, it's important that all of the adults in your child's life have consistent expectations. If the babysitter is still spoon-feeding your child while you're encouraging him to use his own spoon to eat cereal, he'll be receiving very confusing messages. You'll need to check in with relatives, teachers, and caregivers on a regular basis to tell them about your child's progress and find out what they've observed. All the adults in your child's life need to feel confident that he can move to the next level and that with a little help and encouragement, he'll quickly adapt.

• Break It Down •

The simplest self-help skill can seem immensely complicated to a small child and it helps enormously if you break it down into small components. Think about how hard it is to put on a pair of shoes. You have to match your foot to the right shoe. You have to understand that the sock goes on first. You have to begin to understand the concept of left and right. You have to use your fingers to open up the shoe to make room for your foot. You have to figure out what it feels like when the wrong shoe is on the wrong foot. You have to switch the shoes around to try again. It's a conundrum that may take many weeks for a young child to solve. When you teach him bit by bit—sock first, then open the shoe, then slide inside—he'll gradually gain the confidence and the dexterity to complete the task.

• Be Patient •

When teaching your child self-help skills, it's important to set aside time and to be patient. It can often take many weeks before your child accomplishes a seemingly simple task. You can support him by allowing him to struggle a little while complimenting him on his attempts. If the task does seem too difficult, you can suggest a way to work through it together and ask him to make suggestions. This way he can feel successful, his self-esteem will build, and he'll try again the next time.

• Resist the Temptation to Do It for Your Child •

It can be hard for parents to break the habit of doing things for a child. One morning, three-year-old Molly arrived at the nursery school and, rather than taking her coat off and putting it on the hook, she dramatically let it fall to the floor. Her well-meaning parent bent over and scooped it up and put it on her hook. The message to Molly was loud and clear: "You don't have to do it. You can't do it. I'll do it for you." If you do something because it's easier for you, it sends the message that you don't think your child is capable and this can actually undermine his confidence in his own abilities.

• Don't Be Afraid to Let Your Child Fail •

It's okay to let your child try to do something for himself, even if this means he fails in the beginning. When we see a child coming to school with his pants or shirt on backward, we never criticize that child or his parents. We know that he dressed himself and that his parents gave him the benefit of learning from his attempts.

Practical Wisdom for Parents

• Send a Positive, Empowering Message to Your Child •

It's very important to keep encouraging your child, even when you're feeling exasperated. When your child wets himself for the fifth time today, the natural reaction is one of despair. However, when you smile, use positive expressions, and remain upbeat—even when your child isn't succeeding—you ensure that your child doesn't become discouraged or ashamed.

• Don't Give Up •

Often we'll hear parents say, "I tried to get my child to do that, but it didn't work." Trying once or twice isn't enough. It can take weeks of practice and repetition to master the most basic skills. Expect resistance—your child won't always want to do these things alone. Don't give up. You need to be clear in your expectations and communicate that this accomplishment is important. When you stick with it, eventually you'll see results.

• Try Not to Take Steps Backward •

It's very important that you set goals and stick to them. Once you have made a decision to move forward, try not to take steps backward as you'll only be sending a confusing message. Once you've decided to have your child give up the bottle, don't be tempted to go back, even when he's crying and whining. This will pass.

• Keep Raising the Bar •

Every few months, it's important to reevaluate your expectations for your child and raise the bar ever so slightly to support his growth. When he begins to use a fork, maybe it's time for him to start drinking from a cup. If your child has been undressing himself every night before bath time, it's time to start teaching him how to put on his pajamas. Keep stepping it up. It's easy to fall into a pattern of behavior where you applaud his accomplishments thus far, forgetting that he's capable of much, much more.

Toilet Training

Most early childhood programs expect or require children to be toilet trained by the age of three. In fact, most children are physically ready by age two and a half to begin the process of training. We always recommend that parents capitalize on the months leading up to age three. We find that when toilet training begins well after age three, parents often run into a lot of resistance. After three, your child may need to feel in control and want to take charge of the situation.

Many pediatricians tell parents that a child will let them know when he's ready to be toilet trained. Some two-and-a-half-year-olds will beg for Spider-man underwear and then basically train themselves. Other children show no interest in toilet training and need adults to lead the way. Although it's unlikely that any child will say the words, "I'm ready now," you can look for the following specific signs.

Your child is showing signs of readiness for toilet training when he:

- Walks and sits

- Pulls his own pants down

- Says no as a way of asserting independence

- Knows where things belong

- Shows an interest in the bathroom

- Wants to watch you or an older child use the toilet

- Has an awareness that he's soiled his diaper

While a child must be ready to toilet train, it's just as important for the parents to be ready as well. Parents often tell us they're worried about toilet training the "correct" way, fearing that the "incorrect" method might harm their child. In our experience, children respond best when parents take a calm and positive approach to training. When a parent is anxious and fearful, a child may sense that he can gain control over the situation, and the training becomes more complicated. The most important thing is to know that your child is capable of toilet training and that by remaining confident you can help increase his ability to master this skill.

Remember that the concept of going to the toilet without adult help needs to be introduced long before the actual training begins. You can start by giving your child an understanding of what's happening to his body and how to talk about it. Developing an awareness and a vocabulary is an important first step.

You can begin by:

- Naming his urine and bowel movements (i.e., pee and poop).

- Calling attention to his progress by commenting when he's eliminating. ("I see you are making a poop. Does your diaper feel wet? Do you need a dry diaper?")

- Praising your child for requesting a diaper change so he's aware that being dry is preferable.

- Reading books and showing videos that introduce toilet training.

- Buying a potty or special seat for the toilet to put in the bathroom.

- Using dolls to show how to use a potty.

- Having your child pick out nice underwear. (Your child's favorite character is usually an incentive.)

- Avoiding pull-ups. Many parents think of "pull-ups" as a transition from diapers to underwear. In fact, absorbent pull-ups often inhibit training because children aren't aware that they're wet. This often delays training. Pull-ups should be considered diapers, not underwear.

Now that you've prepared your child over a period of time, you're both ready to practice. You'll need to have some uninterrupted time at home to begin this process. As with all self-help skills, time and patience are key. If there are other big transitions going on in your family at the same time, then it's best to delay the training—it's very difficult for a child to take this step when he's adjusting to a new baby, a new house, a new caregiver, or a new school. We often suggest that weekends or vacation-time during the summer are good times to begin training, because you'll be able to stay close to home and your child can practice while wearing less clothing. When he's naked, he's likely to be more aware of his urges—he'll feel more uncomfortable when he's wet or soiled and will want to do something about it.

Some other suggestions that parents have found helpful are:

- Get your child to practice sitting on the potty (boys should start by sitting).

- Help your child to recognize the need to go by saying, "It looks like you have to poop or pee. Let's try."

- Expect accidents, but don't overreact when accidents happen. Don't call it an accident or mistake in front of your child as this will give him the impression he's done something wrong. Don't punish or become angry when your child wets or soils himself. Don't accuse your child of being a baby or refer to soiled clothing as messy or dirty. Just say, "I see you're wet; let's get some dry underwear. We'll try again next time."

- Praise successes and compliment attempts.

- Remember that your child won't always have enough time to get to the toilet. When children are very involved in play, they often forget to pay attention to their urges or leave time to get to the bathroom.

- Use a simple reward like a sticker or an M&M (nothing too big).

- Don't remind your child too often as this can annoy him. When you ask if he needs to go, this can result in an automatic no. It's better to say, "Let's try."

- Be aware of your child's bowel movement patterns so you can time a trip to the potty or toilet accordingly.

- Read a book while your child is sitting on the potty so that he has a reason to stay still, but don't have him sitting for too long. If he doesn't have to go, he doesn't have to go.

- Turn on the tap. It sometimes helps a child urinate.

- Avoid giving your child too much liquid, especially before bedtime or before you get in the car for a long trip.

- Always have him go to the bathroom before you leave the house and before bedtime.

- Remember that if you're overly fastidious in public bathrooms, you can make your child feel anxious about going in unfamiliar bathrooms.

- If your child is having trouble going on the potty, remember that some children prefer a step stool and a child's seat on the toilet. Many children are more comfortable with this, as they have seen their parents going this way.

- If your child is very resistant and you're getting involved in constant power struggles, it's best to stop for a while and try again at a later date. Be advised that many parents find their daughters train more easily than their sons.

- Remain calm. The more anxious you become, the more your child will sense that he has control over the situation and the harder it'll become to train him.

- It's true that some children will withhold as a way of maintaining power over you. If your child becomes constipated over a period of days, it's important to seek advice from your pediatrician. Your doctor may prescribe a laxative. If you have given your child a laxative, you need to stay home so that he can get to the bathroom quickly. Don't send your child to school.

• Managing Clothing, Wiping, Flushing, and Hand Washing •

Once your child is on the road to a successful transition from diapers to underwear, it's important to introduce all of the other aspects of toileting—independently managing clothing, wiping, flushing, and hand washing. By the time your child's ready to toilet train, he should already be able to pull down his pants and underwear. You can help your child by dressing him in clothing he can easily manage. Imagine your child has just learned to use the toilet and is feeling very proud of himself. He feels the urge to go and gets to the bathroom only to find he must unbuckle his belt, unbutton his pants, unzip his zipper, and pull down his underwear. Most small children are unable to do this is under twenty seconds—which is usually the amount of time they leave themselves before they have to go. Elastic waistbands are the best way to insure success.

The next step is to teach your child to wipe himself. You may be concerned that your child won't be clean enough and, as a result, may continue wiping him long after he can do this for himself. In fact, if your child is old enough to pee on the potty or the toilet, then he's old enough to learn to wipe himself. In order for him to feel capable, simple steps need to be taught. First, tell him to take enough toilet paper, then show him how to wipe from front to back. Tell him he needs to repeat this using more paper until he sees that the paper is clean. In the beginning, he may want you to check to make sure he's clean, and when you encourage him, he'll feel more confident the next time. Some parents find that having children use baby wipes after the toilet paper helps them to feel clean.

Now it's time to flush. Some children are fearful of flushing at first because of the sound of the water. If this is true of your child, you can tell him to put the seat down so it's less noisy.

Lastly, you need to teach proper hand washing. Tell your child that wetting hands is not the same as washing them and that he needs to use soap as well as water. Show your child how to wash the top and bottom of his hands and in between his fingers. One way to make this more enjoyable—and to teach him how long he should wash—is to sing the "Happy Birthday" song twice. When you buy your child tops with sleeves that push up easily, this will help him to wash his hands without getting his clothing wet.

• Nighttime Training •

When your child starts to wake up with a dry diaper in the morning or goes to the bathroom first thing, it's time to transition to underwear at night. Most children are daytime trained before they accomplish nighttime training. This is very normal. We hear all the time about children who are wearing underpants during the day but still need a diaper at night. Nighttime diapers can be a very hard habit for parents and children to break. When it's 2 a.m. and your child has a wet bed and you have to get up and change his clothing and bed linens, it can seem a lot easier to put him in a diaper. However, children need to feel wet in order to know in the future that they have to go to the bathroom. When you continue to put your child in a diaper, you're not enabling him to feel the discomfort that comes from wetness. As hard as this is, at some stage, you'll have to draw the line and decide to persist until your child adapts. One way to simplify bedding changes at night is to have a rubber sheet, a regular sheet, another rubber sheet, and another regular sheet on top of that. By having two sets of sheets you can simply remove the top set.

Another good idea is to limit your child's liquids after dinner and to make sure he goes to the bathroom just before bedtime. You can also put him on the toilet before you go to bed, as most children usually go right back to sleep afterward. Despite your best efforts, however, children will have nighttime accidents, so don't become upset when this happens. If you criticize your child for wetting the bed, he'll think he's done something wrong and this may make him anxious and can even perpetuate the problem. If his bed-wetting persists over a period of months, you may want to check with your pediatrician to see if there's a medical reason that he's unable to train at night.

Blankets, Pacifiers, Bottles, and Sippy Cups

A few months before your child begins school is a good time to start sending the message that he's no longer a baby and that "baby things" need to be left at home. School is not a place for security blankets, pacifiers, bottles, or sippy cups. In the classroom, he won't be allowed to walk around with a "blankie" or "passie." Now that your child is beginning school, it's important that you send him clear messages that match those he's receiving from his teachers.

It's true that giving up security objects can be very hard for children—and their parents. Many children are both emotionally and physically attached to security objects; they may be very accustomed to soothing themselves using a blanket or a bottle. For parents, letting go of security objects marks the end of the "baby phase," and you may discover you feel surprisingly reluctant for your child to let go of these comforts. However, you do need to support your child's growth and maturity as he begins school. When you think and talk about growing up in positive terms, your child will respond to the clarity of your expectations. It may help you if you keep in mind that prolonged use of bottles, pacifiers, and sippy cups is known to cause dental and speech problems.

Some children will naturally give up blankets and bottles as they grow, especially if they see that their older siblings or cousins don't use these anymore. Other children will need you to lead the way. Again, changes should not happen concurrently. If you're moving your child from a crib to a bed, this isn't the time to eliminate a pacifier. If you're weaning him from the bottle and he also uses a pacifier, don't take both away.

At first, you can gradually reduce the time and limit the places that your child is allowed to use these baby items. This way the transition can be gradual, and your child will more easily adjust. A way to begin the weaning is to leave these things at home whenever you leave the house. With a blanket, you can gradually trim it down to a smaller size or cut off a piece that could fit in your child's pocket so he can take some of it to school. If it's a toy your child won't part with, suggest that he take it to school but leave it in his backpack. If a child does bring a toy from home into the classroom, he usually becomes preoccupied with it, making it difficult for him to engage in other activities, which is why most teachers don't allow this.

When weaning from a bottle, you may want to begin by reducing the size of the bottle. You could transition to water instead of milk or juice—this will have the added effect of reducing the risk of cavities. While you're weaning, make the rule that bottles or pacifiers stay at home. If you don't take these things out of the house, children will acclimate more quickly and easily. Make it simple; "It's the rule. Bottles and/or pacifiers stay home." Remember that nighttime bottles are one of the greatest causes of tooth decay and also interfere with sleep routines and toilet training.

We do not recommend that parents use a sippy cup when transitioning from a bottle to a cup. Sippy cups, like pull-ups, have been introduced by manufacturers as an "in-between" step that children really don't need. Many parents give their children a sippy cup in the stroller, allowing the child to hold on to a drink for hours at a time. In addition to interfering with toilet training—and potentially causing cavities because the child is constantly drinking—sippy cups can be detrimental in another way. Some speech pathologists have told us that prolonged use of a sippy cup can cause speech problems due to the shape of its spout.

Children can often be surprisingly mature about giving up baby things if you make the rules clear to them. At one of our meetings, we told parents that it was time for their three-year-olds to give up sippy cups. We suggested they could tell their children, "It's the school rule; Nancy and Ellen say no sippy cups." The meeting was on Friday. The following Monday, a grandparent told us that she was watching her grandson for the weekend and when she went to give him a sippy cup, he'd said, "No, Grandma, I can't have that. Nancy and Ellen say no sippy cups!" This was the case of the mother teaching the child, who taught the grandmother.

A better alternative to a sippy cup when you're on the go is a flip-top cup with a straw. However, there's no reason to use a flip-top instead of a cup at home. In general, it's a good idea to get into the habit of only offering your child a drink when he asks for one. When you let your child become thirsty, you're allowing him to become aware of his own needs rather than always relying on you.

If you are struggling with weaning, it's important to remember that, although it can all seem very traumatic, your child will adjust. When Nancy's daughter, Alissa, was giving up her bottle, she was down to one four-ounce bottle that stayed at home and only had water in it. One day Alissa announced that she was ready to give up that last bottle. She happily threw it in the garbage with great pride. Nancy, knowing she would probably relent if

Alissa made a big fuss, quickly took the garbage out of the house. The next day Alissa screamed and cried for her lost bottle, but knowing that it was really gone helped both mother and child. By the next day, the panic was over, and Alissa was able to move on. When your child whines, "But I need my bottle!" try not to get upset. Remain calm. You can acknowledge that you know he wants his bottle and that this is hard for him. Then you can try to distract him by finding a fun activity or maybe offering a chewy but healthy food substitute instead. We've often seen that when children give up these security objects, they quickly learn new ways of expressing their needs and receiving comfort.

Other Self-Help Expectations for Your Preschooler

• In the Bathroom •

Brushing teeth, combing hair, and washing himself in the bath can all be introduced around the age of three. It helps if you can make these tasks fun by having your child pick out a special toothbrush or toothpaste. Fun soaps like foamy liquid soaps and sponges will help encourage your child to wash himself. You can sing a song or count along while he brushes his teeth or washes his hands to make sure he spends a little extra time: "This is the way we brush our teeth, brush our teeth, brush our teeth . . ." or "I'm gonna wash that dirt right off of my hands and send it on its way . . ."

• On the Go •

There's always the temptation to push your child in a stroller rather than expect him to walk short distances. We discourage parents from using strollers once children turn four years old.

• Dressing Independently •

One of the ways that children will assert their independence is by insisting on choosing their own clothes and wanting to dress and undress themselves. If you want your child to dress independently, you need to make things easier for him by ensuring that clothing fits properly. We often see children struggling to manage pants that are too small or tights that are falling down. When teaching children to dress themselves, time and patience are key. If your child insists on zipping his own jacket but doesn't yet have the dexterity to put the zipper together, you can suggest that you start it for him and allow him to pull it up by himself. You can help him get started with other clothing this way. You can put his socks on his toes before having him pull them over his foot. You can place his legs in the pants and then let him pull them up the rest of the way.

Some other helpful suggestions:

- Start by letting your child undress himself as this is easier than getting dressed.

- Learn to put on pajamas first as these are easy to pull on.

- Line shoes up in front of the proper foot.

- Buy slip-on shoes and shoes that close with Velcro straps. Tying laces is a kindergarten skill.

- Buy skirts and pants with Velcro closures and elastic waists, and mittens instead of gloves, all of which are easier to put on.

- Make sure zippers aren't broken.

- Buy toys that teach buttoning, snapping, and zipping.

- Avoid belts, buckles, overalls, or any other complicated clothing.

- Give either/or clothing choices when asking your child what to wear so that he doesn't become overwhelmed.

- Resist the urge to do it for him.

Teachers use a tried-and-true method for teaching young children to put on their coats. It's called "flipping the coat." Without this trick, it would take hours to get the whole class ready to go outdoors. Here's how your child can "flip the coat."

1. Place the coat faceup on the floor at the child's feet. The coat label should be at the child's feet as he looks down.
2. The child bends over, putting both arms into the sleeves at the same time.
3. Then he lifts up his arms so that the coat is above his head.
4. He flips the coat behind him and lets it slip down his back.
5. Ta-da!

• Eating and Drinking Independently •

If your child's old enough to go to school, he's ready to feed himself. We once witnessed a parent spoon-feeding yogurt to her four-year-old before a tennis lesson. This sent a confusing message to the child, who was old enough to play tennis and more than capable of feeding himself. In fact, as soon as your child has enough dexterity to pick up Cheerios, you can begin to encourage him to eat independently. At first, food needs to be served in small, manageable pieces that can be picked up with fingers. Gradually a spoon and fork can be introduced. Expect a mess as your child practices getting the food onto the spoon and then into his mouth. By three, he should be able to use a fork and spoon—a four-year-old eating spaghetti with his fingers is not a pretty sight.

The dinner table is also a good place to begin training your child to use a cup. You can tell him that he can drink from a cup like Mom, Dad, big sister, or cousin, and even let him choose a special cup. Children are most successful when the cup is half filled and when it has a wide base like a mug. Don't overreact to a spill; your child will feel discouraged. Children spill. It's just part of learning how to use a cup.

During mealtimes, you can encourage your child to experiment with pouring. At school, he'll be practicing this skill at the snack table using a small pitcher or measuring cup. Children take great pride in mastering this difficult task, which involves carefully picking up the pitcher, then tilting it just far enough so that the liquid comes out slowly and smoothly rather than in a big slosh, and then setting the pitcher down again. You only have to watch the look of intense concentration on your child's face as he attempts to pour to understand just how important it is to him that he acquires self-help skills. There's nothing that gives a child more confidence and self-esteem than being able to say the words, "I did it!" The joy on a child's face when he finally succeeds is always lovely to behold.

Recommended Children's Books

SELF-HELP AND INDEPENDENCE

The Berenstain Bears and the Messy Room	Stan and Jan Berenstain
The Potty Book for Boys	Alyssa Satin Capucilli
The Potty Book for Girls	Alyssa Satin Capucilli
Your New Potty	Joanna Cole
I'm Good at Building	Eileen Day
I'm Good at Helping	Eileen Day
I'm Good at Making Art	Eileen Day
I'm Good at Making Music	Eileen Day
I'm Good at Math	Eileen Day
Froggy Gets Dressed	Jonathan London
Just a Mess	Mercer Mayer
Uh Oh! Gotta Go!	Bob McGrath
First Experiences: It's Potty Time	Roger Priddy
Going to the Potty	Fred Rogers
You Can Go to the Potty	William and Martha Sears and Christie Watts Kelly
Time to Pee!	Mo Willems

SELF-ESTEEM

I Like Myself!	Karen Beaumont
Olivia	Ian Falconer
Elmer	David McKee
The Little Engine That Could	Wally Piper

Chapter Twelve

PLAY:

Why, What, and How?

When our sons, Charles and Michael, were young, they spent countless hours playing together. The boys were the same age, had many of the same interests, and because they lived in the same building, there was never far to go if they wanted to play. The Matchbox cars and trains would soon take over the living room floor, quickly expanding into cities and worlds of their own. Sheets and blankets thrown over tables became cozy pretend homes with a family of stuffed animals hiding inside. Sometimes their sisters would be given supporting roles in the imaginary play. Even their mothers were occasionally invited into the game. We can still remember being customers at Charles and Michael's "shoe store," which was stocked with shoes from our closets that we paid for with paper money the boys had made themselves.

None of this creativity, fun, and learning would have been possible if our children weren't given the time and space to simply play. Sadly, this type of unstructured play has become much less valued by parents in recent times. Preschoolers these days are busy. After school, they take dance and gym classes. When they get home, they watch educational DVDs and interact with computer software especially designed for their age group. The result is that there are fewer hours in the day when children can feel free to play and create without adult direction. Many loving and well-meaning parents become fixated on keeping their children busy after school because they assume that they're promoting learning and helping their children to use their time productively. Some parents tell us that they must keep their children busy or their children will be bored. In fact, the opposite is true. If a child says she's bored, this often means that she's been so overstimulated that she doesn't have the resources to amuse herself anymore. We often see these children at a loss in the classroom, turning to the teacher for direction rather than relying on their own imagination and abilities.

Play: Why, What, and How?

Never underestimate how much a child benefits from play. The American Academy of Pediatrics recently issued a very strong statement about the importance of play in the lives of young children. In order for a child to develop and be healthy, and for strong parent-child bonds to be maintained, the AAP says, children need to spend less time in structured activities and more time playing. While enrichment activities and educational videos can be beneficial in small doses, these must be balanced with lots of play if children are to develop to their full potential. Too many programmed activities can actually be stressful and unhealthy for young children—not to mention overtaxing for their parents who must organize and pay for them.

The good news is that you don't have to do much to help your child become an enthusiastic learner, be more creative, and feel more confident. Simply set aside time and space, supply a variety of toys and props, and then enthusiastically support your child's natural inclination for play. Your child will do the rest. When children set their own agenda, they stretch themselves in unimaginable ways. They get to test new skills, strengthen muscles, and increase their resilience. They learn to get along with others and see other points of view. They try out new ideas and invent novel ways of doing things. They use trial and error to solve problems, then take their new discoveries and relate them to things they've previously done. The repetition of play gives children a sense of competency that builds self-esteem and increases their willingness to take risks the next time. Skills acquired during play help children navigate their world at the present time, while also forming the foundation for academic learning in the future.

Although play has enormous educational value, there's no need to become overly focused on your child's play as a vehicle for learning. The fact is children love to play; they find it intrinsically rewarding and relaxing. Play is one of the great joys of childhood. It's the doing of play, not the outcome, that gives young children the most pleasure. A child may spend a long time creating an elaborate clay figure of a person, and the moment she finishes it, she squishes it into a ball and happily moves on to the next activity. It's the process that matters. In play, nothing motivates a child more than setting her own goals, whether it's making the tallest pile of blocks or hanging from the climbing equipment. Remember how determined you were as a child to learn to ride your bike and the satisfaction that came from each level of mastery? It's the same with young children and play. They do it because they want to.

We often hear parents say of a child, "Oh, she's *just* playing." Always remember that "just" in this context is a four-letter word. By saying "just," you're diminishing the importance of play in the lives of children. For adults, play is recreation, something to be squeezed in when everything else is accomplished. For children, play isn't secondary to other activities—it's essential. Play is their work, a way of exploring and understanding the world.

How Parents Can Support Play

Although children will certainly play without any help from adults, there are many things you can do to facilitate and encourage play. You can:

• Create Designated Spaces for Play •

Set aside a safe space in your home where your child can create, explore, and have fun without worrying about making a mess. This can be in your child's room or a corner of your living room or family room. It's a good thing for the whole family if there are clear boundaries as to where your child can play. If you look up one day and realize that toys have taken over your entire home, you know it's time to create designated play spaces. Children feel special when they have their own areas, and it's respectful of adults to have some toy-free zones. After your child is finished playing, you should encourage her to clean up her toys. This is an age-appropriate task that will help your child take responsibility for her things and learn to value them. In order for your child to be able to put toys away easily, it's a good idea to use clear bins labeled with pictures to help her understand where things belong and where to find them the next time.

• Limit Your Child's Scheduled Activities •

Make sure you're giving your child enough time for play. If your child is three years old and in more than one scheduled after-school activity a week, she won't have enough time for play. In the same way, your four-year-old should be in no more than two after-school activities a week. When you limit your child's scheduled activities, you're not only benefiting your child, you're also saving money and time for yourself.

• Choose Open-Ended Toys and Materials •

Always think about how many ways a toy can be used. Open-ended toys are usually the ones that children find the most stimulating, that they like the best, and that they will play with for the longest period of time. A good rule of thumb is to ask yourself, can this toy be played with in at least three different ways? A battery-operated toy car only does a limited number of things and depends on batteries to make it work. Now think about how your child plays with a toy truck that depends on *her* to make it work. She decides where the truck is going; she loads it with toy animals and drives them to a zoo; she takes the animals out of the truck; she drives back to pick up the blocks she needs to build the zoo. This toy has allowed your child to make decisions and use her imagination. The next time she takes the truck out to play, she may play in an entirely different way. Toys and materials that are open ended are simply more satisfying, interesting, and educational. Of course, there's no need to buy toys only from a toy store. Most young children will play happily with a carton, pieces of string, or a stick. And as parents throughout the generations will confirm, the very greatest toy of all time is a very large cardboard appliance box.

• Select a Variety of Safe, Age-Appropriate Toys •

When choosing toys for your child, here are some other things to keep in mind:

- **Variety**
  Are the toys you've chosen designed to inspire different types of play (pretend play, physical play, building, art, science, puzzles, games)?

- **Safety**
  Toys and materials should be nontoxic, without small pieces that could be swallowed, and have no sharp edges. Parts should be secure and made of a sturdy, nonbrittle material. If you have a younger child in your home and your older child has toys with very small pieces, you'll have to create a designated space and storage place for this type of toy.

- **Age appropriateness**
  Is it too frustrating? Does it have too many pieces or too many rules? Is it beyond your child's physical ability? Conversely, is it not stimulating

enough? Not challenging enough? Although it's important to introduce new toys as your child grows, it's a good idea to resist the temptation to buy products labeled for children far beyond her age. Even if your child loves building with Legos, the next level may require her to follow very specific directions—to build a rocket ship, for example—and this may be too frustrating so that it becomes your project instead of your child's. Of course your child will have a favorite toy that she plays with long after it's age appropriate, and there's nothing wrong with this.

- **Gender**
  Would you classify the toy as "male" or "female"? Do you have a balance of both types of toys? Do you have toys that are gender neutral?

• Limit Your Child's Toys •

Thanks to a combination of birthdays, holidays, and visits from grandparents and other relatives, most children have enough toys to fill a small garage. Remember that toys don't make play happen. Children do. Toys provide the stimulus for play, but they are not the play itself. While it's important for your child to play with a variety of toys and materials—since each activity will engage her in different kinds of play—you should beware of overloading her with toys. Children become overwhelmed when they have too many things to play with. It's always helpful to limit your child's choices by putting some toys away for a short time. Then, when you bring out an old toy that's been out of sight for a while, as far as your child is concerned, it's new.

Tips for Toy Shopping

If you go into a toy store with your child, you must expect that your child will want to buy a toy. No child is able to resist the many temptations of the toy store, so it's foolish to go inside unless you have a conversation about what can or can't be bought beforehand. It's always a good idea to set the rules prior to going inside. Are you buying something for your child or for a friend? How many toys are you buying? Once inside the toy store, don't try to reason when your child wants to rewrite the rules. If a tantrum ensues, just leave. If your child keeps asking for a specific toy that's too large or expensive, you can postpone buying it. Tell your child she can make a wish list for a birthday or special occasion.

When Nancy's children were very young, she used to tell them that FAO Schwarz was a toy museum and that they could play with anything they wanted, but they had to leave it behind in the museum. For a while, at least, it worked!

Toys, Games, Materials, and Activities

Children learn by doing. When you give your child hands-on experiences with a range of toys, games, materials, and activities, she has wonderful opportunities to grow and learn. Some toys will inspire more solitary play (like sewing cards or shape sorters) and others (like balls or doctor's kits) invite more collaborative play. If you notice your child is always engaged in imaginary play, you can encourage her to play with other toys like puzzles or art activities. If your child is more sedentary, you might want to play a ball game or ride a tricycle. All of the following types of play, toys, games, materials, and activities are tried, tested, and guaranteed to keep your child both engaged and entertained.

• Building and Constructing •

When children use building materials such as blocks, sand, or wood, they can create everything from a road or a zoo to a house or a town. When they do this, they're learning basic information about how components function and how to change and manipulate materials to accomplish an idea. Sometimes these constructions succeed and sometimes they fall apart—it's only through experimentation with these materials that children can learn how things work. If your child has spent a long time building a very elaborate structure, it's possible she'll be reluctant to take it apart and put it away. In this case, it helps to take a photograph of the structure so she can "save it."

Building and construction toys include:

- Blocks of various sizes. Cardboard, wood, plastic, foam, Bristle Blocks and Flexiblocks.

- Duplos and Legos

- Playmobil toys

- Interlocking cubes
- Peg-Boards

- Gear toys
- Trains and train tracks

• Art Materials •

Parents are sometimes reluctant to give children "messy" art materials at home, which is a shame. It's essential for children to have this opportunity to experiment and create as much as possible. If finger painting seems too messy, you can always use foamy bathtub paints to provide a similarly tactile experience without the mess. If you can't tolerate an easel in your living room, you could allow your child to sit at a kitchen table with watercolor and paper or beads and pipe cleaners. At this age, it'll be necessary to supervise your child while she uses art materials so that her creation doesn't spread to the walls and scissors aren't used to give her little sister a haircut.

Art materials and craft ideas include:

- Paper. Construction paper, tissue paper, butcher-block paper, wrapping paper.
- Scissors and hole punchers.
- Glue, glue sticks, and tape.
- Drawing materials. Thick and thin crayons, markers, pencils, colored pencils, chalk, Cray-pas.
- Paint. Finger paint, watercolors, washable tempera, brushes (bristle and foam), sponges cut in shapes.

- Stamp pads and stamps.
- Other fun materials such as sequins, beads, stickers, pom-poms, feathers, wooden sticks, small wood pieces, yarn, wiggle eyes, brown paper bags, paper plates, boxes, cardboard tubes, cloth, ribbon, buttons, magazine pictures, picture frames, chalkboards, colored sand.

• Physical Play •

Physical play is essential so that children can let off steam and develop healthy bodies and a sense of well-being. So much is going on when a child plays physically. Her large and small motor strength is being built, and her muscles, nerves, and brain function are becoming better integrated. During physical activity, she becomes more aware of how her body moves through space. Can I fit through that tunnel? Will I bump into my friend coming down the slide? Do I need to slow down before I crash into that playhouse? When you encourage your child to ride a tricycle, the steering and peddling involved will require her to coordinate her visual and muscle functions with her spatial awareness. By throwing or kicking a ball, she improves her eye-hand coordination as well as the muscles in her arms and legs. Playground equipment is specifically designed to help children develop their sense of balance. By climbing, lifting, and carrying objects, she'll gain better upper body strength. Try to have your child play outdoors each day, weather permitting. You'll probably find your child sleeps much better and is more relaxed when she has had a chance to play physically, particularly if the activity takes place outdoors. Even if you're stuck in the house on a rainy day, you can put on music and dance around, or do yoga or aerobic moves.

Ideas for physical play include:

- Balls. Large and small for kicking, bouncing, and catching.

- Riding toys. Scooters and tricycles. Bicycle helmet.

- Child-sized basketball hoop.

- Child-sized padded soccer goal.

- Fat plastic bat and ball.

- Small bean bags and a container. (Use the container as a target.)

- Anything that involves being in the backyard, park, or playground.

• Music •

Children find music joyful, relaxing, and stimulating all at the same time. If you want your child to love music, it's important to play all kinds of music in your home, not just music created with children in mind. Give your child the time and space to move as the music plays. Give her shakers or pots to bang out rhythms—it's amazing how much pleasure children derive from making music with everyday objects. Music is also a great way to expose your child to different cultures and parts of the world.

Musical toys and instruments and activities for preschoolers include:

• Shakers	• Sand blocks
• Drums	• Wooden spoon and a pot
• Tambourines	• Tapes, records, and CDs
• Bells	• Space to dance
• Rhythm sticks	• Playing DJ
• Triangle	• Forming a family band

• Science •

Young children are naturally curious about nature and the world around them. When your child plays with soil, plants, insects, water, and other materials found in nature, she can take her curiosity to the next level. She'll be able to observe, predict, and draw conclusions from her hands-on experiences. Children love to take the seeds out of fruit or vegetables, to plant them, and then to water them each day and watch them grow. One of the all-time favorite school trips at the nursery school is going to the park to dig for worms.

Ideas and equipment for science play include:

• Bubble blowers.	• Toy binoculars.
• Magnifying glass.	• Insect nets and jars.
• Food coloring, water, and eyedroppers for experimenting with colored water.	• Shovels for digging in dirt.
	• Pails, cups, funnels, sieves, and wheels for playing with water.

Children love to see what sinks and what floats.

- Magnets. Go around the house and see what attracts.

- Freezing water in different containers to see the shapes they form.

- Collecting shells, rocks, and leaves.

- Planting seeds and bulbs. Popcorn kernels and lima beans are foolproof seeds for growing.

- Larvae for hatching butterflies and tadpoles for frogs (these can be ordered online).

• Small Manipulative Toys •

Small manipulative toys such as puzzles and shape sorters build dexterity and teach children about planning, spatial relationships, sorting, categorizing, and comparative relationships (big/small, many/few, high/low). By using different sized and shaped containers to pour water or sand back and forth, your child begins to grasp concepts of volume and size. All of the above activities teach ideas that are basic to math and science.

Small manipulative toys include:

- Puzzles of differing levels of difficulty

- Peg-Boards

- Parquetry blocks like Mighty Mind

- Shape sorters

- Magnetic boards with magnetic shapes, letters, and numbers

- Magnadoodle

- Colorforms

- Lacing cards

• Play Dough and Clay •

When play dough or clay is molded, squeezed, rolled, and shaped, the small muscles of the hands are developed and eye-hand coordination is improved. This is also an activity that's soothing and relaxing for your child. When you add rolling pins, cookie cutters, a garlic press, plastic knives, scissors, or sticks, you help extend the play and get your child ready for cooking.

• The Very Best Play Dough Recipe

6 cups water

6 cups flour

3 cups salt

A few drops of food coloring

4 tablespoons cream of tartar

12 tablespoons oil

Mix together all the ingredients with a hand mixer. A Pyrex bowl works best. Microwave for five minutes on high. Take out and stir very well. Microwave five more minutes. Stir very well again. Microwave seven more minutes. Allow the mixture to cool and then store in an airtight container.

• Organized Games •

In order to play organized games, children need to be mature enough to understand that they must follow the rules. This will require your child to move beyond her own individual desires and to grasp that everyone needs to comply with the parameters of the game, a life lesson that must be internalized in order for her to become a responsible member of a group. At first, younger children won't want to wait their turn, they won't want to play in the prescribed manner, and they're unlikely to accept that they have lost a game. You may want your child to play a board game or ball game the "correct" way, but you may also need to be flexible. Take into consideration your child's particular level of maturity and ability. Sometimes a game isn't appropriate for a child's skill level or has directions that are too complicated. It's fine to stop the game, change to another game, or simplify the rules in order to make the experience more enjoyable for your child.

Parents often ask us whether they should let their child win a game. It's only natural to want to allow your child to win, but it's also important that children experience what it feels like to lose as well. You can help your child understand this by modeling how to be a good loser. You might say, "I lost this time but maybe next time I'll win," or "Wow, you really played that game well. Let's play again." If your child refuses to lose, she might not be emotionally ready for the game in question. You might want to put the game away and try again in a few months. Ultimately, the goal for young children should be to finish the game rather than focusing on winning or losing. There are a number of games you can buy that use cooperative play to achieve the goal of the game, such as Hi Ho! Cherry-O, Orchard, and Snail's Pace Race. These can be more satisfying for young children.

Some other good games include:

- Dominos (with pictures and numbers)
- Lotto (with pictures)
- A "Memory" game
- Bingo (with colors, shapes, pictures, letters, and numbers)
- Board games. Some of our favorite board games for ages three to five include Ravensburger's 4 First Games, Things in My House, Pizza Parlor, and What's My Name
- Card games such as Go Fish, Old Maid, and War
- Hide-and-seek, relay races, and Duck, duck, goose

• Pretend Play and Dress Up •

When you give your child a hard hat, a stethoscope, or toy animals, she may pretend to be a construction worker, a doctor, or a veterinarian. During pretend play, she learns about her own identity and experiments with language ideas, roles, concepts, and feelings in a risk-free environment.

Stimuli for pretend play and dress up include:

- Toy vehicles
- Dolls, doll clothing, dollhouses, and furniture
- Farmhouses
- Toy people
- Toy food
- Pots, pans, plates, cups, utensils
- Mirrors
- Costume box
- Cash registers and play money
- Flashlights
- Sheets or blankets
- Shopping bags
- Clothing and accessories such as purses, briefcases, hats, shoes, jewelry, eyeglasses, and pieces of fabric; telephones; empty, clean

food containers, pizza boxes, and milk and juice cartons; menus, receipt pads, measuring cups and spoons, office supplies, computer keyboards, notepads, memo pads, envelopes, stickers, toy construction tools, doctor kits (complete with Band-Aids, cotton gauze, and cotton balls), puppets, and stuffed animals

---

• Bath Time •

Bath time is about so much more than just getting clean. Children love water play and the relaxation that being in water provides. When you give your child cups, funnels, floating toys, and sponges, she'll spend long periods of time experimenting and pretending.

Fun ideas for bath-time play include:

- Boats
- Foamy bathtub paints and crayons
- Goggles
- Snorkling mask and tube
- Bubble blower
- Pretend fishing rod
- Glove-puppet bath mits

• Other Fun Ideas •

Children love real things in addition to toys. Everyday objects can be just as much fun as a toy purchased in a toy store. Ellen remembers making cardboard houses from cartons with Alice, then painting the walls and creating cardboard furniture. This was one of Alice's favorite activities.

Some other fun ideas:

- Staple paper together to form a book, then have your child draw pictures while you write down the words of her story.
- Before you throw out broken appliances such as telephones, clocks, or computers, you can take them apart with your child

(supervise closely as small parts can easily be swallowed).

- Make a kite and fly it.

- Dissect flowers, fruits, and vegetables.

- Make a lemonade stand and sell lemonade to passers-by.

- Put on a family play.

- Give your child powder, baby shampoo, and bubble bath so she can make potions.

- Give your child a big bowl with cups of flour, water, and salt to experiment with.

- Make chocolate pudding finger paint.

- Create a treasure hunt. You can hunt for shapes, colors, or things that begin with a certain letter.

- Go on a pretend trip.

- Make up silly words for things.

- Play reverse roles.

How Children Play

Once you have provided your child with a space to play and a variety of toys, you can further support play by giving her a balance of time to play alone, with others, and with you. All of these types of play encourage skills, creativity, and fun.

• Independent Play •

In the rush to keep children busy and occupied, many parents forget the importance of independent play. If you think back to your own childhood, you may remember the pleasure you took in playing alone in your room, completely absorbed in your own world. Your dolls were your pretend students in your school. You made a city with pillows for your action figures. You spent hours engaged in making up stories and figuring out scenarios. In the same way, when your child plays alone, she has a chance to make her own choices and figure out the activities she enjoys. She gets to determine the pace and length of time spent doing an activity. When a child plays alone, she's learning how to be independent of adult direction and to keep herself occupied.

Never underestimate the importance of this type of play. Independent play prepares a young child for life in the future—a child who is unable to play alone is often the child who has difficulty doing her homework without assistance and may lack the confidence needed to make decisions. To support independent play, you can surround your child with a variety of toys and materials such as puzzles, art materials, books, dolls, cars, Legos, and blocks. If your child doesn't enjoy being alone, you can be near your child, sitting in the same room reading.

• Play with Others •

Children need to have lots of time playing with other children. Social skills can't be taught from books, videos, or lessons. They're learned when children spend time together. When children play with others on a regular basis, they begin to understand concepts of sharing and compromise and the reciprocal nature of relationships. They learn new vocabulary and new ideas. They extend their play and become more imaginative when they observe and interact with others.

At first, children tend to play near one another but not necessarily together. Even if your child isn't mature enough to actively engage with a playmate, it's still important to expose him to others as this will lead to greater interaction down the line. You can support your child by observing and making suggestions. When you see one child making sand castles next to your child in the sandbox, you can help extend the play by saying, "I see you are both making castles. Can we make a road to connect them?"

When two or more children begin playing together—sharing ideas and interacting with one another—they are now at the next level of play. This is a time for adults to stay in the background and supervise without stepping in too much. Sometimes you'll want to leave the children to explore on their own, and sometimes you may want to direct them a little more by setting up a simple game such as tag or Duck, duck, goose. However, children will often be able to come up with their own ideas and solve problems if left to their own devices.

For most children, cooperative play is the most exciting and the most challenging. Now your child needs to accommodate another child's ideas in order to have fun. When disagreements arise between playmates, the children acquire vital problem-solving skills. They learn to talk things through and how to cope when things don't go their way. Negotiating a game is a highly sophisticated process that teaches resilience and flexibility. When children play together, the play becomes increasingly elaborate, with each child drawing on the other's experience and imagination. One child has just gone on his first airplane trip and now wants to take his friend to California. His friend has read a book about outer space, and so when the playmates get to California, they take a trip to the moon. This requires an ability to think abstractly and more flexibly, which in turn leads to higher levels of understanding for both children.

As early childhood educators and experts have observed, children who spend time playing with others and developing healthy social relationships tend to be more successful in school. Think about some of the adults you know who are successful at their jobs. It's often because they are adept at relating to the people they're working with, not necessarily because they're the smartest person in the room. We believe that this ability to interact well with others is given a better chance to flourish when it's fostered at a very young age.

• Play with You •

When you take the time to play with your child, you're developing an understanding of how she thinks and how she relates to her world. You may not be aware that your child is interested in science until you see her playing a game that involves imaginary dinosaurs. You might discover your child tells wonderful stories when she plays, acting out the roles of different characters in different voices. You may learn that your child is afraid of the dark or going to the doctor when you overhear her conversations with her dolls. By taking this time to listen to your child's ideas, you gain a better knowledge of her interests and needs, and she gets a clear message that you value her thinking, which in turn helps to build her self-esteem.

You need to set aside time to play with your child. Modern life is busy, and most parents are guilty of telling their children, "Not now, later." If you can, try to carve out a block of time on the weekend or cancel one of your child's structured activities so that you can play together. If you're going to get involved, you need to come down to your child's level, slow your pace, and give her your undivided attention. Let the machine answer the phone, turn off the television, and mentally set aside your "to do" list. When you focus, listen, and observe, you can actively encourage and participate.

Some parents have told us that they feel uncomfortable playing—they simply don't know how to do it. It's true that play requires a level of spontaneity and lack of inhibition that many adults no longer possess. It's probably been a long time since you pretended to be a pirate or an astronaut. If you do feel self-conscious, try to follow your child's lead. Remember no one's watching and your child will love to see you being silly, fun, and free. Other parents can go too far with their involvement. They overdirect their child's play or feel compelled to use playtime as a teaching time: "Can you count the cars you lined up?" "What shape is that block?" "Let me show you how to draw a real tree." When you play with your child, there's no need to teach or become focused on making a finished product—in fact, your direction might inhibit your child's imagination and creativity. We find that when children are accustomed to being overly directed, they often wander around a classroom looking lost and overwhelmed by their choices. They may say to a teacher, "I don't know what to do."

Instead of directing your child's play, you can step back and observe what your child is doing and how she's using the toys or materials. Sometimes you'll just need to be physically close without talking or participating—this way you can know what she's playing and if there's a role for you either as a facilitator or a player. In general, it's best to think of yourself as a supporting player rather than the director of the game, and let your child tell you the role she wants you to play. Children have very little control over their lives, and this is the one appropriate, safe place for them to be in charge. As you observe and listen, you'll find natural ways to involve yourself. If your child is playing with her dolls, you could ask, "Is your baby hungry?" Wait for your child to respond and, if she answers, you can continue the conversation. You can also speak in the voice of the character you're playing. Don't feel the need to overtalk, however. The idea is to be supportive rather than dominant.

It's a good idea to suggest ways to extend the play. If your child is pretending to go camping, you can throw a sheet over a table and hand her a flashlight. If she's getting ready to take off for outer space, you can give her a bike helmet to ensure a safe landing. Don't be surprised or offended, however, if you don't get invited into the tent or if your idea of the helmet is rejected.

Many parents find it difficult to see a child struggling or experiencing frustration when playing. In fact, this is an important part of playing and learning. When you allow your child to struggle, you are helping her learn to tolerate her frustration and become a good problem solver. If you and your child are building with blocks, for example, you'll probably be tempted to prop up the structure that's about to tumble. Instead of fixing a problem for your child, however, it's more helpful to say, "Oh, the blocks didn't balance. Let's build it again" or "What do you think would work next time?" Never underestimate your child. She may surprise you with her creative solutions.

If your child is using art materials, your instinct will probably be to show your child how to use them or what to do with them. Bear in mind that it can be intimidating when an adult tells a child what she should be drawing or painting. This is one area where it's very important to take a backseat and allow your child the freedom to be creative. If your child asks you to draw something for her, it can be very hard to say no. Instead of drawing it for her, however, you can help by breaking down the task into small steps that she can do for herself. If your child asks you to draw a face, you can tell her: "First, draw a circle. Where do you think the eyes go? Can you make a line going down for a nose? Can you make a line going across for a mouth?"

Not all of us love all kinds of children's play. If you feel uncomfortable pretending to be a dinosaur or you hate board games, your child will sense this and won't have as much fun. When Nancy's children were little, they loved to play the board game Candyland, which their mother found incredibly tedious. When she mentioned this to a teacher, she got a very liberating reply: "You don't have to play Candyland if you don't like it!" Even if you don't participate directly, you can still be interested and available to your child. You can talk to her about her games and find other activities that you enjoy doing together. Remember, play should be just that, playful, if it's going to be fun. The most important thing is that you find some way to be involved. The preschool years pass very quickly, and soon both child and parent are too self-conscious to share the intimacy of these moments. When you interact with your child in this way, not only are you helping your child, you're letting her do something wonderful for you. You're allowing her to let you share in the pure, innocent fun of play.

Play and Gender

The issue of gender often arises when we talk about play with parents. Many parents are concerned that their daughters will only play pretend games even when they have Legos and puzzles or that their sons avoid art materials in favor of action figures. The reality is that boys and girls are different. As they grow, girls and boys often segregate their play into "feminine" and "masculine" choices, gravitating naturally toward certain toys and activities. Boys may be more active and exploratory, while girls are more likely to engage in cooperative play where verbal interaction determines the game. Boys may develop spatial abilities earlier, while girls often develop fine motor abilities earlier.

If children's play is limited to their areas of strength, however, it follows that they will be less evenly developed. While it's important to respect natural sex role differences, you can still encourage your child to engage in broader ways of playing using a wider range of materials. If your daughter only wants to dress up as a princess, you can play princess for a little while and then bring out a princess puzzle or use her blocks to build a castle. If your son only wants to play soccer, you could bring chalk outside for drawing when he takes a break. Make sure you keep an eye on the gender bias of your child's toys as well. Are they oriented toward girls? boys? neither? If one category predominates, you can introduce a variety of toys including those that are gender neutral.

During this period in your child's life, her ideas about what's male and female are beginning to be formed. As she grows, she's surrounded by powerful cultural and societal stereotypes that overtly and subtly influence her role and sense of identity. Young children think in absolute terms—if they've only seen Mommy cook, then for them, mommies are the ones who cook. Your attitude regarding gender is critical to your child's development. What you say, what you do, and the choices you make for your children will be the most important influence in this respect. Be aware of subtle messages in your own life. We've often observed children emulating the roles of their parents in the classroom. They'll say, "Daddies don't cook," or "Mommies can't go out to work." One child will tell another child, "You can't be the doctor; only boys can be doctors," because his pediatrician happens to be a man. When teachers hear and see play that's dominated by sexist themes, they'll use this as an opportunity to talk about stereotypes and to suggest alternatives: "Did you know Susie's mommy is a doctor?" If you consciously choose nontraditional activities when playing with your child—Mom pretends to be the firefighter and Dad diapers the baby doll—you're helping her to develop a sense of equality between the sexes.

Some other good techniques for facilitating nonsexist play include:

- Mixing boys and girls for group activities.

- Adding pretend tools to the dress-up box and introducing toy people when your child is building with Legos or blocks.

- Using language that enables girls to assert themselves ("Tell Scott that girls are allowed to play this game") and boys to communicate a need for affection ("I see you need a hug. Are you feeling sad?").

- Encouraging girls to use toys that develop spatial skills and boys to use art materials.

- Reading books and other materials that demonstrate nonstereotypical roles and have inclusive messages such as *Sheila Rae, the Brave* by Kevin Henkes and *William's Doll* by Charlotte Zolotow. Books like these show that girls can be courageous and boys can be gentle. If you don't like the gender bias of a more traditional story, you can revise the story as you read, switching the sex roles.

- Being aware of subtle messages of encouragement or discouragement such as telling your daughter not to climb too high while admiring your son's strength and agility.

- Knowing it's okay to roughhouse with your girls and cuddle with your boys.

- Saving special clothing for special occasions. Dressing your daughter in a long dress and party shoes for school means that she'll feel inhibited playing physically or in messy situations. A boy wearing a superhero shirt and cape will probably limit his play to this specific scenario.

At the same time, don't become concerned if your child wants to engage in nontraditional gender play. At this age, children are only just beginning to understand that gender identity is stable and consistent over time. This is often the time when boys will play at being mommies and girls will play at being daddies. Sometimes parents find this type of play upsetting, but keep in mind that it's an important part of normal development. If your son wants to dress up as a bride or your daughter wants to be a superhero, there's no need to react negatively. Children gain an understanding of different roles by playing and experimenting in this way.

Superhero Play

When your child turns four, it's almost inevitable that sweet little Jonathan is going to transform overnight into Batman or Superman or the superhero of the moment. This can happen even if he's never seen a DVD or television show, or owned an action figure. Preschool-age boys—and some girls, but primarily boys—will be drawn to this kind of play. This is not a new phenomenon. Cowboys and Indians, cops and robbers, GI Joe, and toy soldiers have been favorite activities and toys for generations of children. Many parents feel ambivalent about this type of aggressive play, and while it's only natural to be concerned about your child acting out seemingly violent scenarios, there are various reasons why this type of play is so appealing to your child:

- Superhero play helps your child build relationships with his peers because they're playing a common game with a common theme that everyone can understand.

- As your child grows and becomes more independent, he's also aware of how small he is in a very large world. He may begin to look for ways to feel powerful at a time when he's quite vulnerable. When he takes on the role of a superhero with magical powers and great strength, this helps him to feel more in control of his world, giving him a safe way of working out very big feelings. When he's Batman, he can assert himself in ways that may not feel comfortable otherwise; he can try out new words and expressions that are more aggressive and manage his fears with greater confidence. You can sometimes turn this type of play to your advantage. When your child is fearful of monsters under his bed, you can suggest he play at being a "super monster catcher."

- This is an age when children struggle with controlling their impulses. They're learning rules of behavior in school and at home but are still working to internalize them. Superhero play helps your child to define right and wrong in very concrete terms. Superhero narratives revolve around the battle of good and evil. When good guys win, they gain mastery over their "bad" impulses, and this can be a constructive way to channel a child's natural tendencies. Girls will often deal with similar feelings by acting out fairy tales where the good witch overpowers the wicked witch.

Even though there are some real benefits to superhero play, it can easily become overstimulating and lead to real fighting and harmful physical aggression. We remember a particular class where the boys were obsessed with Power Rangers. They wore Power Ranger shirts, brought their lunches in Power Ranger lunch bags, and had Power Ranger backpacks. Their play centered around karate kicks and chops and every object they touched was morphed into a weapon. Other children were frightened or excluded if they didn't want to play in this way. We talked to the parents and suggested that they limit television shows and videos of this kind and that they stop sending the children to school with Power Ranger items. Although the rough play didn't completely disappear, the children became less preoccupied with Power Rangers and were able to engage in other kinds of play that were more inclusive and less aggressive.

You can usually tell when superhero play is spiraling out of control. At first, the children are running around the playground saving people. Soon, the play becomes more physical. The tone of the play changes. The children's voices sound angry or fearful. The pretend karate chops in the air change to actual physical contact. Spiderman starts wrestling Batman to the ground. Batman begins to cry and hits Spiderman. Soon both children are in tears. These children need an adult to help redirect their play and to give them words to express their feelings. An adult who is supervising can anticipate when things are escalating and someone might get hurt. Superman and Batman might not end up in tears if they're given another energetic game or activity to play. You can suggest that the boys see how fast they can run or if they can climb to the top of the monkey bars to "save the kitten stuck in the tree." You can use the children's action figures to act out the story or write a book about a superhero. If the children are too overstimulated by their play, it's best to take a short break or change the activity altogether. You can also teach your child what to say when he becomes frightened by another child's play, that it's okay to tell his friend, "I don't like this game. That hurts me. I don't like when you make that scary face."

Another issue parents often struggle with is whether to allow their children to play with toy guns or other pretend weapons. You'll need to decide if you'll allow this in your home, depending on how strongly you feel about this issue. In any case, you have a responsibility to let your child know that real weapons hurt people. This is a good opportunity to share your feelings about violent behavior and to let your child know that there's a difference between a real gun or sword and one that's pretend or comes from someone's imagination. Even if you don't allow toy guns in your home, it's possible that your child will make a pretend gun out of Legos, pretzels, or his fingers. When this happens, it's advisable not to make a big deal out of this behavior or you'll only increase its appeal for your child. When the play becomes excessively hostile or someone gets upset, of course you'll want to intervene.

If your child has become preoccupied with aggressive play, and it's difficult to engage him in other forms of play, you'll have to set clear limits. Here are some things you can do:

- Limit how long and how often he engages in superhero play.

- Set ground rules—no hurting, no weapons.

- End the play if anyone is getting frightened, bullied, or hurt.

- Limit exposure to television, DVDs, movies, and toys that promote violence.

- Tell your child that superhero clothing isn't appropriate for school. You need to set limits on how often and where your child is allowed to dress up like this.

- If your child engages you in superhero play, use it as an opportunity to introduce ways of solving problems in ways other than fighting.

- You don't need to call your child by his superhero name even if he insists. "I know you like to pretend you are Batman, but at the dinner table you're Jonathan."

- Positively reinforce his other accomplishments and praise his kind and gentle actions.

- Introduce the idea of real-life heroes to your child. "Firefighters and police are the true superheroes. They're brave; they help people and keep them safe."

Screen Time

• TV and Videos/DVDs •

When you were a child, your parents probably worried about how much television you watched. Today, in addition to TV, there are so many ways that your child can spend time in front of a screen. More and more TV programs, videos/DVDs, and computer games are geared toward preschoolers, tempting parents to expose their children to a large amount of screen time at very young ages. According to recent studies, the average child watches television four hours a day. Evidently this is far too much. The American Academy of Pediatrics recommends that children under the age of two have no screen time and older children have no more than one to two hours of quality TV per day.

Most parents are instinctively aware that TV isn't good for their children. When a child is in front of a screen, she's sedentary and passive, she's not using any special skills, and she's not interacting with anyone. TV is a one-dimensional experience that doesn't allow for firsthand experimentation or exploration, which is the way children learn best. Although children may look happy and relaxed while watching TV, they're often cranky or irritable when it's turned off. We've seen that children who are exposed to TV for long periods each day tend to have difficulty focusing their attention and have less patience for listening without stimulating visuals. The immediate gratification of TV can actually impede a child's tolerance of frustration. This can cause problems at school where the pace is slower and where teachers require children to focus for longer periods of time in order to complete a task.

Let's be realistic. There are times in your day when a TV program or a DVD is a lifesaver. When the baby is crying and your three-year-old is whining while you're trying to make dinner, putting on your child's favorite movie is the only thing that will save your sanity. Although there's nothing inherently wrong with turning on the TV, you do need to pay attention to how much time your child is sitting in front of a TV or computer and what your child is watching. These early years in your child's life are the time when you can have the greatest influence in helping to establish lifelong habits.

Here are some other good things to keep in mind:

- Think about how much time you spend in meaningful conversation with your child compared to the time your family spends with the television on. Make sure the ratio is heavily slanted toward meaningful time with your family. Overall, screen time should be limited to one to two hours maximum per day, and that includes computer time.

- Tell your child she needs to ask permission to turn on the TV. Then you can set the limit before she begins to watch, select a specific TV show, and turn the TV off when it's over. Some parents prefer to have only videos/DVDs for their children so that no one gets lured into arguments about watching the next show. You could always use a timer if your child is having trouble ending a TV session: "When the bell rings, that means it's time to play." If your child continues to whine once the program is over, then plan to have fun activities ready to distract her.

- Keep the TV turned off during mealtimes and transition times. Sometimes parents will turn the TV on for "company" while the children are eating. Even if you're not eating with your child, you should still treat mealtimes as a social experience. If you want your child to be able to converse and have good manners at the dinner table, you need to set the expectation and practice it. On school days, it's a good idea to avoid turning on the TV when you're trying to get your child dressed, fed, and out of the house. This will help avoid arguments about turning off the TV when it's time to leave.

- Remember that young children have difficulty separating fantasy and reality. For your child, what she sees on TV seems real and she may become frightened or upset by the programs she watches. Your child may ask, "Is the witch really coming to my house?" "Is the lion under the bed?" "Did the mommy really get hurt?" These fears are real and should be taken seriously. You can help your child by reminding her that the program is make-believe, that the story was made up, and that grown-ups wrote it down and made it into a film for TV. In general, you should avoid programs with scary or violent content, and make sure your child doesn't watch TV just before bedtime.

- From time to time, you should watch with your child and talk about what you see. Many children's programs, especially cartoons and superhero shows, contain aggressive and violent content. These programs rarely show the real consequences of violence, so you'll need to talk about these with your child. Many TV shows and commercials perpetuate subtle stereotypes about gender and race, and over time, these can influence your child's attitudes. Have you ever seen a man cleaning a bathroom or doing the laundry in a commercial? When you sit and watch with your child, you can use programs and commercials as teaching tools, encouraging her to become a critical viewer. You can ask her questions, explain actions that you see, and elicit her ideas about what she's seen. Another way of counteracting negative stereotypes on TV is to expose your child to nonbiased examples in books and activities. When you extend the ideas you've seen on TV in this way, you're turning the passive experience into something more active.

Play: Why, What, and How?

- Try to have your child watch videos/DVDs or noncommercial TV as often as possible. This way you can avoid advertisements aimed at young children that usually promote materialism and unhealthy eating habits. If your child sees the latest sugary cereal on TV, you can guarantee she's going to plead for it when you're at the supermarket. Too much exposure to commercials can create conflicts between you and your child as you try to establish healthy values and good nutrition. You need to explain that commercials are for selling things and talk about the messages with your child. She'll most likely still hear about these things from her friends, but you can lessen the impact of the marketing in this way.

- Plan ahead and pick programs that are geared to young children and that have socially positive themes. Programs such as *Dora the Explorer, Go, Diego, Go!,* and *Sesame Street* promote concepts like sharing, cooperating, and dealing with feelings or new situations, and they expose children to number and letter concepts. Nature and science programs are great ways to introduce your child to new ideas and different parts of the world. Although digging for worms in the backyard is always a better alternative to watching TV, your child won't be able to see penguins in Antarctica or monkeys in the rainforest unless she watches Animal Planet. Quality programming can actively stimulate your child's imagination and fantasy life—after watching a fictional film or TV show, she may take the parts of the characters she's seen and act out scenarios. Many children we know enjoy watching the Food Network because the pace of the programs is slower, and they find the step-by-step process of making the food interesting.

- Bear in mind that the news can be incredibly disturbing for young children. Reports of fires, extreme weather, killings, shootings, abductions, and violent crime are regular stories on local news programs. These can terrify children who take everything they see at face value. After September 11, the news repeatedly showed the twin towers collapsing; young children had no understanding that this was a single event and thought that the towers were falling over and over again. When the newscaster talks about a hurricane in Florida, your child in New York may get the impression that the hurricane is happening here and now.

- Don't use TV time as a reward or treat it as an illegal pleasure. This will only increase its appeal for your child. However, when you threaten to take TV time away, this can be an effective incentive. Instead of saying, "If you clean up your room, you get to watch TV," you can say, "If you don't clean up your room, there's no TV today." When you use the latter phrasing, it usually gets results.

- Be a good role model for your child in your own TV-watching habits. As with everything else you do as a parent, what you do influences your child as much as anything you say. Think about your own viewing habits. Adults are in the habit of turning on the television as background noise while getting dressed, making meals, or talking on the phone. Remember that even when your young child seems to be busy playing, she's aware of what is being shown and said on TV. Unlike you, she can't filter out something that's right in front of her. We've heard children talking about inappropriate things they've seen on soap operas or other adult programs that are very confusing and upsetting to them. Ellen once saw a four-year-old boy and girl kissing in a very adult way. She asked them what they were doing, and they said, "We saw a man and a lady kissing on TV."

- If all else fails, unplug the TV and tell your child it's broken. This really works.

• Computers •

When you're calculating the amount of time your child is spending in front of a screen, you need to take into account computer time as well. Although playing on the computer is more interactive than watching TV, it's still a sedentary activity where your child is staring at two-dimensional images.

Parents often ask us, "Does my child need to learn how to use the computer?" Although children as young as three can use a mouse and may enjoy playing a computer game, it's important to think about how a child actually benefits from this. By playing on a computer, children can develop skills such as memory, eye-hand coordination, visual perception, small muscle control, planning, classifying, or number and letter recognition. Some children will feel freer to take risks with the less threatening interaction a computer offers. However, as any early childhood educator or expert will tell you, children learn best through hands-on experience. To truly learn, a child needs to play with a range of different materials that stimulate all her senses. In other words, computer time should never be valued over playtime.

Play: Why, What, and How?

There are various negative aspects to computer play. No matter which software you choose, ultimately, the computer determines the outcome. Computer games can actually limit creative thinking, problem solving, and language experience. Regular play, by comparison, offers a far greater degree of flexibility and many more opportunities for experimentation. The other problem with the computer, especially at home, is that it can easily become a solitary activity. In a classroom, children rarely use a computer alone. You'll see several children taking turns and working cooperatively. If your child likes to play on the computer, it's a good idea to participate with her.

In the final analysis, there's really no need to rush out to buy a special computer or software for your three- to five-year-old. By kindergarten-age, most schools will introduce computers to children. That's early enough for your child to become computer savvy.

If you are going to allow your child time at the computer, however, here are some things to keep in mind:

- Don't use the computer as a babysitter.

- Be very selective when choosing software. Make sure it's age appropriate.

- Differentiate between your need for your child to be computer literate and your child's actual needs.

- Let your child proceed at her own pace.

- Encourage your child to experience hands-on activities that will enable her to use a computer in a more meaningful way as she grows. Anything to do with eye-hand coordination or using her small hand muscles will help her to develop the skills she'll need for computer use when she's older.

- Don't put a computer in your child's room.

Young children can learn everything a computer can teach them—and more—by engaging in active play. The most brilliant computer program could never simulate the actual experience of making a tent from bedcovers, climbing inside, and seeing flashlight patterns in the dark. And no matter how much fun your child derives from the virtual world, nothing trumps the look on her face when she sees her first customer at her real-life lemonade stand. Even the best computer games and educational TV programs won't ever be able to match the fun of that.

Recommended Books for Children

NONBIASED BOOKS

People	Aliki
We Are All Alike/We Are All Different	Cheltenham Elementary School kindergartners
The Brand New Kid	Katie Couric
A Kaleidoscope of Kids	Emma Damon
Whoever You Are	Mem Fox
I'm Like You, You're Like Me	Cindy Gainer
Sheila Rae, the Brave	Kevin Henkes
Two Eyes, a Nose, and a Mouth	Roberta Grobel Intrater
The Colors of Us	Karen Katz
Here Are My Hands	Bill Martin Jr. and John Archambault
We All Sing with the Same Voice	J. Philip Miller and Sheppard M. Greene
The Daddy Book	Todd Parr
It's Okay to Be Different	Todd Parr
The Mommy Book	Todd Parr
Martin's Big Words	Doreen Rappaport
Yo! Yes?	Chris Raschka
If We Were All the Same	Fred Rogers
Brave Irene	William Steig
The Skin You Live In	Michael Tyler
William's Doll	Charlotte Zolotow

ACTIVITY BOOKS

Wonderplay	Fretta Reitzes and Beth Teitelman
Playing Together	Wendy Smolen

Chapter Thirteen

TALKING ABOUT DIFFICULT TOPICS

At some point in your child's early years, you're going to have to talk to him about topics that you may find difficult or that you sense he finds upsetting. Your first response is going to be to protect him from these issues. If this is an "adult" topic such as death, sex, illness, or divorce, you may want to avoid the subject altogether. Despite your feelings of unease, however, it's important that you talk to your child in an age-appropriate way about these things as they come up. If you withhold information, you run the risk that your child may overhear a conversation or somehow find out the very information that you're trying to keep from him. Many times, a child will report to a teacher, "My mommy's having a baby," or "My grandma's sick in the hospital," when the school has been informed that the child "doesn't know" about these things. Instead of concealing sensitive issues from your child, you need to think about how and when to talk to him so that he doesn't misinterpret what's going on and become anxious as a result.

You may worry that you don't have the words to adequately explain the subject. You may think your child is too young. You won't want to upset him. It can help to remember that you have a very different level of understanding and usually some "baggage" that you bring with you to these difficult topics. Keep in mind that children are new to the world and see things in their own way. Your child may react to your explanations in ways you couldn't have anticipated. When Michael was five, he asked Nancy, "Do you have to have sex to have a baby?" Nancy thought this was a very straightforward question that needed a simple, straightforward answer. She responded confidently, "Yes." Michael looked at her and said, "Oh . . . What's sex?" It's always a good idea to ask your child, "What do you think?" before giving your own answer so that you can assess his actual level of understanding.

In other instances, you may forget that something that's easy for you can be difficult for your child. At this age, children are experiencing everything for the first time. For under-fives, transitions and new experiences of all kinds can be stressful. Many times parents assume that children will "just handle" these new situations, failing to remember how confusing and unsettling it can be to do something you've never done before. Things that your child may find difficult include starting a new school, moving, having a new sibling, getting a new caregiver, or even just going to the dentist. As you won't always be able to predict the nature of your child's concerns, you'll need to listen and provide the necessary reassurance. When Charles was about to start summer camp for the first time, he anxiously asked Ellen, "How will they know my name?" Ellen couldn't have guessed that her son would worry about this. She tried not to show her own concern and told him all of the children would be wearing name tags and the counselor had a list of names for each child in the group. Then Charles asked, "How will I know where to go when I get off the bus?" Ellen explained that Dave, the bus counselor, would take him to his group. By breaking it down and addressing each one of his worries with a concrete answer, Ellen helped Charles feel more confident about going to camp.

Your child will benefit greatly when you take the time to calmly answer his questions without transmitting your own anxiety. When you're clear and honest and when you explain a little but not too much, your child will most likely accept your explanation without becoming too upset. If you resist telling your child or anxiously tell him too much, you may find that he becomes perplexed or overly concerned. These are topics that you'll need to talk about at each stage of his development. The ways in which you support him now will form the basis for future conversations as he grows.

Dealing with Difficult Topics as They Arise

Here are some good rules of thumb for talking about difficult topics with your child:

- Be sensitive to your child's age, temperament, and degree of interest. A three-year-old cannot fully understand things in the same way an older child might. A highly anxious child may overreact if you give him too much information too soon. An inquisitive child may look for more information. You'll need to tailor your explanations and answers accordingly.

Talking About Difficult Topics

- Use books to open the door to conversation and to help your child find the words to express his concerns. If you have time, you can make your own book. A personalized story about visiting a sick relative, for example, can be very comforting to a young child encountering someone with a serious illness for the first time.

- Avoid anxiously saying too much. Although it's important to talk to your child, you should always be cautious of overdoing it. If your child is going to the doctor and you know he's going to need three injections, it's best to keep your explanation brief. You can simply say, "The doctor needs to give you shots to keep you healthy. I'll be here to hold you, and it will be over very fast."

- Don't give information too far in advance. There's no point in telling your three-year-old that he's going to the dentist "next week." For a child, a week is an eternity. It's better to wait until the morning of the dentist visit to prepare him. You're better off dealing with the situation shortly before it happens rather than telling your child in advance about something that you know is going to upset him.

- Remember that any difficult topic has to be doled out in very small amounts. Rather than overwhelming your child with information, tell him a little bit, and add more when he seems ready to hear it. He'll ask as much as he needs to know at each stage of his development. As he grows, you can tailor the conversation to his next level of understanding.

- Try role-playing with your child. Many children benefit from role-playing a new situation before it happens. You can act out a scenario or play with dolls or puppets to demonstrate what's going to take place. A child who's fearful of going to the doctor can give his teddy bear an examination with his doctor kit. He can practice giving a shot and tell his doll that it'll only feel like a pinch.

- Remember that your facial expression and tone of voice will express more than the words you use. It can take a lot of self-control and self-awareness to keep a calm demeanor when you're feeling worried, anxious, upset, or uncomfortable. But by showing your child that you're coping and by being a good role model, you're making him feel secure in your strength.

- Pause before answering. It's important that you take the time to think through what you want to say and how you are going to say it before giving information or responding to your child's questions. If a sensitive topic comes up at the supermarket checkout or you need time to consider your answer, it's okay to wait until later. Children will accept it when you say, "I have to think about that," or "Let's talk about it later or tomorrow." This will also give you the opportunity to discuss with your partner how you're going to explain these issues. Just remember to bring it up again with your child within a short period of time so that he knows you're responsive to his questions and concerns. If you avoid the subject, your child will surely raise it with you.

- Maintain routines and be there for your child. During times of transition or new experiences, you need to give your child lots of attention and plenty of hugs. Routines and clear limits will be comforting and necessary to a child who feels that things are out of his control. Simplifying his life with fewer activities and more time for play and relaxation can also be helpful.

- Keep your child's school informed. If something has happened in your family's life that might affect a child—such as the death of a relative, a move, or some other major change—it's very helpful to share that information with your child's school. Let relatives and teachers know exactly how much you have told your child about the situation so that the information he receives is consistent.

Transitions and New Experiences

If your child is going to a new school or to camp for the first time, you'll be aware that these experiences may be unsettling for him. But it may not be so obvious when your child reacts fearfully to things that seem straightforward to adults. One year at the nursery school's summer camp, we'd planned a "Teddy Bear Picnic" day where each child brought his teddy bear from home. One parent told us that her four-year-old, Noah, had been afraid to come to camp that morning. When his mother asked Noah what was wrong, he told her that he was afraid there would be real bears at the picnic.

Many things that are apparently easy for adults—such as going on vacation or to a movie—can trigger intense fears and emotion in a child. Perhaps your child is worried because he doesn't know where he's going to sleep on vacation or because he doesn't like being in the dark at the movie theater. Remember that every child will react differently according to his degree of sensitivity, and you'll need to tune in to his individual worries and address these specifically in order to reassure him.

Young children aren't always able to put their feelings into words. When children can't identify or explain their emotions, their discomfort will often manifest itself in behavioral or physical symptoms. When Danny, a child in one of the nursery school classrooms, was five years old, he began persistently blinking his eyes. This tic coincided with the end of the school year, so we assumed that Danny was feeling anxious about leaving nursery school. Danny's pediatrician reassured his parents that there was nothing physically wrong and that instead of calling attention to the blinking, they should give their child more frequent hugs. The blinking stopped after a short time.

Other physical symptoms of unease in children include stomachaches, headaches, facial tics, stuttering, and chewing on clothing. Some children may become overstimulated, aggressive, or irritable. Others may regress to younger behaviors such as toilet accidents, sleep disturbances, or baby talk. When a child becomes fearful of things that never bothered him before, such as going to bed in a dark room, this may be another sign that he's anxious or upset. The first thing you can do is to ask your child's teacher if she's seen any change in your child recently. Then you can take a look at what's going on in your family and in your child's daily life to see if you can identify a specific cause. Often it's the case that young children display uncharacteristic behaviors during developmental growth spurts and usually there's no reason to be concerned. Most of the time your child's reactions are transitory and will pass once he's adjusted. We tell parents that a typical period of adjustment is six to eight weeks. If any of these behaviors continue or intensify, you may want to consult your pediatrician.

Some things that may trigger anxiety in young children and that adults often overlook include:

- Moving to a new classroom within the same school.

- Going to a movie or a concert.

- The transition from school to camp or camp to school.

- Getting a haircut.

- Staying at a hotel.

- Going on an airplane.

- Staying overnight in someone else's home, even if it's a close relative or friend.

Moving

Whether you're moving across the street or across the country, moving is stressful for the entire family. Many parents become so preoccupied with packing and organizing that they forget how confusing this experience can be for a young child. At this age, your child doesn't have the benefit of prior experience and probably won't be able to comprehend what moving actually means. One family told us about their four-year-old daughter, who turned to her parents on the day of the move and said, "You mean my toys are coming with us?" Often children won't automatically understand that their toys and furniture are moving too. Another common misunderstanding we've heard about is the child who doesn't realize that the whole family is moving together.

Things you can do to help your child transition during a move:

- Wait to tell your child. Most young children don't understand the concept of time. When you tell your child that the family's moving, he'll probably assume that this is happening tomorrow at the latest. Once your plans are definite—in other words when the contracts are signed and the movers are booked—this is a good time to tell your child. Certainly once you start packing, your child needs to be told.

- Although you may be excited or anxious about this transition, it's important that you remain as outwardly calm as you can during the time leading up to the move. Be aware of the things you say, as well as your tone, manner, and facial expressions when your child is in the room. If your child feels that things are under control, he's less likely to become worried or confused.

- Break it down into simple terms and explain what's going to take place. As you begin to pack, you can tell your child that you're going to put everything in boxes and that a big truck is going to come and take the things to your new home. You can explain that the whole family will follow the truck in the car together. Children are concrete thinkers and will be able to understand the concept of moving if they can picture where they're going. If you can visit or show your child photos of his new home, he'll be able to create a mental image.

- Instead of focusing on the things that are going to change, remind your child about all the things that will stay the same. "The family is going to be together. Grandma and Grandpa will still visit on Sunday. I'll still take you to school every day." Children are comforted by things that are familiar to them.

- Involve your child in the packing. Your child will need to be reassured that his things are moving too. The day before you move, you can give your child a box and tell him to put his favorite toys inside. This way he won't feel that his possessions have mysteriously disappeared. Instead of putting this box in the truck, you can keep it with you so that your child can unpack his things as soon as you arrive.

- Ask the moving people to put your child's furniture in the truck last so that it can be unpacked first. It helps if you can arrange to have your child's room set up before all the other rooms in the house so that your child has a chance to play while you finish the move.

- During this period of transition, routines and schedules should remain stable so that your child feels secure. Keep other transitions to a minimum. Toilet training or moving your child from a crib to a bed should definitely be postponed, as these will only further unsettle your child. Although you may want to buy a new bed or sheets for your child's new room, it's a good idea to use his old bed and bedding during this early stage. His familiar things will help him to feel more at home.

- If your child is moving to a new school at the same time, schedule your move before the start of a new school year if possible. This way your child will have the opportunity to transition to a new class along with the other children. Once you've moved, you should contact your child's new school and get one or two names of children who'll be in your child's class. Although they may not end up as friends, a familiar face and name can help ease the adjustment. If you invite old friends to visit you in your new home or write letters or make phone calls with your child to old friends, this will create continuity and make him feel special.

- Expect that your child may regress or show changes in behavior such as baby talk, sleep disturbances, bed-wetting, and clinginess. In our experience, it can take children at least six to eight weeks to adjust to a new school or home. After this period, if your child is still showing signs of distress, you should consult your pediatrician.

- Stay home. While your child is adjusting to his new environment, it helps if at least one parent stays home as much as possible. It's not a good idea to schedule a babysitter in the evenings for at least the first few weeks. Remember, it will take time for the whole family to adjust.

Sex

It's usually a good idea to start talking about sex much earlier than you might assume is necessary. Nancy's sister-in-law, Margie, didn't talk about sex with her twin sons until they were twelve years old, assuming that they weren't old enough until they were nearly teenagers. She asked her husband, Ronnie, to speak to them since she was uncomfortable doing this herself. She waited anxiously for Ronnie to come back and tell her what had happened. After a considerable length of time, her husband returned and announced, "Well, I just learned a lot of new things!"

It's a fact that children will begin discussing sex with each other at very young ages, and this includes preschool-age children. Sex is a subject that all children are curious about and find interesting. We believe that it's always best when children learn about sex from their parents rather than from friends or someone else's older sibling. Children are naturally intrigued by their bodies. At different stages in your child's development, he's going to ask you questions about his body or show an interest in how bodies work. How you answer these questions will set the stage for all future communication about sex. While it's only natural to feel conflicted about how best to reply, if you are evasive or seem embarrassed, you're sending your child the message that he was wrong to ask you the question. This may lead him to avoid coming to you when he needs information in the future.

Talking About Difficult Topics

Some good things to bear in mind when answering your child's questions about sex:

- Use correct anatomical terms for body parts. Young children's first questions about sex usually center around their bodies, how boys and girls look different, and questions about pregnancy and childbirth. When you use anatomically correct vocabulary, your child will learn words that he can use when he needs to ask you questions later on. Instead of telling your child that "Mommy has a baby in her tummy," you can use this opportunity to teach the words "womb" or "uterus," which are more accurate and less confusing. If you grew up calling your penis a "pee pee" or you refer to your vagina as "down there," it might take time to get comfortable using anatomical words with your child.

- Answer directly and honestly in a straightforward manner. When your child wants to know, "How did the baby get in your uterus?" there's no need to overcomplicate things or overwhelm him with too much information. Instead of embarking on a long-winded explanation about "the birds and the bees," you can tell him, "Because a uterus is where babies grow." Then wait until he asks the next question. Your child will ask for more information when he's ready to know more.

- Try to discover your child's existing level of understanding. If your child wants to know where babies come from, you can respond by asking him, "How do you think babies are born?" You'll discover by his answer how much he knows and where he is developmentally. There's the well-known story about the child who asked his parent, "Where did I come from?" The parent went into a detailed explanation of how babies are born. The child looked quizzically at the parent and said, "No, I mean, was I born in Philadelphia?"

- Read age-appropriate books about this subject and share them with your child. When five-year-old Michael began asking questions about sex, Nancy told him, "Let me think about that." She went to a bookstore and read up on the subject. She bought Michael a book she felt comfortable with that was suitable for his age. She told Michael that the book was something that they could read together and talk about. Of course that didn't keep him from calling his friend Charles to share his new information.

Practical Wisdom for Parents

• Overstimulation •

When children reach age four, they usually become much more aware of their bodies and curious about sexuality. As a result, they can become easily overstimulated. A parent came to us with an issue that's very typical for children this age. Her four-year-old daughter, Catherine, had been on a playdate with a boy in her class. Later that day, Catherine told her mother that she showed Alexander her vagina and he showed her his penis while they were playing dress up. The mother's instinct was to tell her daughter calmly and clearly that boys and girls do not show each other their private parts. This incident made her think about whether Catherine should still bathe with her six-year-old brother and be in the bathroom with her father when he was naked. This mother wisely understood that her daughter was overstimulated by her exposure to their nudity and it was time to change the way the family handled this.

If your child seems overly interested in a friend's or sibling's body—whether they're the same or opposite sex—it's a good idea to start having separate bath times. If you're used to bathing with your child, walking around undressed, or having your child accompany you to the bathroom, you may decide that you need to introduce the idea of privacy around age four. You can start by closing the door when you're showering or naked. Tell your child: "When people are naked or bathing or using the bathroom, they sometimes like to have privacy. As you get older, you'll need privacy too." Although you don't want your child to feel self-conscious or ashamed of his sexual curiosity, you do want him to learn that touching someone's "private parts" or being touched is inappropriate. If your child is touching your breasts, you can gently redirect him with more appropriate physical affection.

It's very common for young children to masturbate. From the time they're born, children can derive pleasure from touching their genitals. If you see your child masturbating, you can teach him that touching himself is fine, but he needs to do this in a private place like his room. Even if you're uncomfortable about it, it's important that you handle this in a nonjudgmental way so your child won't feel embarrassed or ashamed of his actions. If your child is masturbating very frequently or his teacher mentions that it's occurring in school, this may be a sign that he's experiencing tension. Try to identify the causes—there may be issues at home or at school that are creating stress.

• Being a Good Role Model •

Unfortunately, young children are exposed to many sexually provocative images and messages long before they're ready to understand them. On any given day, a child walking along a street is likely to see scantily clad mannequins in store windows, images of men and women embracing on billboards and buses, and half-naked women on the covers of magazines at the newsstand. Although it's impossible to protect your child from these outside influences, remember that you and your partner are your child's most important influences. What you wear, what you buy for your child to wear, what you watch on television, the magazines you read, the language you use, how you treat your partner and members of the opposite sex—all of these will inform your child about healthy relationships and set the example. When you're respectful of your partner, show affection, and take pleasure in each other's company, you're providing a positive model for your child's future relationships. It's also a very good idea to avoid adult-style clothing for your daughter. It can be very confusing for a four-year-old if her parents decide to dress her like a mini-teenager.

Divorce

It's well-known that 40 to 50 percent of all marriages in this country end in divorce. Whatever a couple's reasons for separating, this can be highly stressful and emotionally charged for the whole family. You may be feeling angry, sad, or guilty, and your energy and reserves will be low. Meanwhile, your child needs you to be strong during a period when you're feeling extremely vulnerable. A change of this magnitude can only be unsettling and upsetting for young children. Typical reactions to divorce in children include anger, sadness, confusion, anxiety, and feelings of rejection or guilt. During this time your child's behavior may regress. He may test limits or become aggressive or anxious to please. You may find he becomes easily distressed when separating from you. He'll most likely act out as a way of getting your attention.

The best thing you can do for your child during this period is to maintain your regular expectations and routines. Your child will get through this if he feels loved and secure. Now more than ever, you need to find the strength to support your child's physical and emotional well-being. Listen to him and make time to observe his behavior and reactions. Be there for him and be consistent in your attention and approach. Although there's no "easy" way to separate, if you're sensitive to your child, you'll help to ease the way. You may find that you actually derive strength from knowing that your child needs you to be strong during this time.

Some other ideas that you may find helpful:

- Your child doesn't need to be told about a separation or divorce until you know for certain that you'll be separating and have made plans for other living arrangements. If possible, it's best for both parents to be present when telling a child.

- When you talk to your child about the divorce, bear in mind that he won't have any context for this information. Children under five have a very limited understanding of adult relationships. Simple, direct, and honest language is best: "Mommy and Daddy are getting a divorce. A divorce means that Mommy and Daddy won't be living together anymore. I will still be your Mommy and Daddy will still be your Daddy. We'll always love you and take care of you." Reassure your child by letting him know that this isn't his fault and that he did nothing to cause this.

- Keep in mind the egocentric perspective of a child at this age. Your child will worry about who'll take care of him, where he'll live, what'll happen to him, or whether it was his fault. Children think in concrete terms, and you'll need to address fears specifically. What your child doesn't need to know are the details of *why* this is happening. It won't help to say to your child, "Mommy and Daddy don't want to live together anymore." Instead, your child needs to know specifically how the divorce will affect him: "You will be living with Mommy during the week and with Daddy on the weekends."

- It can help to point out all the things that will be staying the same. When you tell your child that school, friends, family visits, and caregivers will stay the same, this will be comforting to him.

- Remember that this is only the first of many conversations you'll have with your child about the separation. As he grows, he may need different information and explanations. You can revisit his questions and have conversations at each developmental stage and as his understanding of the situation changes. Both parents should regularly set aside time for talking and answering questions.

- Although your words are important, physical affection and spending time with your child are just as important during this time. Lots of hugs are the best way to comfort and reassure him. You may decide to cancel some of your child's structured activities so that you have more time to be together.

- Maintain routines and expectations. During this transition, you may suffer from guilt or feel that you need to protect your child from any other kind of hurt. This may lead you to believe that it's okay to relax your usual routines and expectations. You might allow your child to stay up late to watch TV because you don't want to get into a conflict about bedtime. You might permit him to behave impolitely around others, excusing him by saying, "He's going through a difficult time." In fact, by indulging your child, you're only further undermining his sense of security. It's extremely important that you continue to set limits, give responsibilities, and hold him accountable for his actions during this period of change so that he can feel safe and loved.

- Be positive with your child. Tell him he can feel sad but that he can have fun too. Explain to him that it'll take time to get used to the changes but he'll grow accustomed to them soon. When you plan fun activities with your child that you can do together, you're actively reminding him that some things change, but many things remain the same.

- Make certain that you save your disputes with your partner for the times when your child isn't around. Certainly blaming one parent, talking negatively, or shouting in front of your child is extremely undermining to his stability.

- Don't use your child to obtain information about the other parent. Don't try to communicate with the other parent through your child or ask for details about his time with the other parent. When you do these things, you're putting your child in a very difficult position.

- Avoid discussing your problems or feelings with your child. Remember, you're the adult, and your child needs to see that you are strong and in charge. It's not fair if you confide in him as if he were a friend.

Practical Wisdom for Parents

- When the separation has taken place and you're living in different spaces, it's helpful to have favorite toys in each home or ones that go back and forth. Something as simple as having the same bedding in both your child's bedrooms is comforting to him. You can hang your child's artwork in both homes as well.

- Maintain the same routines—such as bedtime and mealtimes—in both homes. Basic rules such as brushing teeth before bed or only reading two books before bedtime should be consistent with both parents if possible.

- Set up a calendar to show what the visitation schedule will be so that your child feels that there's a routine that everyone in the family is going to follow. In this respect, it's extremely important that both parents are dependable and are on time for visits and pickups. Don't refer to time with the other parent as a "visit," however. Spending time with a parent isn't visiting. It's spending time with a parent.

- Try to maintain good communication with your partner if you can. We've seen instances of divorced parents who have managed to put their children's needs first and cooperate with each other in their children's best interests. As a result, their children were much less likely to display the signs of distress usually associated with children going through a divorce. If you can attend school conferences together, keep similar bedtimes and other routines consistent in both homes, and agree upon basic rules, you'll effectively lessen the negative impact of the divorce.

- Make sure you communicate positive things as well as concerns about your child when speaking to the other parent. It's nice to be able to share your pride with someone who's connected to your child in the same way as you.

- Accept your child's love of the other parent. Your child needs to know that you actually approve of his love of the other parent. You can help by encouraging his contact with the other parent: allowing him to make regular phone calls, exchange drawings and pictures, or have a photograph of the other parent in his room.

- Observe your child's behavior as he adjusts. If you see over time that your child's still exhibiting a great deal of regression and negative behavior, if he's having sleeping or eating problems, or if he's taking less pleasure in activities he used to enjoy at home or at school, you should consider seeking professional guidance.

- If you're having trouble coping with your own feelings and the needs of your child, reach out to friends or family for support. Get professional help if you're feeling overwhelmed.

- Of course, you should let your child's teacher know what's happening in your family and what the schedule is for visitation.

Illness

• When Your Child Needs to Go to the Hospital •

When a child needs to be hospitalized, it's only natural for parents to feel worried and upset. It can help to know that hospital staff members are usually very sensitive to the emotional needs of families in this situation and that there will be doctors, nurses, and programs available to support you throughout this experience.

If you know in advance that your child needs to go to the hospital, there are a number of things you can do to prepare. First, get as much information as you can about the hospital and the medical procedures your child will be receiving. By preparing in this way, you're giving yourself a greater sense of control, and this can help to alleviate some of your anxiety so that you'll be better able to reassure your child. Some hospitals offer orientation tours for families and will have specially trained professionals who can give you information and language to help your child. If you do choose to take a tour with your child, make sure it's only a few days before the hospital stay so that you don't give him too much time to worry beforehand.

Sometimes hospitalizations are necessary in cases of emergency and you won't have the time to prepare your child. When you stay as calm as possible and explain what's happening, your child will feel calmer. You can tell him that the doctors and nurses are there to make him better.

When talking to your child about his hospital stay, here are a few things to keep in mind:

Practical Wisdom for Parents

- Wait until a few days beforehand if you can before telling your child so that you don't cause him any unnecessary anxiety. When you do tell him, you need to be truthful and use simple language. Give him enough information without overwhelming him with too many details. Avoid using frightening words and phrases like "cut," "sew you up," or "put you to sleep." Maintain a calm facial expression and tone of voice. Even if your words are reassuring, when your face looks worried, your child will worry. You can say: "You've been getting lots of earaches. I know how much that hurts you. Dr. Abramson knows how to make you feel better. Many children who have earaches need to have special tubes put in their ears so they won't hurt anymore."

- Your child will benefit from a simple step-by-step explanation about what's going to happen. He may be fearful of possible pain and might worry about not knowing where you're going to be. You can say: "We'll be going to the hospital so that Dr. Abramson can put the tubes in your ears to stop your earaches. The hospital is a place where doctors and nurses help people feel better. We'll be sleeping there overnight, and I will stay in your room with you. We can take your teddy bear and favorite books to read. The doctor will give you a special sleeping medicine so it won't hurt, and I'll be there when you wake up. Is there anything else you want to know?"

- If your child is being hospitalized overnight, make sure at least one parent stays in his room. If you need to leave your child's room, don't sneak out. Tell him where you're going so that he doesn't wake up and find you gone. Reassure your child by holding him and being with him. Congratulate him for being brave.

- Many children regress after they return home from the hospital. Your child may express anger, demonstrate separation anxiety, or have sleep disruptions. You'll need to be around as much as possible while your child is recuperating.

- It's very important to remain positive with your child. Young children are immensely resilient and have tremendous facility for healing. Although it's only natural to want to protect your child at this time, try not to become overly protective. If you handle him with kid gloves, you'll be sending the message that he's fragile and unable to cope. Keep reassuring him that he can do all the things that he did before—if not now, then soon. This will send the message that he's strong and capable. Another way of letting him know that everything is okay is to maintain his daily routines and expectations. This will help him bounce back more readily.

• When a Parent Needs to Go to the Hospital •

If you know in advance that a parent needs to go to the hospital, here are some things you can do to help prepare your child:

- Tell your child a few days before you'll be admitted. Don't give him time to worry beforehand.

- Explain to your child in simple terms why you have to go to the hospital. Don't elaborate. Wait for his questions.

- Tell him how many days you'll be there and mark a calendar with stickers for each day you'll be away.

- Let him know who'll be taking care of him while you're away and discuss when and how you'll be able to talk to one another.

- Write a little note to your child to be given to him each day.

- Make sure that his routines remain the same while you're away.

- Don't talk about your illness in front of your child and don't let others talk about it in front of him.

- Depending on the hospital rules and your condition, you need to decide whether a visit would be beneficial. When a parent doesn't look like himself or herself, it can be very upsetting for a young child.

- When you come home, explain to your child that the doctor wants you to rest. You can suggest quiet activities you can do together like reading, games, drawing, or watching videos.

- Let your child's school know that you'll be going to the hospital so the teachers can give your child some extra care and attention.

Death

For a young child, everything is interesting and worth investigating. We often see four-year-olds lying down on the playground playing dead, even though they're too young to have fully absorbed the meaning of the word. Even if your child has no direct experience of a relative or pet dying, it's likely that at some point he'll ask you about death and what it means to die. Although children under the age of five have a limited understanding of death, they're also naturally curious about this subject and, even if this causes you some discomfort, you'll have to answer your child's questions.

For most of us, talking about death is extremely difficult under any circumstance. When your child asks you questions about death, your every instinct will be to protect him from the knowledge that people die. You may be afraid of saying the wrong thing. You may be wary of projecting adult feelings about death onto your child. Despite your natural discomfort, it's very important to give your child calm and truthful answers to his questions. If you avoid answering or make up stories, your child will only become confused. Bear in mind that this subject will come up at various stages of your child's development and the information you give him now will serve as a basis for a deeper understanding as he grows.

Here are some other things to keep in mind:

- Be aware of the language that you use and how much you say. Children are very literal and when adults use euphemisms like "went to sleep," "passed away," or "lost," this can be confusing and frightening. You can tell your child that dying means that a body stops working; it doesn't breathe or move anymore. Listen and wait for further questions. Your child's questions will help you understand his level of comprehension. Answer specifically without elaboration.

- Your child may want to know, "Are you going to die?" If this question comes up, you need to reassure your child while being honest. You can say, "Yes, but not for a long, long time. I will be here until you're very, very, very old. I'll still be here when you're a daddy and you have children of your own."

- One way to help your child understand death is to use nature as a teaching tool. When your child sees a dying plant or a dead bug, you have a chance to explain to him about "things not living anymore." We recommend that parents keep a goldfish so that children can observe firsthand what "dead" means. By the age of three, your child has the ability to understand that when a fish doesn't move, breathe, or eat, it's not alive. This can help him to grasp that death means the loss of life functions. When you have a ceremony to bury the fish, you're helping your child to handle the transition from life to death through ritual.

- Young children are often quite matter of fact about this natural process. At the nursery school, we were very concerned about the children's reaction when the classroom pet rabbit died. The teachers sensitively talked to the children about their feelings and asked what they liked best about Fluffy. After a few minutes, one of the children raised his hand and said, "Can we play now?" We've often heard four-year-olds announcing at lunchtime, "Did you know my grandpa died?" and then quickly moving on to the business of eating a sandwich.

- If someone close to you dies, your instinct may be to hide your feelings from your child so that you don't cause him any additional anxiety. It won't harm your child to see that you're upset. You'll need to explain why you're feeling sad and reassure him that you're okay. You may discover that your child is an enormous source of strength and consolation to you during this difficult time.

- If your child was close to the person who died, you need to explain in clear terms what happened: "Grandma was very old and sick. Her body stopped working and she died. We're going to miss her very much, and we feel sad we won't see her anymore. We can look at pictures of her and think about all the wonderful things we did together. We can always talk about her."

- Take your cues from your child. Just like adults, children will grieve in different ways. Some children show sadness or cry. Others will be clingy or fearful. Your child may become uncomfortable and act silly or misbehave. Some children don't show any emotion at all. Your child's reaction will be influenced by his age, personality, and relationship to the person who died.

- Children will often want to know where the person who's died has gone. It's very hard for a young child to understand that death means never seeing someone again. When Ellen's father died, Alice asked,

Practical Wisdom for Parents

"Where is Grandpa?" Ellen wanted to give her five-year-old daughter an answer that would be comforting. After thinking about it for a moment, Ellen told Alice, "He's in heaven." Although heaven wasn't something Ellen necessarily believed in, the answer proved very comforting to Alice. When you're five years old, it can be a relief to imagine there's a place where Grandpa has gone. Since young children are concrete thinkers, the idea of heaven is usually very reassuring. If your personal beliefs about what happens after death are more complicated, you can always talk about these with your child when he's older and able to understand more complex concepts.

- Children under the age of five can't really understand or benefit from attending a funeral. There are other ways that are more age appropriate to have closure when someone close to your family dies. You can look at photos, draw pictures, and write down memories of favorite things you did with that person. You can plant a flowering plant that blooms yearly and becomes a lasting memorial—this can help a child to understand the cycle of life. One parent we know sends helium balloons into the sky with her children on her mother's birthday.

- When you talk about the person who's died—rather than avoiding the subject because you feel uncomfortable—you're helping to keep that person's memory alive and meaningful for your child. If your child has traits that remind you of a grandparent or another relative, you can point this out to him, making a comforting connection between the generations.

Remember, as adults, we all approach death and grieving in our own way, bringing our own set of experiences and attitudes. But for young children, who don't have any prior experience, death, like everything else, is new. The best way to deal with the subject is by being direct, simple, and reassuring. By being open and honest and by showing your child that death is a part of life, you're building a foundation for his own attitude toward death and grieving in the future.

Talking About Difficult Topics

Recommended Children's Books

TRANSITIONS AND NEW EXPERIENCES

It's Going to Be Perfect!	Nancy Carlson
Moving House	Anne Civardi
Just a New Neighbor	Gina and Mercer Mayer
Getting a Haircut	Melinda Beth Radabaugh
Going on an Airplane	Melinda Beth Radabaugh
Going to a Concert	Melinda Beth Radabaugh
Going to the Library	Melinda Beth Radabaugh
Going to a Restaurant	Melinda Beth Radabaugh
No Haircut Today!	Elivia Savadier

FEARS

Berenstain Bears Learn about Strangers	Stan and Jan Berenstain
Go Away, Big Green Monster!	Ed Emberley
Wemberley Worried	Kevin Henkes
Swimmy	Leo Lionni
Froggy Goes to the Doctor	Jonathan London
There's a Nightmare in My Closet	Mercer Mayer
Brave Irene	William Steig

SEX AND BIOLOGY

What's the Big Secret	Laurie Krasny Brown and Marc Brown
How You Were Born	Joanna Cole
When You Were Inside Mommy	Joanna Cole
Amazing You!	Gail Saltz
How Are Babies Made?	Alastair Smith
Your Body Belongs to You	Cornelia Maude Spelman

DIVORCE

Dinosaurs Divorce	Laurene Krasny Brown and Marc Brown
Two Homes	Claire Masurel
When My Parents Forgot How to Be Friends	Jennifer Moore-Mallinos
Let's Talk About It: Divorce	Fred Rogers
Missing Rabbit	Roni Schotter
Mama and Daddy Bear's Divorce	Cornelia Maude Spelman
My Family's Changing	Pat Thomas

Practical Wisdom for Parents

Chapter Fourteen

TIME TOGETHER:

Weekends, Holidays, Traditions,

and Vacations

Many parents worry about not spending enough time with their children. It's true that for most families, the weekdays are hectic. Monday to Friday is spent racing around, getting to school and to work in the mornings, then rushing home or to activities in the afternoons. Life today is busy, and it's not always possible to set aside family time during the week. This makes it all the more important that you slow the pace when weekends, vacations, and holidays come around. These times provide families with wonderful opportunities to let go of the "to do" list and to allow for more spontaneity and fun. Children benefit so much when they have time with their parents without the pressure of having to be someplace in the next five minutes. When you spend a lazy Saturday afternoon lying in the grass watching clouds forming shapes in the sky or taking walks around the neighborhood talking about the things you see, you have a chance to connect and enjoy each other's company. If your weekends and vacations are completely crammed with planned activities, you'll be missing out on the opportunity to simply spend time with your children and to create family memories together.

When we think back to weekend, holiday, and vacation mornings with our children, we remember how pleasurable it was to relax the pace. These were times to snuggle in bed without having to be anywhere else. Breakfast could be a leisurely affair where everyone pitched in to help. We could spend these days sharing special interests as a family or with each parent doing something individually with each child. On the weekends, we found that we inadvertently created special family rituals, such as having French toast every Saturday for breakfast or going for lunch at Grandma's on Sunday. Children love to participate in special rituals—they feel stable and safe when doing something familiar and thoughtful. It's always gratifying when our grown-up children remind us of the weekly and annual events that we participated in together.

Your preschool child is now at an age when she can really begin to appreciate the rituals and holidays that divide up the year and bring a family together. When you do something on a weekly or annual basis, this helps create a wonderful sense of belonging within a family. Some families reject ritual because they assume it needs to be religious, but rituals don't necessarily need to be grounded in a spiritual practice or even a holiday. A tradition can be something as simple as taking a trip to the ice-cream parlor once a month, having pizza on Thursday nights, or a family movie night. Many families find special ways to celebrate birthdays—the birthday person chooses what's for dinner or sits at a coveted place at the table. Your child will remember these special privileges long after she forgets the gifts she was given.

It's often the case that rituals—whether secular or religious—center around mealtimes. Eating together is the most effective way of creating a feeling of cohesion within a family. If you make time to plan, shop, and prepare meals together—even if it's only once a week—this regular routine creates its own ritual. Each family member can be given a designated task such as setting out a special tablecloth for "family Sunday brunch" or putting fresh flowers in the "brunch vase." It's the details of everyday life that your children will remember with the most fondness: helping to decorate turkey cookies on Thanksgiving or going to the park for a birthday picnic each year.

Now that your child is preschool age, she'll begin to recognize your family's rituals, and these will continue to have meaning for her as she grows. Nancy's family would always go apple picking each fall. After climbing trees and picking the best ones, the family would end the day by making an apple pie and eating it for dinner. Recently, Alissa went apple picking with her college friends, then came home to her apartment to make "Mom's apple pie." She proudly e-mailed a photo of her first pie to Nancy, re-creating a lovely connection between mother and daughter. Ellen's daughter, Alice, always helped her mother and grandmother prepare Thanksgiving dinner. Even when Alice was four years old, she would peel potatoes, tear lettuce for the salad, and stir the ingredients into the stuffing. As she grew, she took on more and more of the cooking responsibility. After Alice was married and Ellen went to visit her daughter's in-laws for Thanksgiving, it was a wonderful surprise to find that the "Birnbaum turkey" was still the centerpiece. Traditions like these create threads of continuity that will draw your children closer to you even as they get older and move away. When you create family rituals, you're building a store of memories that will stay with you and your child, acquiring more meaning with every passing year.

Weekends and School Vacations: Places to Visit and Things to Do

Children do not need expensive organized activities to make them happy. When you set aside time to spend together as a family doing everyday things, you're sending a message that family is important. Often, the simplest activities you do together can be the most pleasurable.

Some great ideas and activities for weekends and school vacations include:

- Going to the vegetable stand or supermarket. You can talk to your child about the names of different vegetables or fruits, their shapes, colors, and size, and explain how they grow. Select some for tasting; then talk about their texture and taste.

- Walking down the street. Point out and talk about the different cars and their colors, types of transportation, street signs, mailboxes, types of stores, construction sites, types of dogs, and different plants and trees.

- Visiting the fire station or post office. Going to these local places helps children learn about the different roles people have in the community and the kinds of work they do.

- Visiting the pet store. Ask a sales person if your child can play with a kitten or puppy. This is a great substitute if you don't have a pet in your home.

- Going to the library or bookstore. Find out if there's a regular story time at your library or local bookstore and sign your child up for a library card. Children love to know that they have a card that lets them borrow books.

- Going to a pick-your-own farm to pick strawberries and raspberries in the summer, and pumpkins and apples in the fall. Afterward, you can go home and cook something with the ingredients that you gathered.

- Collecting leaves, flowers, and pinecones in the park or forest.

- Going for a picnic, whether it's in the park, the local playground, or your backyard.

• Visiting Museums •

For young children, museums can either be incredibly fun and interesting or overwhelming and boring. Here are some helpful hints for keeping your child engaged while visiting museums:

- Ask yourself, "Is this exhibition something my child will enjoy, or is it just that I want to see this exhibition?"

- Before you go, talk about museum etiquette—using quiet voices, walking not running, looking not touching.

- Before you go, show your child pictures of what she might see. Children are always more interested when they see something familiar. "I know that picture. I saw it in my book."

- Don't plan to stay too long. Forty-five minutes to an hour is enough for under-fives.

- Go at a time of day when your child will be well rested so that she has more stamina.

- Choose a few things to see rather than attempting to see an entire exhibit in one visit.

- Bring along pencil and paper so your child can draw her own version of what she sees. This is a way of helping her to become more actively involved in the experience.

- Take a break or have a snack while you're there. Young children don't have very long attention spans and will easily tire or become cranky without a break.

- Stay only as long as your child continues to show interest.

- Be aware that your child may be more interested in the staircase or the water fountain rather than the sculptures or paintings.

Some questions or points you can highlight during your visit include:

- What do you see?
- What do you think they're doing?
- Where are they?
- What did the artist use to make this?
- What colors did the artist use?
- What shapes or lines do you see?
- Does it look real or does it look like the artist used his imagination?
- Tell your child the artists' names and something about them.
- How does the sculpture look different when you look at it from different perspectives? What are the shapes and spaces that a sculpture creates?
- Suggest that your child replicate a sculpture by imitating the pose.

Holidays

For the first few years of your child's life, she was too young to appreciate the rituals that accompany the holidays. As a preschooler, she'll naturally become more involved, and it's possible that some of her most powerful future memories will center around the holidays.

For your part, you may have the expectation that Thanksgiving or Christmas should be the "happiest time of the year," especially now that you have a child. If your experience of family holidays in the past has been at all negative, you may decide to wipe the slate clean and create a different experience for your child. It's important to remember that holidays are rarely simple and that you'll need to maintain realistic expectations. You may find these are emotionally charged times, bringing up powerful feelings and memories from your own past. When you're aware that these issues may come up, you can be better prepared to deal with them.

Here are some other things to keep in mind when dealing with the holidays and young children:

- Try to give up the idea of perfection. Holidays can be stressful, and it always helps to lower your expectations in order to maintain sanity.

Practical Wisdom for Parents

One of the parents at the nursery school once asked us how to make a Passover seder, as this wasn't a tradition in her own family. We shared with her the basic elements, including a favorite matzoh ball soup recipe. She came back after Passover and reported that she cooked all day, prepared the table beautifully, and was exhausted by the time the seder began. After all her efforts, her children picked at the unfamiliar food and were ready to leave the table after twenty minutes. We told her, "That sounds just about right."

- Try to do less. When you have young children, you'll most likely have to do less around holiday times. If you're hosting, you may not have the time to prepare all the food yourself. It's okay to ask other family members or friends to bring food or order some prepared foods. It's more important that your holiday time is relaxed and enjoyable than it is to have a gourmet dinner with twenty elegant place settings. Your child will remember these times as fun and happy if you can find ways to reduce your stress levels.

- Involve your child. When you encourage your child to help prepare the meal or decorate the table, you're ensuring she'll feel that she's an important part of the celebration. Children often enjoy decorating place cards or making other decorations for the table.

- Create simple but meaningful rituals that your child can remember as she grows. Baking cookies for her teachers and neighbors or putting out cookies and a glass of milk for Santa can be fun. Everyone can make a special wish on New Year's Eve for the year ahead, and these can be read out loud the following year. These are the kinds of things that your child will recall with the most pleasure when she's older.

- Limit the number of special events you attend. Bear in mind that most young children become excited, overstimulated, and exhausted when surrounded by lots of people, presents, and activities. Both sets of grandparents may wish to see the children, but you need to be clear about how many people you can realistically visit in a single day. If you can limit the number of special events, it's likely that you'll have a more enjoyable holiday. A big brunch followed by a visit to Grandma and Grandpa's, then a large dinner party at your home will surely invite meltdowns from your three-year-old.

- Maintain routines. On the day of the holiday, attempt to balance all the excitement by sticking to a familiar schedule as much as possible. Look ahead and plan the day accordingly. If you can fit in a quiet time before going out to a family dinner, you may be able to prevent a meltdown later in the day. It's always a good idea to carry a favorite snack with you in case the holiday meal doesn't include child-friendly food. If you're going to stay out later than bedtime, bring pajamas and a favorite snuggly so your child can fall asleep in the car on the way home. Be prepared to leave early if you have to.

- Pace the gift giving. When children receive too many gifts all at once, they quickly become overwhelmed and can lose their sense of enjoyment. It's helpful to pace the gift giving by only allowing children to open a few presents at a time. If your child is given a chance to delay her gratification, it will help increase her pleasure in her presents. You can even put some gifts away, saving them for a rainy day.

- Stay home if you want to. If you live far away from extended family and the idea of traveling is too overwhelming, you can always stay home and celebrate with your immediate family or with close friends instead. We know many families at the nursery school, including ours, who have holiday celebrations with friends.

• Combining Traditions •

When you create a family, it follows that you're going to be blending your own holiday traditions and those of your partner. You need to think about what's most important and meaningful for each of you—it would be overwhelming to try to incorporate everything. Although it's a good idea to introduce rituals from both sides of the family, you'll certainly want to create traditions that are unique to your family. Some of your inherited traditions may no longer reflect who you are or your new family's lifestyle. For example, if you grew up in a more formal home where everyone dressed up for dinner but your home is more casual, you might want to let go of these past expectations.

Holidays can be particularly challenging for families in which the parents come from different religious or cultural backgrounds. It's important that you talk about your beliefs with your partner and how you want to impart your traditions to your children. This may mean celebrating each holiday separately, combining both traditions, or choosing one tradition or the other. When you're celebrating with extended family, it's important that you show respect for traditions and beliefs that are not your own. You can celebrate one tradition at home and enjoy another tradition with extended family without this becoming confusing for your child. Your child needs to feel a strong sense of connection to both sides of her family.

One family we know always celebrates both Christmas and Hanukkah. When their daughter Abigail was four years old, she asked her Jewish mother to read her a book about Christmas. She asked her Christian father to read her a book about Hanukkah. It was important to Abigail that her parents understood the meaning of each tradition. Reading these books became part of their family ritual. When you read books about different holidays to your child, you have a chance to talk to her about cultural differences and traditions.

• Finding Meaning •

In recent times, holidays have become increasingly commercialized, with families feeling the pressure to devote large amounts of time and money to shopping for gifts. What you choose to emphasize about the holidays will teach your children something about your values. Your child needs to know that the holidays aren't just about receiving presents. If you can make time to create handmade cards or bake cookies to give to friends or family members, this will help your child to appreciate the pleasure of giving as well as receiving. Another good idea is to involve your child in choosing gifts for family and friends so that the giving becomes more meaningful to her.

If you want to help your child value the gifts she receives, you need to teach her the importance of saying thank you. Your preschool child is old enough to acknowledge each gift she receives, either in the moment, or at a later date by sending a thank-you card or making a special phone call. This will establish a good habit that can last throughout life.

If holidays only revolve around gifts and eating, however, you're depriving your child of the opportunity to appreciate her privileges. Volunteering is one way of creating meaning during the holidays. Many charities rely on volunteers and donors around this time of year. When you involve your child in giving to those in need, you show her that helping others is something your family values. Young children enjoy volunteering. Ellen's family used to bring food to an elderly homebound woman at holiday time. This was organized through her synagogue, and her children would come along, bringing the cards they had made as their contribution. Other families we know cook food for a homeless shelter and deliver it the day before the holiday.

Vacations

As you've probably already discovered, family vacations are not vacations for parents. Family vacations can be a fun opportunity to experience a new place and to be with each other without the distractions and demands of everyday life, but they are never completely relaxing for the grown-ups involved. When our children were young, both of our families went on a vacation to a family resort in Pennsylvania. We arrived late on Christmas Eve, and the restaurant was understaffed. The children were exhausted and very hungry. The wait for the food was excruciating, as was the whining. When the waitress finally came out of the kitchen, we heard a loud crash. All of our meals were on the floor. Out of sheer desperation, we salvaged what we could so that the children could eat. It was truly a humbling experience, but we still look back and laugh with our husbands and children about the "worst vacation of all time."

It's important to be realistic when planning family vacations. Young children usually become unsettled in new locations. When your three-year-old wakes up at 5 a.m., then refuses to nap and is cranky for most of the day, you may find it hard to remember exactly why you left home in the first place. Most families aren't used to spending more than two or three whole days in each other's company, and it can take a few days for everyone to wind down and get used to the new setting. If you plan in advance and take into consideration the age, interests, and needs of your children, you're likely to have a more pleasurable time. Vacations work best when young children are able to take part in age-appropriate activities. Locations such as the beach, the lake, a house or hotel with a pool, or resorts that include activities for children are going to be the most fun. By far the most interesting and exciting vacation activities for under-fives include playing in the pool, digging in the sand, looking for shells, and collecting rocks and bugs.

Some other tips for family vacations:

- Divide up the journey. Generations of children have asked the same question: "When are we going to beeeeeeee there?" For young children, even a few hours in a car, train, or plane can seem like an eternity. When you reply, "We'll be there in two hours," this means nothing to a young child, who wants to know what she'll be doing for the next five minutes. Instead you can say, "We'll be there after lunch," or "We'll be there when this CD and then the next CD is over." Snacks can be dispensed at intervals to give children something to anticipate and to distract them from the long journey time. "When we get to the next bridge, you can have a cookie."

- Be prepared. We don't need to remind you that children have limited patience for long trips and dislike sitting in one spot for extended periods of time. It's a good idea to take along a special bag of fun activities for each child to help pass the time. Paper, crayons, stickers, and books are useful for keeping young children entertained. Games like I Spy or How many blue cars can you see? are also valuable distractions. Singing your favorite songs or having story tapes or music playing will also help keep everyone occupied. If different children want to listen to different things, bring headsets. If all else fails, you can always try playing "the quiet contest." Although this usually only works for a short time, it will give you some peace for a few minutes. If two children are fighting in the backseat, and there are two adults in the front, one adult can get in the backseat and sit between them.

- Take rest stops. It's an inescapable fact that children on long car trips will need to stop and move their bodies or go to the bathroom periodically. As much as you'd like to get to your destination speedily, you'll have to pull over at intervals to give the children a chance to let off steam and use the restroom.

- Remember that young children take time to adjust to new places and are most comfortable when you maintain routines and familiarity by bringing a few toys or a favorite blanket or pillow. (Whatever you do, don't leave "blankie" at the hotel unless you have a duplicate.)

- Try not to feel pressured to do too much in a day or think you must do something interesting every day during your vacation. Your children will quickly burn out and so will you. If you pace yourself and balance the days with busy activities and things that are relaxing, everyone will have a better time. Parents or other adults in the group can split up and go separate ways, especially if your children are different ages. If you have a preconceived plan for the day but your children only want to play in the pool, you need to be flexible. You can always visit "Butterfly World" another day.

- Try to find restaurants that seem child friendly and serve food that your child enjoys. Unless you are staying in a hotel or house with a kitchen, being on vacation means eating in a lot of restaurants. This may mean you have to succumb to the local fast-food chain at least once or twice during your trip. It's okay. Your child will understand that vacations are special and that you get to do things that you wouldn't do at home.

- Bear in mind that other diners in restaurants are unlikely to appreciate your loud and messy children. If your child is becoming unruly, be considerate of the people around you and take her outside for a walk. Bring crayons or books so she has something to do while she's waiting for her food. Ask the waiter to bring your child's food as soon as it's ready so she won't have to wait. If you can stay at a place that has kitchen amenities, you will eliminate some of these restaurant meals, which can be stressful for families.

- Decide to stay home instead. If you can't or don't choose to leave home for a vacation, you can still have fun doing things together in your city or town. You may decide that this is actually the preferable option for you. Instead of spending a large sum of money going to a fancy resort where your child spends the whole week in the pool, you can stay home and go to the local pool or lake instead. One vacation, Nancy's family pretended that they were tourists in New York City. They went to all the attractions, visiting places they'd never been to before and doing things they'd never done. They went to the top of the Empire State Building and took a horse-drawn-carriage ride through Central Park. This still counts as one of their most enjoyable and stress-free family vacations.

- Make memories together afterward. Part of the fun of the family time is recalling your memories—good or bad—when your children grow older. It can be enjoyable to involve your child in making a photo album or a scrapbook of your trip to create a lasting record of the experience.

A Final Word: This Time Together Is Shorter Than You Think

As we write this, our children are in their twenties and thirties; yet it seems like such a short time ago that they were preschoolers, still making a mess at mealtimes, running races in the hallways, feuding with their siblings, sharing bubble baths, and waking us up at dawn on a Sunday morning. When you're in the midst of raising young children, it can seem as if this time will last forever. After all, a single day is a very long time when you're woken up at sunrise by a child who wants your undivided attention until she finally closes her eyes at night. Even so, this period in your child's life is remarkably brief. When she grows to be six and seven, she's no longer going to need you in the same way she did when she was three and four. Before you know it, her focus will shift from you to her own world of school and friends.

During these preschool years, you're still at the very center of your child's life. This is an enormous responsibility, and it can be extremely challenging. But it's also a wonderful time in the life of your family. The way your child instinctively reaches for you at the end of the day or climbs into bed with you in the morning or joyfully smiles to see you returning from work—these are the things that make being a parent of a young child so heartwarming and fulfilling. When you look back on this period, it's the everyday things that you'll remember the most: the feeling of wrapping your child in a towel as she comes out of the bath, the silly games you played together, the worn-out stuffed animal that she couldn't be without.

One parent recently told us that if she could relive her children's early years, she would try to be less focused on the next thing and more appreciative of the moment. If you turn being a parent into some kind of race to the finish line, then you'll pay less attention to the here and now. It's always going to be worthwhile to slow down and savor these very special years. When you're rushing to the supermarket and your child stops to notice the tulip plant pushing up through the ground, stop and look with her. Observe what your child observes and let her guide you. During the preschool years, you have a tremendous opportunity to relive the wonder of discovering the world alongside your child. If you're distracted because you're thinking about what you need to do next, you'll miss out on these magical moments as they occur.

Your child will help you do this. Her mischievous giggle when you're having a stressful day can lift your spirits like nothing else. When she's dancing unselfconsciously to her favorite music, she'll draw you into doing the same. If you've asked her to put away her toys ten times in a row and you walk into her room to find her sitting in the middle of her mess wearing her underpants on her head as a "crown," suddenly your exasperation is forgotten.

There's nothing like becoming a parent to humble us so that we recognize we're all human. Parenthood is a long road, and you'll surely make mistakes along the way. Always remember, you'll have many opportunities to guide your child to becoming a confident and competent human being and the results of your efforts won't always be obvious or immediate. It may be many years before you reap the rewards of the hard work of good parenting. Meanwhile, it's all the little things you do that will lay the foundation for your relationship in the years to come. This is the most exhausting and exhilarating work. It's the most frustrating and most satisfying. It's the most tedious and most fun. It's the most challenging and most meaningful. The days seem endless, but these years fly by. Enjoy them while they last.

Acknowledgments

After one of our parent meetings at school, a parent approached us and said, "You two should write a book." Of course we didn't take her too seriously, but she persisted. We had coffee with her, and she told us that we had a unique perspective and convinced us that we could write a book. This book would not have been written without Gretchen Rubin's support, enthusiasm, and belief in us. Gretchen led us to our agent, Christy Fletcher, who from our first meeting understood who we were and skillfully guided us through the new world of publishing. We're also immensely grateful to Emma Parry and the wonderful team at Fletcher & Parry for their hard work on our behalf. Christy very wisely led us to Jordan Pavlin, our editor at Knopf. Jordan appreciated our ideas, respected our perspective, and through her brilliant editing, showed us how to turn our ideas into this book. Her insight and guidance stretched us throughout the writing process. We feel fortunate to have been in her capable hands. Thanks are also due to Carol Rutan for her thoughtful copy edits. We appreciate the enthusiasm and support of Leslie Levine, Sarah Gelman, and everyone at Knopf for this book. For the past year and a half, we have met weekly with Eve Charles, who through her questions and thoughtful comments helped us shape our thinking and express our ideas with clarity. Our meetings with Eve and then with Eve and Grace (our tiny muse) have been a joy beyond description. Eve's sensitivity and talent have been invaluable to us. While we gave birth to this book, Christy, Emma, Jordan, and Eve had babies, making this experience all the more meaningful.

We're so grateful to our friends and family who took the time to read our manuscript and give us important feedback. Alice Roebuck (most enthusiastic fan, along with Andy) and Judy Motzkin (best sister, who with brother Barry, make having siblings fun) were supportive, insightful, and helped us remember things when our own memories failed. We appreciate the expertise and comments of Tracy Birkhahn, Carol Hendin, Dr. Kenneth Katz, Dr. Kenneth and Sandra Covelman, Susan Goldman, Amy Goldberg Michel, Bonnie Muir, Alicia Brackman Munves, Susan Stillman, and of course, Gretchen Rubin.

We're very fortunate to be working at an incredible institution, the 92nd Street Y, under the leadership of Sol Adler. We feel lucky to work with our colleagues, Fretta Reitzes and Sally Tannen, whose commitment to and respect for young children and their parents are admirable.

The 92nd Street Y Nursery School is an extraordinary place to work, with a warm and caring community of teachers and administrators. The dedication and talent of the teachers is exceptional and inspiring. We have so much respect for them and have learned so much by working alongside them. Over the years, we've been privileged to work with so many wonderful parents who have entrusted their children to us and shared their stories with us. Over the years, we've seen more than one thousand children come through the nursery school's classrooms, and we've been motivated, energized, and moved by each and every one of them.

Our wonderful husbands, Richard and Barry, our partners in parenting, have been supportive in so many ways. Their crack legal expertise, the willingness to give us the hours we needed every weekend, holiday, and summers, and their encouragement and pride in this endeavor means so much to us. To our children, Alice, Charles, Michael, and Alissa—you're our inspiration. You taught us what it meant to be a parent, to experience the joys and challenges along the way. You never failed to let us know if we went astray, but we are confident that we did a good job because we not only love you, we are so proud of the adults you've become.

Index

Index

Index

Index